D0757783

THE 1980 BOOK OF THE OLYMPICS

THE 1980 BOOK OF THE
OLYMPICS

OMEGA   OMEGA   OMEGA   OMEGA   OMEGA

THE GAMES SINCE 1896
A PICTORIAL RECORD
by James Coote

NEW YORK

First published in USA by
Exeter Books
Distributed by Bookthrift
New York, New York

Copyright © James Coote and London Editions 1980

This book was designed and produced in Great Britain by
London Editions Limited, 9 Long Acre, London WC2E 9LH

Printed in Italy

All rights reserved. No part of this publication may be
reproduced or transmitted, in any form or by any means,
without permission.

LC 79-56643

ISBN 0-89673-042-5

Picture Credits
H. Abrahams – Associated Press – British Lion Films Ltd –
Brown Bros – Ken Regan/Camera 5 – Camera Press – Bryn
Campbell – Central Press – Rich Clarkson – Collection Viollet –
Colorsport – James Coote – Gerry Cranham – Tony Duffy –
Raymond Depardon (Gamma) – International Olympics
Committee – Keystone Press Agency – Kyodo Picture Service –
E. D. Lacey – London Express – René Burri (Magum) – Mansell
Collection – Omega – Paul Popper – Press Association – Race
Recording Company – Radio Times Hulton Picture Library –
Leni Riefenstahl – Chris Smith – Swedish Olympic Committee –
Syndication International – Time/Life – Transworld – UPI – .
Eric Wimbolt-Lewis

Contents

Ancient Greek Olympics

The torch, lit from the rays of the sun, ignites the flame which will burn throughout the celebrations, signifying that peace should prevail—at least until the closing ceremony.

According to Homer, Pelops, the god of fertility, staged the most memorable games in antiquity at a date calculated to be roughly 1370 BC. Later on, Achilles organized games in honour of his friend Patroclus, hero of the Trojan War, which took place about 1250 BC. It is recorded that these games consisted of chariot-racing, boxing, wrestling, running, archery, discus and javelin throwing. In addition to the ritual sacrifice and eating of a small boy on the anniversary of Patroclus' death, duels to the death were also held which in later antiquity were to become the *Pankration* event – a no-holds-barred fight with gouging, strangling and limb-breaking allowed. It seems that this entertainment was to persuade Patroclus to reappear. We also know that Clymenos, descendent of Hercules, erected an altar to his ancestor at Olympia and promoted games there, only to be deposed by Aethlios, who offered his crown to whichever of his sons excelled in running at the Olympic games. Aethlios, first King of Elis, is the origin of the word 'athlete'.

Setting aside Homer, Hercules and Patroclus, we come to the first date that has any degree of certainty – 776 BC. In that year Coroebus of Elis won the Stade race. Long established as a principal running event in the pre-history of the Olympics, the Stade (hence 'stadium') was the length of a running track, said to have been measured out by Hercules himself as being the distance he could walk while holding his breath. It would seem that Hercules had to draw breath after walking 600 Olympic feet, or 192.28 metres (210 yards), judging by the dimensions of the remains of the Stadia in Greece. But from 776 BC the Olympics were fully recorded until the Emperor Theodosius banned pagan religions in 381 AD, by which time Christianity had been adopted as the official faith of the Roman Empire. The Olympics were indeed a pagan religious festival. They were discontinued having enjoyed an unbroken run of 1,168 years – the last, the 293rd Olympiad, being celebrated in AD 393.

The most important feature of the Olympic Games, said to have been revived, after hundreds of years' lapse, in the reign of King Iphitus of Elis around 884 BC, was the sacred truce: no-one was allowed to take up arms, all legal disputes were suspended and no death penalties were carried out during the Games. The personal safety of everyone was guaranteed. Pilgrims and official delegates flocked to Olympia in the Kingdom of Elis under the terms of truce inscribed on the sacred discus of Iphitus, set out in five concentric rings – hence the five-ringed altar at Delphi. The design was later adopted in 1920 as the Olympic symbol standing for the five continents of the world. Elis remained permanently neutral under the terms of the truce – an advantage that proved fatal later on as the apolitical farming community grew rich on the sidelines of the city-states, acquiring the reputation and vigour of mere bucolic pleasure seekers. It was at this time that the quadrennial cycle was established where formerly the Games had been held every eight years when the linear year and the solar year coincided.

The Greek idea was to practise sport not for its own sake but in pursuit of physical perfection and military proficiency. Competitors had to agree to train under

The sculpture (above left) shows the torch used to light ceremonial fires, often for sacrificial purposes; (above right) a close-up of the starting lines.

strict supervision for ten months of which the last had to be spent at Elis in one of the three superb gymnasia, complete with steam baths and facilities the equal of most training centres today. Foreigners and slaves being generally despised, only men of pure Greek descent were allowed to compete. Married women were not allowed as spectators, probably a rule dating from former times when fertility rites played a big part in the ceremonies. Those unlucky to be detected were thrown down a steep mountain side – a fate escaped by Callipatira who trained her son Pisidorus after her husband died, and attended the games in disguise as her son's trainer. When her son won his event, she gave herself away in her joy by jumping over the barrier dividing the spectators from the judges, exposing her guilty secret. But as she came from a great family of athletes, her brothers all being champions and her father the famous boxer Diagorus of Rhodes, the judges forgave her. But to avoid similar impostures in the future it was decreed that all contestants and trainers had to appear naked.

The games eventually grew from one race to a full five-day programme. The first day was devoted to the opening ceremony and the taking of a solemn oath against cheating – the judges, the *Hellanodikai*, dipping their hands in sacrificial blood and swearing to referee the events impartially. They were known for their honesty throughout Greece and had the power to impose fines, disqualify, banish or even order a beating – a penalty sometimes awarded for false starts.

The second day saw the Pentathlon (discus, javelin, running, wrestling and jumping), eulogies to Pelops and the two- and four-horse chariot races.

The third day started with a sacrifice to Zeus followed by three races: the *Stade* and two longer races – the *Diaulos*, two lengths of the stadium, and the *Dolichos*, 24 lengths, *i.e.* 4,614·72 metres. A triple victor earned the title *Triastes*, once won by Leonidas of Rhodes four Olympiads in succession.

The fourth day was given over to wrestling, boxing and *Pankration*. This last event was particularly dangerous. It was not unheard of for a dead man to be proclaimed winner. Arrhichion of Phigalia was declared the winner after dying in a stranglehold – having just broken his opponent's toe. The final day was the prizegiving, the thanksgiving and the banquet.

This happy stage of the Olympic Games continued until Elis involved itself in the Peloponnesian wars (431-404 BC) between Athens and Sparta, losing neutral status and weakening the value of the Olympic oath which transcended wars. The decline of the Games coincided with the collapse of the political independence of the Greek states until the Roman legions imposed their own peace on the heirs of Alexander. The Roman period is notable for the bribery in AD 65 of the judges by the Emperor Nero to postpone the 211th Olympiad to coincide with what he hoped would be the flowering of his own talent. Despite being thrown from his ten-horse chariot and being unable to remount he was still awarded the olive wreath, picking up the contests for singing and acting as well. For the first and only time an Olympiad was declared invalid, after Nero's enforced suicide the following year.

The Olympics may have died in Greece in AD 393 but

The altar at Delphi with the five rings later to be adopted as the symbol of the modern Olympics.

the poems of Pindar and the writings of Pausanias
lingered to remind posterity of the beauty of the ancient
Games. With the revival of classical Greek learning in
the Renaissance, the memory of the Olympics found an
echo in Britain. In 1636 Robert Dover held his own
Cotswold Olympic Games in the heart of rural England
and these continued till 1850, the year of the founding
of the Much Wenlock Olympian Society by Dr Penny
Brooke. The seed was sown and Major Zappas held his
first modern 'Pan Hellenic Olympics' in 1859, seven
years after a German archaeologist Ernst Curtius had
given a lecture suggesting the Olympics be re-established
– events that were to bring forth a world-wide movement
in only a few years.

An artist's impression, dated 1819, of the Ancient
Olympics, shows chariot racing, discus throwing and
boxing.

THE MODERN OLYMPICS

The founder of the modern Olympics in the nine-
teenth century was a Frenchman, Pierre de Frédy,
Baron de Coubertin. Obsessed by the mental and moral
condition of his people, a reason for France's defeat by
the Germans in 1870, he studied widely, and came to
the Platonic conclusion that the success of Victorian
Britain was due to the character of its ruling class, whose
attitude to life was formed by an educational system in
which the physical counted above the intellectual, and
the moral above both. De Coubertin saw in this a way
of re-establishing France.

He discovered Dr Arnold, the famous Headmaster of

Rugby, through *Tom Brown's Schooldays*, a book much quoted in the French philosopher Taine's *Notes sur L'Angleterre*. A visit to Rugby School persuaded him that the English public school system, built on team sports rather than Latin verse, would be particularly beneficial for the French. As the originator of organized games in French schools and of inter-school competition, it was naturally to him that the government turned to organize an international conference on physical education in 1889. Inspired by the newspaper campaign in *Le Temps* led by Pascal Grousset who proposed the idea of holding the Olympic Games, de Coubertin preached the Olympic scheme in a US lecture tour and in London. His efforts were rewarded in 1894 by the first international Olympic Congress, attended by seventy-nine delegates from thirteen countries, with a further twenty-one sending messages of support. It was unanimously decided that the Olympic Games be renewed. Later that year de Coubertin published his famous *Edict on Professionalism*, in which he declared 'the supreme importance of preserving the noble and chivalrous character of athletics against professionalism'.

In keeping with the romantic notion of the Olympic revival, it was decided to hold the first Games in Athens, Greece, in 1896 – the original date of 1900 being brought forward at the suggestion of the Greek delegate. As a practical consideration it had little to recommend it. Greece was on the verge of bankruptcy and its government unable and unwilling to help. But the Crown Prince was enthusiastic, forming a committee under his chairmanship to grapple with the problems, the chief of which was the absence of any money. Some committee members thought the position was hopeless. Hungary was proposed as an alternative, but declined. De Coubertin travelled to Athens to advise and rally support – the Crown Prince remaining enthusiastic. At his suggestion each Greek municipality was asked to raise funds, and the diplomatic missions abroad were ordered to get money by whatever means possible. Rich and poor were asked to donate. Even though these efforts realized twice as much money as was at first thought necessary, there was still not enough to undertake the reconstruction of the Pan-Athenian Stadium and all the other buildings needed to house the competitors and their attendants. So a delegation was sent to Alexandria to beg funds from a rich merchant, George Averoff, a most generous benefactor of Greek causes. The delegation came back with a million drachmas to pay for the entire cost of restoration of the Stadium, built around 300 BC. Despite the neglect of centuries, the limited time available and the enormous problem of organizing the first truly international sports meeting for 1,500 years, the Greeks, to their eternal credit, managed to complete a shooting gallery, a velodrome, a pier for the spectators of nautical sports and, of course, the Stadium.

On March 25, 1896, a sad rainy Wednesday morning, cannons were fired, doves released, and, after a gap of 1,503 years, the Olympics were reborn. The dream of one man had become reality.

The magnificent stadium at Epidaurus, Greece, was unusual in that the ends were square, rather than rounded as at Olympia. It was laid out in the fifth century BC and had particularly interesting starting arrangements. The start (the line in the foreground) and the finish were marked by a pair of stone pillars between which lay a line of grooved stone slabs. In front of the stone slabs were five pillars which formed the basis of a starting gate.

1896 Athens

Although thirty-four countries took the initiative to revive the Olympics, only thirteen countries were represented. The reason may largely have been that no invitations were sent out until December 1895, and as the Games had been fixed for early April it did not give competitors much time. Over sixty per cent of the entries came from Greece, with Germany, France and the United States sending twenty-one, nineteen and fourteen people respectively. Britain's total entry was eight.

Everything was weighted against the runner, for the track consisted of a very long straight of 206 metres, extremely sharp bends and a circumference of 333·5 metres – which meant the runners had to slow down almost to walking pace to avoid landing in the laps of the spectators. The 200 metres event was dispensed with on the grounds of safety. Races were run clockwise rather than the customary anti-clockwise. The track was laid by Charles Perry, groundsman at Stamford Bridge football ground, London, but he was given too little time and had trouble in finding the right materials, and the result was a loose, dry surface.

The Americans were to start a subsequent trend by winning all but three of the twelve athletics events, the exceptions being the Marathon which went to Spiridon Louis of Greece, and the 800 metres and 1,500 metres which were won by Edwin Flack, an Australian who went not as a representative of his country initially but as a member of London Athletic Club. Flack, a 22-year-old accountant, had moved to England to work and when he heard about the new Olympics, took a month's holiday and made his own way to Greece.

Despite the Americans' success their team was by no means a representative one. They included only one national champion, Thomas Burke, a quarter-miler from Boston, while the New York Athletic Club, the leading club in America, did not bother to send anyone.

It was a Games noted for odd episodes rather than for athletic performances. The French sprinter competing in the 100 metres heats wore kid gloves because he was running before royalty. Grantley Goulding from London finished second in the hurdles and it was said at the time that he had never before hurdled on cinders and therefore was at a great disadvantage!

Consider the case of Robert Garrett, a Princeton University student, who heard about the discus event back at home and decided to try for it. A class-mate designed a discus for him in steel and he practised throwing for a couple of weeks before sailing for Athens. Not surprisingly he had difficulty in flighting it correctly, but he was pleasantly surprised when he arrived in Athens to find that the standard two kilogram discus used in the Games was far lighter and a far more aerodynamically designed implement. Although he did not display the same grace of movement as the other competitors, he won the event, defeating three Greeks.

Shattered at losing this most classical of events, the Greek crowd could only count on the final event, the Marathon, which took place on 10th April. This event had been suggested by the French delegate, Monsieur Breal, who submitted the idea of the race to commemorate the heroic feat of Pheidippides in 490 BC. Pheidippides, an Athenian soldier and an Olympic champion, was in Athens when news came that the Persians were about to land on Greek soil at Marathon. He travelled two days and two nights to seek aid from the Spartans, more than 150 miles away. The Spartans refused immediate help since it was the eve of a religious festival. His mission having failed, he returned to fight at the great battle of Marathon. After the Greeks had

Far left Crowds mill around the newly built Pan Athenaic Stadium shortly before the opening ceremony.

Left and right The memorial at Olympia where lies the heart of Pierre de Frédy, Baron de Coubertin (right), father of the modern Olympics.

defeated the Persians, he ran to Athens to bring the city elders news of the victory. His message was brief. 'Rejoice, we conquer'—and he dropped dead.

As an inducement to a local runner to salve their national pride, the Greeks offered all sorts of gifts to any Greek winner. Averoff offered the hand of his daughter and a dowry of a million drachmas—exactly the cost of the reconstruction of the Stadium—a Dr Teoflaxos offered a large barrel of sweet vintage wine, and a tailor offered to clothe the winner for life. A barber offered a life-time of free shaves. The owner of a chocolate factory promised over 2,000lb of chocolate, and even the peasants arrived on the day with cattle and sheep destined for the winners.

At two o'clock, twenty-five runners, including four foreigners, contested this first race over 40 kilometres (25 miles) from Marathon to Athens, but of the four only the Hungarian, Gyula Kellner, had trained with the Marathon specifically in mind. The Frenchman, Albin Lermusiaux, who had finished third in the 1,500 metres was the early pace setter. After covering 22 kilometres he actually led by 3 kilometres and stayed ahead until a steep hill, shortly after the 32-kilometre mark, when he got cramp and gave up. Flack then took over the lead, but within 5 kilometres he too had dropped out exhausted and had to be taken back to Athens by ambulance. Meanwhile Louis, a 25-year-old postman from Greece, went ahead. The racing ability of Louis has been greatly underrated for it must have been very tempting to go with the Frenchman and Flack, the kind of temptation that many great runners have fallen into since then. In fact Louis is supposed to have drunk one or two glasses of wine en route, though the effect of the acid on the human stomach makes it unlikely.

Another victim of the race was Arthur Blake, runner-up in the 1,500 metres, who began to have hallucinations and toppled into a ditch. At the village of Ampelokipi, Louis accelerated smoothly, followed by Harlambos Vassilakos and the Hungarian, Kellner. To wild cheers from the 100,000 crowd he headed for the Stadium. The largely Greek crowd had been kept posted by progress reports; having started out depressed when the foreigners took the lead, they were ready and waiting to see their dream of a Greek winner fulfilled. The excitement was unbelievable. As Louis entered the Stadium, the whole arena was in pandemonium. Women tore off their jewellery to throw at his feet. A mounted band followed him into the Stadium, and the two Crown Princes of Greece, Constantine and George, both well over 6ft, ran alongside the 5ft 4in Louis to the finishing line. Fortunately for Averoff, Louis was already married, but he was still able to accept a voucher for 365 free meals, free shoe polishing for life and a field known henceforth as 'the field of Marathon'.

Nor surprisingly, in view of de Coubertin's *Edict on Professionalism*, Louis never ran again. As if this was not enough, there was the first of many controversies in connection with marathons. Two minutes after Louis came the second runner, Vassilakos, followed by another Greek, Dimitries Velokas. Unfortunately for him, Kellner, the fourth man to finish, complained to the jury that he had seen Velokas get out of a carriage.

Bob Garrett, of the US, winner of the discus, poses in the classic position made famous by the Discobolus of Myron about 450 BC.

The scene at the stadium when Spiridon Louis approached the winning lines accompanied by the Greek Crown Princes. In the picture above, he is level with the two posts which represent the old finishing lines; later (above right), he poses with his prizes—a gold medal and an olive branch—which he received from King George.

Velokas could not deny it. He knew every detail of the route, hid a carriage in one of the parks, and used it. Disqualification was automatic and his singlet with the national blue and white colours was ripped off his back. Kellner took the bronze medal and was given a gold watch as 'compensation'.

The swimming took place at Phaleron, near the Bay of Piraeus. Unfortunately for the swimmers the thermometer had dropped abruptly and with it the temperature of the water to 13°C. After winning the 100 metres freestyle, Alfred Hajos took the precaution of liberally coating his body with grease for a later event, which was just as well. The swimmers were taken 1,200 metres out into the open sea and were forced to dive into the water from the boats, which then scurried for the safety of the harbour. Alas the competitors had to contend with 12ft waves and the boats reluctantly left the security of the pier to fish out of the water three-quarters of the numbed competitors who were in danger of drowning. Hajos' cunning paid off for he won a second gold medal.

Varying start styles for the 110 metres hurdles, with the eventual winner, Tom Curtis of the US (third from left), using the method which was then current of balancing the front of the body on sticks.

1900 Paris

Despite the many problems that had arisen in Athens, the Olympic Games had come to stay. In 1897 the Olympic Congress held a meeting in Le Havre, France, where de Coubertin said that the resuscitation of the Olympic Games proved the moral and international value of physical training. It was at this meeting too, incidentally, that the words *Citius, Altius, Fortius* (faster, higher, stronger) were adopted as the Olympic motto. This was adapted from *Citius, Fortius, Altius,* the motto of Friar Didon's college at Arceuil, not far from Le Havre.

Although the Congress wanted the Olympics to be held only in Athens, de Coubertin's influence swayed the voting and the second meeting was scheduled for Paris in 1900 and thereafter on a world-wide rota basis. From then on nothing went right. Like so many great international figures de Coubertin was not accepted in his own country. The French were indifferent to the Games. Their interest was centred solely on the World Fair and the Eiffel Tower being built at the time. The organization was minimal, publicity non-existent and poor de Coubertin finally had to resign from the Organization Committee with the others of his group who had helped to found the Games. Even the title 'Olympic Games' was removed and the name of this competition was changed to *Concours Internationaux Exercises Physiques et du Sport.* Angling in the Seine was included as an official event. The fencing competitions started on May 14 at different venues, and were not finished until June 24. Foreign competitors arrived haphazardly to find nobody to meet them and no information of where the competition was to be held.

The athletics were held at the Bois de Boulogne in the grounds of the Racing Club de France. The track was basically a 500 metres oval with a heavy dip at the 100 metres stretch. The track itself was bumpy, the take-off for the jumps loose, and there was no check on the spectators who wandered among the competitors. Not surprisingly, the competition dragged on for two months.

The outstanding competitors were two Americans, Alvin Kraenzlein, who won the 60 metres, 110 and 200 metres hurdles and the long jump, and Ray Ewry, winner of the standing high jump, standing long jump and hop-step and jump. Ewry won another five gold medals at later Olympics. His was a classic example of de Coubertin's point that sport helped health, for as a child Ewry suffered from rheumatic fever and was advised by a doctor to run and jump to help regain his strength.

Above Michel Théato, a baker's roundsman, receives a welcome hosing from a kindly official en route to winning the Marathon for France. Using local knowledge, gleaned during his bread deliveries, Théato won by nearly $4\frac{1}{2}$ minutes from another Frenchman. The race took place during extremely hot weather conditions with dust thrown up by horse-drawn vehicles and the crowds.

Far left and left The long-legged Ewry of the US, who dominated the standing jump events between 1900 and 1904, displays his virtuosity and later poses shyly for the camera. Even by today's standards Ewry would not lag far behind in these now discontinued contests, for he had a remarkable ability in these difficult events. His eight individual gold medals was still an Olympic record over seventy years later, and he also won two golds at the unofficial 1906 Games.

1904 St Louis

While not one of the 1896 winners retained his athletics title in Paris, several, including Ray Ewry and John Flanagan (in the hammer), did so in the 1904 Games at St Louis. Again the organization coincided with a World Fair which meant that the Olympic Games were very much in a subsidiary role. The Americans had promised to supply a ship to visit all the European ports to gather up competitors; but it failed to arrive and very few overseas countries were represented.

Although there were many good athletics performances, it is the memory of the Marathon that lingers. William Garcia, a local runner, suffered a cerebral haemorrhage and almost died in the frightful heat. The Cuban postman Felix Carjaval took up a collection for himself in Havana and arrived in St Louis still penniless, having lost his money to gamblers. Yet he hitchhiked 3,000 miles to St Louis and arrived in sufficient time to start. He had never before run a Marathon and had it not been for the fact that he appropriated a couple of unripe apples from an orchard, he could have finished higher than fourth. It was the first and last time he was ever seen at an Olympic meeting.

Many of the runners dropped out because of the thick dust stirred up by the passing cars – a recent invention – on unsurfaced roads, belching out poisonous fumes. One such man was Fred Lorz, who retired after ten miles, then obtained a lift in a truck for another nine miles before the truck broke down. He continued to run, telling the officials en route that he wanted to get home in a hurry. Unfortunately no-one told the crowd, and when he arrived first in the Stadium he was acclaimed and congratulated by President Roosevelt. The medal ceremony was under way when British-born Thomas Hicks, competing for America and by profession a clown, tottered into the Stadium. Lorz's deception was at once apparent. All hell broke loose and Lorz was banned for a year for his 'joke'.

The organization for the swimmers was just as primitive. The swimming was held in an asymmetrical lake, making it impossible for the competitors to keep to their lanes. The starting line was a raft which sank from time to time.

From all accounts the most lasting memories of the competitors were of the diet: the sole fare on the menu was buffalo meat which was so unpalatable for the Europeans that they survived largely on boiled potatoes and milk.

Above and top right Two contrasting styles of 'heavy man': Perikles Kakoukis of Greece displays his strength in the one-arm lift, while the 20-stone Ralph Rose, winner of three successive gold medals for the US, tucks the shot into his chin before setting an Olympic and world record.

Below and bottom right Tom Hicks receives some illegal assistance from his attendants during the Marathon. Although he went on to win, the first man into the stadium was the hoaxer Fred Lorz, who had hitched a lift. He is fourth from the left wearing a dark vest in the line-up.

1906 Athens

Top In the only unofficial Olympic Games to be held—in 1906—the swimming events took place in the centre of a pontoon of boats. The long-distance events started further out to sea.

Above The Greek organizing committee achieved considerable attendances for their Games, as this picture of the gymnastic display, given by the German team, shows.

1908 London

Queen Alexandra has given the starting signal and already the Marathon runners are well strung out (above) as they leave Windsor Castle on their way to Shepherds Bush. When Dorando (right) passed the Jubilee Clock Tower, Harlesden, he was apparently still fresh, but the effort needed to catch Charles Hefferon of South Africa, who was two minutes ahead at this point, was to prove too great.

Although the London Olympiad followed on officially after St Louis, an unofficial Games had in fact taken place in 1906. The Greeks had seen 'their' Olympics slipping away from them and passed a law which stated that every four years, beginning in 1906, they would organize an Olympics. Thus the first and last Athens Olympic Games were held. Twenty countries sent nearly 900 competitors, but there were many problems with sleeping accommodation, food and poor organization, not to mention accusations of cheating by umpires and complaints over the roughness of the water at Phaleron. Ewry won another two gold medals, but generally standards were far lower than in St Louis.

All this tended to detract from the fourth Olympiad, which had been scheduled for Rome. During the Athens meeting the Italian delegation let it be known that they could not act as hosts. Thus the scene of the Games was shifted to London, and despite the shortness of time available for building they were successfully staged. The most advanced stadium of its type was built in the outskirts of London – the White City – for what seems now an infinitesimal sum of £40,000. The stadium had a 603·5 metres (660yd) banked concrete cycling track, 536·45 metres (586yd 2ft) running track which in turn included an open air 100 metres swimming pool.

The London presentation of the fourth Olympic Games was outstandingly the finest international sports meeting up to that time. The competition, facilities, judging and organization were of the highest order and set an example for future sports meetings. Pietri Dorando is the name blazoned on the memory of the

1908 Olympics. Dorando's Marathon run from Windsor to the White City Stadium was scarcely less dramatic than Pheidippides' original Marathon run. Watched by the largest recorded sports crowd in history up to that time, the frail little Italian tottered first into the Stadium and ran some way in the wrong direction. The officials told him his mistake but, in the final stages of exhaustion, he had to be helped when he fell and was supported over the line, an action which led to disqualification and the loss of the gold medal. However, a sympathetic Queen Alexandra gave Dorando a special gold cup. As the story flashed erratically round the world, so the world's sporting bodies came to realize the enormous potential and advantage of sending their competitors to international competitions.

The Games are remembered also for a sentence in the Bishop of Pennsylvania's sermon – mis-attributed to de Coubertin: 'The important thing in the Olympic Games is not winning but taking part. The essential thing in life is not conquering but fighting well'. What de Coubertin did was to take up these words and on July 24 at a banquet in London say 'Last Sunday during the sermon organized at St Paul's in honour of the athletes, the Bishop of Pennsylvania made the point that "the important thing in these Olympics is not so much winning as taking part". The important thing in life is not the victory but the battle. The essential thing is not to have conquered but to have been a good loser'.

Two men who must certainly have pondered these words were the American 400 metres runners Taylor and Robbins. In the four-man final, the Scotsman Wyndham Halswelle was 'wilfully obstructed' by their compatriot Carpenter, and when the latter crossed the line first he found that the British judge had already snapped the tape crying 'foul'. Carpenter was disqualified and a rerun was ordered, but the other Americans refused to turn out and Halswelle won a unique gold medal – racing against no opponents. His time of 50 seconds was remarkable.

Above Wyndham Halswelle of Great Britain won the 400 metres race on a walk-over—the only time this has ever happened.

Right The previous day John Carpenter of the US, seen walking disconsolately off the track, had been disqualified, after coming in first, for wilfully obstructing Halswelle.

Top right Martin Sheridan, a team-mate of Carpenter, ensures proper decorum by wearing sock-suspenders.

Above The swimming was held in a pool built within the stadium and for the first time inside the athletics track. Standards were generally very good and well ahead of those of previous Olympics, no doubt helped by the excellent design of the pool.

Right One of Ray Ewry's chief rivals in the two standing jumps was the Greek Constantine Tsiklitiras who finished second in both events. In the standing long jump the competitor leaned as far forward as he could, keeping the body straight, and, at the moment of losing control, brought the legs up and leaped as far as possible.

Dorando collapsed shortly after entering the stadium. He was helped to his feet and after this second collapse he was half carried across the winning line. He was then put on a stretcher and rushed to hospital, where it was found that his 'heart had been displaced by half an inch', according to contemporary reports. Not surprisingly, he was disqualified, and the gold medal was awarded to the next man home, Johnny Hayes of the US. Dorando later gained some consolation in the magnificent gold cup which was given to him by Queen Alexandra. He turned professional before returning home to Italy. His signature is at the bottom of the souvenir photograph.

Left Johnny Hayes was carried round the stadium by his team-mates but was almost ignored in the excitement caused by Dorando's collapse.

Dorando with the Queen's Cup.

A Souvenir of
The Marathon Race 1908.

Pietro Dorando
Carpi Italia

1912 Stockholm

One of the greatest sportsmen the twentieth century has seen is Jim Thorpe, half Sac-Fox Indian, half Irishman, who was the first Olympic competitor to suffer from the harsh and wordy rules with which de Coubertin had saddled the Olympics. Thorpe, whose favourite sport was catching wild ponies, enjoyed a remarkable sporting record at Carlisle Indian School in Pennsylvania.

It was early in 1912 that Wa-tho-huck (Bright Path), his Indian name, first achieved immortality at an athletics meeting. When the team arrived at the station the Lafayette College officials pointed out that they had forty-eight competitors to Carlisle's seven. Wa-tho-huck finished third in the 100 yards, won the high jump, long jump, shot, discus, and both 120 yards and 220 yards hurdles. Not surprisingly, Carlisle won. Another interesting competitor on that day was a team-mate of Thorpe, Lewis Tewanima, a Hopi Indian, who won two events, went on to finish second in the 10,000 metres at Stockholm and surprisingly was the *only* American to win an Olympic medal in this event until 1964.

In 1912 Thorpe competed against West Point at football, playing the full sixty minutes, and moved one observer, a certain Cadet Dwight Eisenhower, to describe him as 'the greatest football player I have ever seen'. Thorpe was naturally selected for the 1912 Olympics in Stockholm and dominated both the Decathlon and the now discontinued Pentathlon. He was not just a good all-rounder but had a remarkable aptitude for acquiring the necessary techniques for the throwing and jumping events.

He overwhelmed Hugo Wieslander of Sweden in the Decathlon by the ridiculous margin of 688 points. He was also placed seventh in the individual long jump and fourth in the individual high jump. At a time when the world high jump record was 6ft 7in he was supposed to have cleared 6ft 5in. In the 110 metres hurdles shortly after the Stockholm Olympics he actually defeated the new gold medallist Fred Kelly in 15 seconds, a time which equalled the world record. A year after his return to the United States it was found that Thorpe had accepted payment for holiday work in playing baseball during college vacations. The total amounted to cents rather than dollars, and there is no doubt that Thorpe never even realized that the pittance he was accepting to help pay for his food and clothes would later render

Above Britain's winning 4 x 100 metres freestyle relay team of Bella Moore, Jennie Fletcher, Annie Spiers and Irene Steer, with their chaperone Miss Jarvis.

Top left The Swedish coxed fours: Ture Rosvall, Willie Bruhn-Möller, Conrad Brunkman, Hermann Dahlbäck and Wilhelm Wilkens.

him a *cause célèbre*. Thorpe was ordered to forfeit his gold medals but to the credit of Wieslander and Ferdinand Bie, runner-up in the Pentathlon, they refused the medals. Thorpe went on to fulfil a top-class role in football as well as playing major league baseball. In 1932, however, he was too short of money even to buy a ticket for the Los Angeles Olympics. He died in 1953, a poor man with perhaps the consolation that he had been voted three years earlier the greatest male athlete of the first half of the century and the greatest American footballer. An indication of his uncomplicated attitude is his greeting of 'Hi! King' when about to be presented to King Gustav of Sweden.

Stockholm will also be remembered for the first death in an Olympics: Lazaro of Portugal, who collapsed during the Marathon which was held in the most unbearable conditions. Stockholm had a heat-wave on the day and the runners were obliged to compete when the sun was at its highest.

Just as Avery Brundage fought during the 1960s and 1970s to keep the Olympics 100 per cent amateur and to limit the number of events, so in 1909 de Coubertin was asking that the programme be shortened, no doubt influenced by the London Games where tennis, racquets, rugby football, and three women's events—tennis, archery, and skating—had been included. Yet although one or two events were dropped, the Swedes still included such esoteric events as left- and right-handed javelin and discus throwing. For the first time competitors were entered on a national basis and individuals were refused.

As a portent of the future, Hannes Kolhemainen became Finland's first Olympic champion, winning the 5,000 metres, 10,000 metres and 8,000 metres cross-country. Yet Finland were not fully independent, being within the jurisdiction of Russia, whose colours they were forced to accept as their own flag for the Games.

Technically these Games were well ahead of their time, using such aids as electric timing and photo-finish equipment. (It is only since 1964 that the judges have accepted the evidence of the electric timer rather than the human hand.) Charles Perry, the London groundsman who had constructed the original track in 1896, was asked to do the same at Stockholm and it is a credit to his work that even up to the 1970s the same cinder track was still producing world class times when many others had been changed to artificial surfaces.

The two 'forgotten' winners of the Pentathlon and Decathlon are seen in action above—Hugo Wieslander of Sweden (top) and Ferdinand Bie, who refused to accept Thorpe's medal after his disqualification.

The peerless Jim Thorpe of the US displays some of his
talents as he crosses the line after winning the 200 metres,
prepares to throw the discus, leaps in the long jump and
poses in the dress of the sport, baseball, at which he was
to excel after being banned from the athletics he had
dominated for such a brief period.

Kenneth McArthur (South Africa) struggles to the finish of the Marathon after being prematurely garlanded with a laurel wreath at the end of his 26 miles 385 yards ordeal.

There are only four recorded instances of father and son competing in the same Olympics; three times in yachting and once in shooting, where Alfred and Oscar Swahn (first and third from left) gained many successes for Sweden. Between them they competed in every Olympics from 1908 to 1924, being team colleagues in 1908, 1912 and 1920. They won a total of fifteen medals: three gold, one silver and two bronze were won by the father, Oscar, and three gold, three silver and three bronze were won by the son. Swahn senior was seventy-three when he made his last appearance, Swahn junior forty-five. Alfred won two gold medals and finished fourth twice in the Stockholm Games compared with one gold, one bronze and one fifth place gained by his father. The other marksmen are Ake Lundeberg (second from left) and Per Olof Arvidsson (right).

Above An unusually fine action picture taken during the foil final between the Italians Nedo Nadi, the winner (left), and Pietro Speciale.

Below A judge gets down to the heart of the action in the 10km walk, where George Goulding (Canada), the eventual winner, is fractionally ahead of the silver medallist-to-be, Ernest Webb (left).

1920 Antwerp

Between 1912 and 1920 the world was turned upside down by war and its aftermath. For the first time, a modern Olympics had to be cancelled. It was to have been staged at Berlin in 1916. Curiously enough when in 1940 another Olympics had to be cancelled because of war, the venue was to have been Japan.

In April 1919 the IOC (International Olympic Committee) decided in favour of Antwerp, Belgium, instead of the first choice of Hungary, one of the defeated nations. Antwerp could scarcely have been (from a sporting point of view) a less apt decision, with few facilities and little athletic tradition. Austria, Bulgaria, Germany, Hungary and Turkey as defeated nations were not invited and another absentee was Russia. Again the admirable Perry was asked to build the track.

For the first time the Olympic five-ringed flag, which had been chosen in 1913, was on view. De Coubertin adapted the five rings on the altar at Delphi to signify the unity of the five continents; the colours blue, black and red (at the top) and yellow and green (underneath) were selected as at least one of these colours was included in all the member nations' flags. The Olympic oath was also proclaimed for the first time, by Belgian farmer Victor Boin. Credit must be given to the resilience of the Olympic movement in producing 'unity' after the holocaust of 1914-18.

The major talking point of 1920 was not the gold medal won by 14-year-old Aileen Riggin, the American diver, nor the victory of the American rugby team, nor the first appearance of Paavo Nurmi, nor the disqualification of the Czechoslovak soccer team for walking off the pitch, but the 'revolt of the *Matoika*'. The American team travelled across the Atlantic on the *Princess Matoika*, known as the 'death ship', which had been used to return home American dead from the First World War. Conditions were unbearable and the team, many ex-servicemen, formed a committee of protest. The protests were to all intents ignored but there were promises that Antwerp would provide reasonable accommodation. This was not so and what started off as the revolt of the *Matoika* carried through to another revolution in Antwerp. The American living quarters were former barracks, and when Dan Ahearn, the veteran triple jumper, was suspended for refusing to live in official quarters, the entire US team threatened to boycott the Games. These incidents undoubtedly reflected on the American results, and they had far fewer successes than had been expected.

Mon cher Collègue,

Vous ne serez pas surpris que, la guerre se prolongeant, je n'aie pu consentir, malgré mon âge, à n'y point participer. Vous comprendrez aussi que, m'étant engagé, je juge incorrect que notre Comité soit présidé par un soldat. J'ai donc prié notre Collègue et ami, le Baron Godefroy de Blonay, d'exercer les fonctions de président par intérim. Aussi bien est-il rationnel que la direction du Comité dont le siege est à Lausanne, se trouve entre ses mains pendant la durée des hostilités. Vous connaissez sa compétence et son dévouement. Je vous demande de lui donner votre confiance et votre appui ainsi qu'à notre cher secrétaire le Comte Brunetta d'Usseaux.

Ce m'a été un grand réconfort de constater que la plupart d'entre vous êtes en plein accord avec moi en ce qui concerne l'avenir olympique. Nous avons restauré une institution séculaire et non passagère. Quelque terribles que soient les commotions présentes, le cours de l'histoire n'en saurait être interrompu et l'Olympisme est rentré dans l'histoire.

Je compte absolument qu'avec ou sans moi, vous continuerez d'en diriger le développement et je saisis cette occasion de vous dire à tous, avec mon fidèle attachement, ma profonde gratitude pour les vingt années que nous avons vécues en un effort commun.

Votre affectionné

Pierre de Coubertin

Left In the letter written shortly after the outbreak of the First World War, de Coubertin says he intends to join up and that he judges it incorrect that the IOC should be headed by a soldier. He has decided to hand over the presidency *par interim* to Baron Godefroy de Blonay.

Below An exuberant Charles Paddock throws both arms in the air even before he breaks the tape in the 100 metres, ahead of his team colleague Morris Kirksey (left) and Harry Edward of Great Britain.

Right Frank Foss of the US gracefully clears the winning height in the pole vault.

Aileen Riggin (left) of the United States, who won the first women's springboard title a few days after her fourteenth birthday, and was the youngest gold medallist until Marjorie Gestring in 1936. Four years later Aileen became the only competitor to win both swimming and diving medals by coming third in the 100 metres backstroke in Paris, where she was also silver medallist in the springboard diving.

ÉQUIPE NATIONALE DES ÉTATS-UNIS D'AMÉRIQUE
Champions des Olympiades d'Anvers

Above At a time when British rugby was ahead of the world, it seems unthinkable that the United States should win the Olympic title, but no team was entered from Great Britain due to the demands of the domestic rugby programme. Only two teams entered, from the United States and France, the latter still much affected by the loss of personnel due to the war.

Below The middle-distance double of 800 and 1,500 metres is a rare feat in Olympic history. The first man to do it was Albert Hill of Great Britain, seen winning the 800 metres with ease. The second double did not come until forty-four years later, when Peter Snell triumphed for New Zealand in Tokyo.

1924 Paris

After the fiasco in 1900, de Coubertin decided that the thirtieth anniversary of the modern Olympics would be a fine occasion to bring the Games back to Paris. They were dominated by two men, Johnny Weissmuller, later to achieve fame as a film Tarzan, and Paavo Nurmi.

In the face of remarkable opposition Weissmuller won two individual swimming gold medals, the 100 metres and the 400 metres. He also won a gold in the 4 × 200 metres freestyle relay and a bronze medal as a member of the American water polo team. He prevented the Hawaian Duke Kahanamoku from winning a third successive gold medal in the 100 metres; and in what has been described as one of the finest races of all time, defeated the Swede Arne Borg and 'Boy' Charlton of Australia, in the 400 metres.

Nurmi by any account must be the greatest athlete the world has so far seen. In a sport measured critically by medals and against the clock, he comes out top in both. He set twenty-two ratified world records and his haul of nine Olympic titles is approached only by Ray Ewry's eight, all of which he won for the now obsolete standing-jumping events. Nurmi made his debut at the Olympics in 1920, with second place in the 5,000 metres and victories in the 10,000 metres and cross-country individual and team races.

In a deliberate move to break the Finn's monopoly of middle and long distance gold medals, the International Amateur Athletic Federation changed the athletics programme and placed the finals of the 1,500 metres and 5,000 metres within an hour of each other. (Nurmi later set world records for both events under similar conditions.) Even being entered for the 1,500 metres, 3,000 metres team race, 5,000 metres and cross-country was not enough. He was bitterly disappointed when he was told that his main rival and fellow-countryman Ville Ritola would be his country's representative in the 10,000 metres.

Nurmi's week went thus: July 6, while Ritola was winning the 10,000 metres in a world record time, Nurmi in a training session ran faster on his own! July 8 and 9, the 5,000 metres and 1,500 metres heats, which he won easily. July 10, 1,500 metres. He covered the first 500 metres faster than either Herb Elliott or Jim Ryun when setting their world records in 1960 and 1967. At the start of the last lap Nurmi checked the stop watch he always carried when running, tossed it gently on to the grass, and continued at the same unbelievable pace. Within the hour he was lining up for the 5,000 metres final. Nurmi faced Ritola and another old rival in the Swede Edvin Wide. Ritola just managed to hold on until the last lap, when Nurmi inexorably drew ahead to win. The next day, July 11, in the 3,000 metres team race heats, he dropped back time after time to shepherd the rest of his team to the front. The Finns and Nurmi won. July 12 saw possibly his greatest ever race, the 10,000 metres cross-country held in a temperature of over 100°. Twenty-four of the thirty-nine competitors gave up and many of those who finished had their feet heavily bandaged. Nurmi, the comfortable winner, was unbothered, took off his shoes, posed for photographs and as he was about to leave the stadium there was a great shout. The second man was in sight. Nurmi turned round, saw it was Ritola and grinned broadly. On the following day Nurmi won his fifth gold medal, the 3,000 metres team race. It was the greatest week's running by one man before or since.

Both as a swimmer and as a screen star ('Tarzan'), Johnny Weissmuller of the US was something special, bringing a dynamic quality to both roles. In swimming he broke through barriers hitherto thought to be insuperable. He achieved a total of twenty-four world records and is said never to have lost a race from 50 yards to 880 yards in ten years of competition. In two Olympics he won five gold medals and one bronze. In this picture, he stands proudly between 'Boy' Charlton of Australia (left) and Arne Borg of Sweden, third and second in the 400 metres freestyle event.

Left Paavo Nurmi, the Flying Finn, lived by the stop watch and carried one during races. The significance of this was rarely appreciated at the time and there are few recorded instances of his actually checking the dial. Here, during one of his great races in Paris, he appeared unworried about the opposition, the best the world had to offer, as he checked his stop watch to see if he was far enough ahead of record-breaking schedules.

Top right Harold Abrahams dives in perfect style across the line to become the first European titleholder of the 100 metres, despite a poor start by his own standards.

Centre right Lawn tennis was staged for the last time in an Olympics at these Games. The women's doubles champions were Helen Wills (foreground) and Hazel Wightman (right) of America, shown during their finals match against the British pair Phyllis Covell and Kathleen McKane. Mrs Wills also won the singles.

Bottom right Eric Liddell, Scotland's greatest athlete, was almost champion by default. A 200 metres runner, he entered the 400 metres only because the final of the 200 metres was on a Sunday, and won. On his return, still wearing his victor's laurel, he was triumphantly taken on a tour of Edinburgh by University 'Blues'.

Far right John Kelly, father of Princess Grace of Monaco, who was refused membership of Leander on the basis that he was an 'artisan', shakes hands with the American ambassador in Paris after his victory in the double sculls. His partner, Paul Costello, is on the left.

1928 Amsterdam

Nurmi had become something of a recluse in 1927 and 1928. He had been frequently beaten in short distance races – frequently for him that is – and retired from the public eye to meditate on his defeats and to train. He suffered violently from some form of rheumatism, no doubt due to the excessive road training he did, in those days without the advantages of modern medicine. Even the Finnish Olympic Committee did not know if Nurmi would compete and they must have felt relieved when he arrived on the pier, luggage in hand, when the boat taking competitors to Amsterdam was about to leave.

He had definitely reverted to the sombre cast of mind for which he was known. He won the 10,000 metres again, thus regaining the title he won in 1920, but unlike Paris where he received the plaudits of the crowd and the congratulations of the opposition, at the Amsterdam Games he refused to shake hands with anyone or discuss the race. That he finished second in the 5,000 metres to his old rival Ville Ritola is from an athletics standpoint completely logical, for with his background of huge training mileage he was obviously better equipped for a 10,000 metres than a 5,000 metres. This strength-work stood him in good stead when he decided to run in the steeplechase, an event at which he was completely inexperienced. Nevertheless, he finished second, sandwiched between two other Finns.

It was to be Nurmi's last Olympics. He continued to train and race as much as ever, running distances from 1,500 to 20,000 metres both in Europe and America. There was every expectation that he would set the seal on his career by winning the Marathon at Los Angeles in 1932. However, during some of his barn-storming tours he had accepted payments in excess of the permitted legal expenses and the International Amateur Athletic Federation declared him ineligible.

Finnish athletes reached a peak at these 1928 Games, winning all track events from 1,500 metres upward and taking nine out of a possible twelve gold medals, plus victories in the javelin and Decathlon. They were never again to reach such heights.

Johnny Weissmuller, 'Boy' Charlton and Arne Borg dominated the swimming as in 1924. On the track the women's 800 metres caused the greatest controversy. It was the first time the event had been held and so many of the girls finished distressed that it was not to reappear in the Olympics until 1960.

These were the first Games at which de Coubertin was not present. He had given up the Presidency of the IOC in 1925: the years of travelling round the world had taken their toll on his health and on the family exchequer. Sports whose inclusion he had attacked, slipped back in – such as hockey – and more and more women's events, which he had also opposed, were included.

The Dutch had been among the original supporters of the Olympic movement. They had previously applied unsuccessfully for the 1916, 1920 and 1924 Games. The Stadium for 1928 was built on forty acres of swamp in south Amsterdam and 4,500 piles had to be driven into the ground as foundations. These Games set various precedents: an Olympic flame burned throughout the Games, and there was a large results board to inform the spectators what was going on.

Below Some of the greatest duels Paavo Nurmi had were with fellow-countryman Ville Ritola. Nurmi took delight in tormenting him in races, running close at his shoulder, and often drawing away when Ritola thought he had the race won. Here, an already haggard Ritola is attempting to force the pace in the 10,000 metres, but there is nothing he can do and Nurmi will soon accelerate sufficiently to win by three-fifths of a second but with plenty in hand. Ritola, however, had his revenge in the 5,000 metres.

Top Hildegard Shräder (Germany) is a few strokes from setting a world record in the 200 metres breaststroke.

Above and right The start and finish of the women's 800 metres, which was not to take place again until 1960, because of the distressed state of so many of the competitors. The winner was Lina Radke-Batschauer (Germany) from Kinuye Hitomi (Japan).

1932 Los Angeles

For the first time an Olympic village was constructed to house the 1,300 male competitors (the 120 women were separated in a hotel). Although forty countries managed to make the trip, the distance and time involved in travelling meant small entries from European countries. This did not extend to the Japanese who were gradually becoming more and more of a power both in track and field events and in swimming. At Los Angeles they won five of the six men's swimming titles, Yasuji Miyazaki being a dual medal winner, and took second place in the women's 200 metres breaststroke.

By now the Winter Olympics, another innovation which de Coubertin had contested, were well established and the Winter Games at Lake Placid earlier in the year were the third to take place. The Scandinavians and Finns had consistently dominated the ski-ing; this year Norway, Sweden and Finland won all twelve medals in the four events. It was at Lake Placid that the one person who has done more to popularize ice skating than any other swept to international fame. Sonja Henje had competed in the first Winter Olympics at Chamonix in 1924, finishing last of eight in the figure skating. Between 1927 and 1936 she won ten successive world championships, three Olympic gold medals, and six successive European titles from 1931. The theatrical flair that she showed in the Olympics was eventually to bring her a fortune in films and ice shows, perhaps the greatest example of an Olympics amateur exploiting her talents in a commercial market.

At Los Angeles an 18-year-old schoolgirl Mildred Didrikson, one of the greatest of all natural sportswomen, won the 80 metres hurdles and javelin but was placed second in the high jump when her 'dive roll' technique was judged illegal. A girl of remarkable reserves, she had competed in eight events within two and a half hours in the American Women's Championships, winning five of them and gaining enough points to win the team title *on her own*, beating among others a 22-woman club from Illinois. Banned in December 1932 for allowing her name to be used in a sales promotion campaign, 'Babe' as she was always known, became a vaudeville artist. In 1934 she took up competitive golf, winning every major title in the world, including the British Ladies, US Open and World Championships. She had a drive of between 280 and 300 yards, such as most men would envy, and once reached 346 yards.

It is a tragic coincidence that two such great sportswomen should have died of a similar disease. Sonja Henje succumbed to leukaemia aboard an aeroplane from Oslo to Paris, seeking urgent medical treatment; while Babe Zaharias (she had married the famous wrestler, George Zaharias) had her life cut short by cancer.

Above Sonja Henje of Norway, three times winner of the ice skating, seen during one of the cheerfully happy displays which endeared her to spectators—and won her titles too.

Below John Anderson (United States) hurls the discus 162ft 4½in to break the Olympic record.

Right Imre Petnehazy captured in dramatic pose as his horse, Aerounta, appears to land on its nose during the riding event of the modern Pentathlon.

Above The South African, David Carstens, floors Peter Jörgensen of Denmark, during their light-heavyweight semifinal. At the end of a seesaw match Carstens gained the verdict and went on to win the gold medal. Jörgensen was the bronze medallist.

Top right Bob Tidsall, of Ireland, knocks over the hurdle, which under the rules then in force robs him of a world record. His winning time of 51.8 seconds was in fact two-tenths of a second inside the existing record set four years earlier by Morgan Taylor and subsequently equalled by Glenn Hardin.

Right and far right Babe Didrikson (of the US) pictured in the 80 metres hurdles, one of two events she won. She also took second place in the high jump.

1936 Berlin

The 1936 Games were to be held in Berlin, an opportunity of which Adolf Hitler (who had come to power in 1933) was determined to take full political advantage. His intention was to display the discipline his National Socialist régime had imposed on the Germans, and to demonstrate the mastery of the Aryan race, which would defeat any competition, especially from those he considered 'inferior', such as the Negroes. Thanks to Leni Riefenstahl's magnificent film we can see today that the Berlin Olympics were a massive achievement of planning and presentation. It was, incidentally, the first time that details of every single heat, jump or throw were committed to posterity.

At the Winter Games in Garmisch-Partenkirchen and in Berlin, Hitler revealed the extent of his personal backing by approving a virtually open-ended budget. He ordered all Government departments to allow sportsmen in their employment unlimited time off to train. The German Olympic Committee ran a training camp in the Black Forest for months before.

Hitler himself attended both the opening and closing ceremonies and was present at many of the athletics competititions. But a major rebuff was awaiting him.

Jesse Owens, a Negro from Cleveland, Ohio, established himself indelibly as *the* athlete of the Games. Owens won four gold medals – in the 100 metres, 200 metres, long jump and sprint relay – each an Olympic record. He had already, on May 25, 1935, broken or equalled six world records within the space of 75

Top left The closing ceremony and searchlights, soon to be used for warlike purposes, sweep the sky.

The Nazi attitude towards the Olympics is epitomized by the ordered ranks of military uniforms and swastika banners, as the torch enters the last stage of its relay from the sacred grove of Olympia.

minutes. Owens' long jump record stood until 1960. Even his 200 and 220 metres records stayed intact until 1949.

The memory of 1936 will inevitably be one of the Nazi salute (which to their credit the British team refused to make at any time), the rhythmical chanting of the crowds and the remarkable gymnastic displays.

De Coubertin's voice was played over the loud-speaker at the opening of the Games. An old man now, he cannot have been at all happy at this blatant national-ism. It was completely contrary to anything he had envisaged. Just over a year later, de Coubertin died, almost penniless, in Geneva. He was buried in Lausanne where the International Olympic Committee had taken up residence, but his heart was removed and placed in a specially erected monument in the Sacred Grove of Olympia.

The victor of the single sculls, Gustav Schäfer, is an ironical contrast as he thrusts out his right arm while the left hand supports the traditional laurel wreath, signifying, among other things, peace.

Jessie Owens of the US is a study in power and muscle as he prepares to destroy German hopes in the 100 metres (far left), lands well ahead of the existing Games record in the long jump (top), rounds the bend in the 200 metres (left) and leaps high in incomparable style (above).

One of the well-ordered gymnastic displays which were a
feature of the Berlin Games.

Right An extract from Leni Riefenstahl's famous film shows why Forrest Towns of the US was the greatest high hurdler of his time. Using a double-arm shift technique, he won easily from Britain's Don Finlay (foreground). Towns was the first man to crack the 14-second barrier for both 110 metres hurdles and 120 yards hurdles.

1948 London

Fanny Blankers-Koen, the Flying Dutchwoman, wins the 100 metres, beating Dorothy Manley of Great Britain on extreme left and then walks through the rain (right) carrying a bedraggled bouquet. Mrs Blankers-Koen won four gold medals, in the 100 metres, 200 metres, 80 metres hurdles and sprint relay.

The 1940 Games were scheduled for Tokyo, but hostilities intervened and the Games were offered hopefully to Helsinki. They were then finally cancelled. The eighteenth Olympics in 1944 which were offered to London were also cancelled. With the coming of peace, London took on the task of organizing the Games for 1948 – which proved to be the largest Games up until then. The figure of 4,700 competitors was 600 more than at Berlin. There were fifty-nine nations represented compared with forty-nine in Berlin.

The traditional British talent for improvization has never been put to better use than in organizing the Games at Wembley. Everything was against the organizing committee. It was the days of rationing, of 'spivs' dealing in black market goods, of a shortage of most things and the non-availability of others. Austerity was the national keynote of the time. But the Olympics somehow rose above it all.

As in 1920, the defeated 'aggressor nations' were not invited – Germany, Italy and Japan. In Europe, only neutral Sweden and Switzerland had survived with their sporting continuity intact. On the other hand, not one major sports meeting had taken place in London since 1939.

The Games in traditional fashion opened in blazing sunshine, which later gave way to torrential rain. While no male athlete was able to score a double victory, for the first time since 1896 the focus swung to the women. Fanny Blankers-Koen, a Dutch housewife of thirty, took her place alongside the Olympic immortals by winning the 100 metres, 200 metres, 80 metres hurdles and sprint relay.

In contrast to the smooth flowing Scandinavian running there appeared the first hint of Eastern European power in the form of Emil Zatopek, whose best achievement up to that time had been a fifth place in the European 5,000 metres Championships in 1946. If Zatopek's ungainly style and grimacing face may have been painful to the watching crowd, it was soul-destroying for the runners who had no reply to his repeated surges, which won him the 10,000 metres. His method of training in army boots and against the elements was eventually to change the pattern of distance training. Delfo Cabrera who won the Marathon gold medal for Argentina informed the world's press that he trained only 36 miles a week. Soon teenagers were to be training that much each day.

One man who epitomizes Olympic competition is Karoly Takacs, a Hungarian army sergeant who was national pistol champion. Earlier in his career a grenade had exploded in his right hand. He taught himself to shoot with his left, and crowned his career with a gold medal in London. Even this title was hard won for shortly after reloading, his pistol accidentally went off. The umpire counted this as a failure shot. Only after a lengthy deliberation by the jury was he allowed to fire again.

Another gold medallist in London was Humberto Mariles Cortes, a Mexican army officer, who won a gold medal in the individual and team equestrian events of

the Grand Prix des Nations. As a result of this success it was decided in 1965 that Cortes, then a general, would organize the equestrian events for the 1968 Olympics in his home country. In 1967 he was involved in a car accident in which a man was killed. His job was taken from him, but during the Mexico Games he was allowed to receive visitors and watched the entire competitition on a colour television set.

Torbay, where the yachting was held, saw the first of a long series of successes for the Dane Paul Elvström. He was to go on to win in 1952 at Helsinki, in 1956 at Melbourne and finally in 1960 at Rome. He had retired from competitive racing at the time of the Tokyo Games in 1964, but in 1968 he emerged once more and finished fourth in the Star Class.

Another great campaigner of 1948 who was to achieve notable success in other Olympiads was the canoeist Gert Fredriksson of Sweden. Between these Games and Rome in 1960 he totalled six gold, one silver and one bronze medal.

From the aesthetic point of view the peak performance was possibly that in the Decathlon, in which a raw 17-year-old American from Tulare, Bob Mathias, who had not tackled the event before that year, emerged to beat the world's greatest all-rounders. In a sport in which technical brilliance is at a premium, Mathias won with a total of 7,139 points, more than 150 ahead of the second man–an amazing margin considering the conditions and the length of the competition.

Top right and right In a sport where nerves need to be firmer than steel, Nino Bibbia qualifies fully. Winner of the skeleton toboggan event, the Italian competed continuously through to the early seventies, winning many championships.

Right Arthur Wint beats fellow Jamaican, Herb McKenley, in a classic 400 metres final, later to finish second in the 800 metres. Four years later Wint was again to finish runner-up in the 800 metres. By a strange coincidence McKenley again took the silver medal in the 400 metres behind a Jamaican, not Wint, who this time was fifth, but George Rhoden.

Below In weightlifting, where size is important, Joseph de Pietro of the US earns a special mention for becoming the smallest-ever Olympic champion. His height was 1.42 metres (4ft 8in) yet he set a world bantamweight record with his total lift of 307.5kg.

1952 Helsinki

Above Paavo Nurmi, who twenty years earlier had been banned from taking part in the Marathon at Los Angeles, lights the Olympic flame at the opening ceremony.

Right Emil Zatopek grimaces his way to another Olympic record in the 10,000 metres.

Below Chris Chataway of Great Britain has fallen and Emil Zatopek (Czechoslovakia), elbows firmly akimbo, heads for the tape in the 5,000 metres – and his second of three gold medals.

The year 1952 saw the intervention for the first time of a team from the Soviet Union. In the pre-Bolshevik era certain Russians had competed, all from the higher social strata. The Soviet Union had sent observers to the 1948 Olympics, and acted in earnest on their reports. They arrived in Helsinki with a massive contingent, extremely well prepared. They won a hatful of medals, though none were gold, in the men's athletics, but it was their women athletes who really gave a hint of the impending Red dominance. The men proved in weight-lifting, wrestling, boxing, shooting, gymnastics and rowing that there was a source of sporting wealth to be released once international competitions increased.

The new era of distance running was confirmed – epitomized by Emil Zatopek, the Czechoslovakian army officer who had not started competitive running until he was eighteen. Not only did he retain his 10,000 metres title and add to it the 5,000 metres crown, but in his very first Marathon he decimated the world's greatest. A wonderfully open, cheerful man, Zatopek approached Jim Peters from Britain, at that time the world's best Marathon runner, before the race asking for his advice. Peters's answers satisfied Zatopek and he kept pace with him for mile after mile. After sixteen miles he turned to Peters and said 'We go a little faster, yes?' Peters went faster but there was the Czechoslovak shadow, trotting alongside and saying with a grin 'Don't we go faster?' The psychological effect was shattering. Peters did not even finish the race and Zatopek went on to win in an Olympic record. His wife Dana won the javelin to make it a unique husband-wife double.

One decision of significant proportions was taken shortly before the Games opened – just how momentous nobody was to know. It was the election of Avery Brundage, the Chicago millionaire who had started life as a penniless orphan, as President of the IOC – a post he was to hold until 1972. Known as 'Slavery Bondage' for his rigid adherence to de Coubertin's rules, Brundage from that day set out on a one-man campaign fighting the influence of commercialism and the weakening of amateur ideals. In this connection he fought a running war with the International Ski Federation. Unceasingly he attempted to limit the size of the Games and guarded against undue expenses and payment for loss of earnings while training and competing.

It was a pleasant gesture of consolation that the Finnish organizing committee should have selected Paavo Nurmi to carry the torch into the Stadium. Nurmi, who on the eve of another Games twenty years earlier had been declared a tainted professional.

In the football stadium the stylish Hungarians were to win the soccer competition – an event which influenced the whole course of the game. Only a year later almost the same team defeated England at Wembley Stadium, London – the first time they had been beaten by a non-British team.

Above Exhultation comes in a different way for the father of Jean Boiteux, who, like all good Frenchmen, keeps his beret on after leaping into the water to congratulate his son on his 400 metres freestyle victory.

Left Emil Zatopek's wife, Dana, turns a cartwheel after winning the javelin and the family's fourth gold medal in the Games.

Far left 'I'm over!' shouts a delighted Bob Richards of the US after the pole vault that gave him the gold medal. He went on to retain his title in 1956.

Above Britain's women high jumpers finished second in every Olympics from 1936 to 1960. One of the girls who prevented a British victory was Esther Brand of South Africa, seen using the scissors style during the competition.

Right No handicapper could have envisaged a closer finish than this in the 100 metres. The placings from top to bottom were: Vladimir Soukharev (fifth), Herb McKenley (second), Lindy Remigino of the US (first), Dean Smith (fourth), McDonald Bailey of Great Britain (third) and John Treloar (sixth). The first four clocked 10.4 seconds, the last two 10.5 seconds.

Above Avery Brundage was three times all-round champion of the United States and finished fifth in the Pentathlon in Stockholm in 1912. The same determination and dedication he had shown as a competitor were to be displayed when he was elected President of the International Olympic Committee shortly before the Games opened in Helsinki.

1956 Melbourne

Melbourne opened a new chapter in the history of the Olympics. It was the first time a city outside the United States or Europe had been allowed to act as hosts, creating a special problem for the equestrian events. Owing to severe quarantine laws, the horse events were held in Stockholm; the first time the International Olympic Committee allowed any event to be split from the main Games. However, between June when the equestrian events were held and November 22, when the Games opened at Melbourne, a more bitter contest took place in Budapest. Hungarians were fighting the Russian invaders, and such was the confusion that the Hungarian team made their way independently across the world to Melbourne in ones and twos. Many did not return home, preferring to seek asylum abroad, such as Laszlo Tabori, one of the finest 1,500 metres runners of the day. The British team contributed clothes, pocket money, even running spikes and swimming trunks for the exhausted Magyars.

The Hungarians gained a minor revenge in one event, anyway. The water polo match against the Russians was bitterly fought, and those who watched the battle still speak with awe of the conflict. Hungary went on to win the gold medal, the USSR the bronze.

Russia's great hope was their distance champion, the Leningrad sailor Vladimir Kuts, in the 10,000 metres. He was thought to be evenly matched by the British hope Gordon Pirie. Having been the cause of a false start, Pirie held back fractionally for the second 'off' and Kuts rushed to the front. Pirie steadily moved up to his shoulder but after a couple of laps two Australians moved up ahead of Kuts and cut in front of him, almost causing him to stumble. Kuts responded with a fantastic spurt with only the British record holder holding on. The Russian surged time and again, forcing Pirie to break rhythm. The track was in an atrocious state, like sand, but such was their speed that although they were running a lane wide throughout, to avoid the pot holes in the first lane (and the runners they were lapping), Pirie reckons they broke 'world records' for four and five miles. With four (of the twenty-five) laps to go, Pirie thought the medal was his. He was on the inside with Kuts at his shoulder. But he underestimated the Russian who somehow found the energy to put in another burst after Pirie had tactically let him take the lead. Pirie struggled to hang on. But Kuts gradually opened a vital gap, and this time Pirie had no answer. He struggled on to finish eighth at a walking pace. Yet there is no doubt that he was the second best runner in the world on the day.

Kuts said later that had Pirie responded that last time he would have crumbled, and the psychological effect on Pirie would have been quite different. Five days later, Kuts demolished Pirie again, in the 5,000 metres, but this time the Briton managed to hold on to second place.

Another Briton was at the centre of a big track drama. Chris Brasher went to Melbourne as Britain's third string in the steeplechase, never having won even a national title. It was on the last lap that Brasher saw his chance. He was lying a close second to the Hungarian Sandor Rozsnyoi. He and Ernst Larsen of Norway lying third, simultaneously decided to pull out on this last bend, but as Brasher made his last surge, his left arm hit Larsen in the stomach.

Brasher finished first by 2.4 seconds, and Larsen lodged no complaint. But the Australian judges, unfamiliar with international steeplechasing, did. The jury awarded first place to the world record holder Rozsnyoi. The British protested. For three hours the runners endured an agonizing wait. Then came the verdict: his action was not considered 'wilful', Brasher's gold medal was restored. This victory was the supreme example of reaching fitness at the right time, for he ran six seconds faster than he had ever previously achieved.

Charlie Dumas, the first man to high jump more than 7 feet, rounded off a superb season with a victory. Al Oerter won what was to be the first of four successive gold medals in the discus, a unique achievement, and a third American Hal Connolly, despite an arm that a childhood disease had left wasted, won the hammer. At these Games Connolly met a beautiful Czech discus thrower Olgo Fikotova, the Olympic Champion, and after a long and difficult courtship managed to marry 'across the curtain' following the personal intervention of the American and Czech Presidents. Larissa Latynina, of Russia, distinguished herself by winning four gold and one silver medal in the gymnastics, a total almost equalled by her team colleague Viktor Chukarin with three gold, one silver and one bronze. India won the hockey for the sixth successive time, a record for a team game until the Americans won their seventh consecutive basketball title in 1968.

Betty Cuthbert (Australia, No. 466) hurtles down the straight for victory in the 100 metres. She also won the 200 metres and was a member of Australia's sprint relay gold medal squad. After retiring she was to return to the sport eight years later and win the 400 metres in Tokyo.

Above Gerd Potgieter, only a year later to become world record holder in the 440 yards hurdles, crashes over the final barrier in the 400 metres hurdles. He got to his feet again and finished sixth, well behind the winner Glenn Davis (US, right). Shortly before the Rome Olympics Potgieter, then favourite, was forced to withdraw because of injury in a car crash.

Germans and Russians sprawl at the foot of the banking after crashing in the third heat of the 2,000 metres tandem. The Russians were so badly injured that they had to retire.

1960 Rome

Above A barefoot Abebe Bikila of Ethiopia trots down the Appian Way, followed by Rhadi of Morocco, to bring black Africa its first Olympic gold medal.

Right Livio Berruti, in sunglasses as usual, brings the host country their only athletics gold medal, by winning the 200 metres.

Drugs and death in the cycling; frequent cases of heat prostration; a still disputed decision in the 100 metres freestyle swimming and the first African victory in track and field were the outstanding features of the Rome Olympics. For the first time television covered this scene in force – more than 100 television companies seized on the spectacle to present the Games to a massive international audience. The Olympics were staged in the heat of the Italian summer, not a popular time for the tourists, and hotels were filled to advantage without over-straining the capacity of the city. Unfortunately the decision did not take into account the difficulties

raised for the competitors.

A number of teams, the British included, suffered heavily because they arrived too late and were unable to accustom themselves to the sun and temperature. Although Knud Enemark Jensen died after taking a stimulant during the road cycle race, medical evidence suggested that the heat of the day also played a great part in his death.

Electronic timing was available but not made use of in the swimming events, and as a result John Devitt of Australia was wrongly awarded the gold medal over the American Lars Larson in the 100 metres freestyle. Subsequent films confirm the error but the official record has never been changed. Significantly, since then human timing has taken second place to electronics.

The high point of the Games was the dramatic conflict in the Decathlon between Rafer Johnson of America and Yang Chuan-kwang, from Taiwan. Delayed by rain at the start of the first day of this two-day ordeal, Johnson and Yang fought it out until after midnight. The competitors were back at nine o'clock next morning. Thanks to his amazing pole vault ability Yang was a mere 24 points behind after eight events. With one event to go, the 1,500 metres, the American led by a narrow 67 points. Yang therefore had to cover the distance eleven seconds faster than Johnson to win the gold medal. With both men pushing themselves to the limit Yang could only gain one second and had to settle for the silver medal, beaten by 58 points. The American's total of 8,392 points was a new Olympic record.

If it had not been for Wilma Rudolph, the long-legged wonder from the State of Tennessee, the US would have been without a victory in the women's events. Wilma had been so crippled by poliomyelitis as a child that she could not walk properly till she was eight. But she set an Olympic record in the 100 metres dash, set another in her qualifying heat of the 200 metres dash, and won the final going away. She was also the key to the US victory in the 400 metres relay with her tremendous drive in the anchor leg. When the spectators saw the unknown Ethiopian Abebe Bikila waiting with the rest of the runners for the start of the Marathon, the only remarkable thing was that he was barefoot. However, he soon proved his supreme powers by striding out with an extremely fast ten kilometres, to an early lead, and holding off from the established favourites. There were four Africans in the first eight and Bikila's winning time was nearly eight minutes faster than Zatopek's at Helsinki. Bikila followed up this victory with another at Tokyo only a few weeks after an appendectomy. But at the peak of his athletic life he was tragically crippled when his car was turned over, and after spending some years in a wheelchair he died in 1973. What was not appreciated at the time of his triumph was that one of Bikila's great advantages lay in his increased lung capacity resulting from his living at altitude. This knowledge was to alter the entire course of sports training within half a dozen years.

The Winter Games had taken place six months earlier at Squaw Valley, California, and reached a new peak, with 30 nations taking part before 200,000 spectators and more than 100 television companies.

The Russian Press sisters were dominant competitors in the mid-sixties. Tamara (top) was an outstanding shot put and discus thrower, and the younger Irina (above) was the champion of the 80 metres hurdles and the Pentathlon.

Right Another bemedalled Russian was the speed skater, Klara Guseva.

Left 'The Black Gazelle', Wilma Rudolph of the US, youngest of a family of nineteen, wins the 200 metres, one of her three gold medals. Yet at the age of seven she could not walk because of polio.

Left and below Even the photo-finish equipment had trouble in separating the American Otis Davis from the German Carl Kaufmann. They shared the winning time of 44.9 seconds in the 400 metres, a world record, but Davis was just two-hundredths of a second faster.

The powerful control of Bob Hayes of the US, fastest man in the world, as he starts down the 100 metres.

Above and left Vera Caslavska was thrown into the air by her jubilant colleagues after her faultless displays in the gymnastics had won three individual golds for Czechoslovakia.

Overleaf The 400 metres finalists round the bend. The winner was Mike Larrabee of the US (fourth from the left).

Twenty-four years after it had originally been selected as a venue for the Olympics, Tokyo staged the Games. It was to be the last time that women could compete without undergoing an independent sex test to establish their chromosome count, and it saw the end of the mighty Russian muscle women, the sisters Tamara and Irina Press, and the lanky high jumper Iolanda Balas from Rumania. They all won gold medals but retired the following year. Ewa Klobukowska from Poland, who ran the anchor leg in the sprint relay and finished third in the 100 metres, was to suffer the indignity of being found to have an incorrect chromosome count and failed a sex test before the European cup final at Kiev.

The Japanese organization was superb on every count, using technical advances such as computers. In a gesture of international unity, the Olympic flame was lit in the Stadium by Yoshinoro Sakai who was born the same day the atomic bomb was dropped on Hiroshima. The flagpole on which the Olympic flag was raised was exactly 15.21 metres (49ft 10¾ins), the winning length of Mikio Oda's triple jump in 1928.

The Japanese had desperately hoped for one gold medal. Their hopes centred on the Marathon. Kokichi Tsuburaya entered the Stadium behind Abebe Bikila but was overtaken before the tape by Basil Heatley, a British market gardener from Coventry. Tsuburaya suffered mentally so much from this that two years later he was to commit hari kiri, leaving a note apologizing for 'failing' his country. The hosts had the consolation of winning three of the four judo titles, but lost the coveted Open class to the giant Dutchman Anton Geesink.

Don Schollander of America set a record in the swimming by winning four gold medals and, had he been given the chance, could have won a fifth. Two people who were to win a third successive gold medal were Dawn Fraser in the 100 metres freestyle, the forthright Australian who was severely reprimanded for swimming the moat of the Imperial Palace and attempting to haul down the Japanese flag; and Al Oerter of the United States in the discus. Whereas Oerter's achievement was not all that unexpected at his age, 32, Dawn Fraser's success was surprising and unexpected since swimming is a sport where a teenager has a greater physical advantage. Although Dawn Fraser retired shortly after, Oerter continued, and against all odds won a unique fourth gold medal in Mexico City in 1968 while wearing a surgical collar to prevent further damage to the vertebrae at the base of his neck – vertebrae weakened by countless hours of throwing during training.

A few months earlier at Innsbruck, Tony Nash and Robin Dixon won Britain's first Winter gold medal since 1952 and the first ever in a bobsleigh event. Their margin of victory was merely twelve-hundredths of a second over the famous Italians, but it helped to dispel some of the gloom caused by the death in practice of the British tobogganist Kay Skrzpecki and the Australian skier Ross Milne. Lydia Skoblikova, the speed skater, became the first competitor to win four gold medals at a Winter Olympics, setting three records within four days; while Sixten Jernberg, at thirty-five the veteran of one of the toughest of all events, cross-country skiing, won the 50 kilometres marathon and was a member of a winning Swedish 4 × 10 kilometres relay team. This brought his medal tally in three Olympics to four gold, three silver and two bronze.

The US – traditionally dominant on the track and field, but overshadowed in recent Games – scored heavily. Bob Schul from Ohio won the 5,000 metres to become the first US victor in this event. The other outstanding US performances came from Bob Hayes in the 400 metres relay with a final 100 metres time estimated at 9.5 seconds, probably the fastest 100 metres of all time; and the unexpected victory of Billy Mills in the 10,000 metres, another first for the US. Mills, who beat world-record-holder Ron Clarke of Australia into third place, won with a final burst of speed that by this time had become more and more characteristic of the great distance runners, bringing them apparently nearer to sprinters in the handling of the final laps.

Abebe Bikila, the Ethiopian palace guardsman who had won at Rome in 1960 running barefoot, wore shoes this time to repeat his Marathon victory. He broke the record, easily beating the other competitors in 2hr 12min 11sec. After crossing the line he trotted into the midfield to do a few deep knee bends and stretch exercises, more like a man warming up than a competitor who should have been close to exhaustion. As Peter Snell put it later, 'I had thought the cheering for some of the events in the Stadium was enthusiastic but the reception Bikila got at the end of all this made the rest seem like polite applause at a cricket match.' Bikila foreshadowed the problems to face athletes at the next Olympics saying, 'The altitude there (Mexico) is high, just like in Ethiopia. I know I'll do better than in Tokyo.' Perhaps the 1,500 metres showed most clearly the dramatic improvement in standards when the first eight runners all ran faster than the equivalent of a four-minute mile.

Above Penny Snyder (Canada) lies immobile after knocking herself out in the 80 metres hurdles heats.

Right The view seen by the ski jumpers from the 80 metres tower.

1968 Mexico

When the International Olympic Committee voted under rather extraordinary circumstances to allow Mexico City to stage the 1968 Games, not one IOC member realized that a sea-level competitor would be at a disadvantage over those who were born or lived at a high altitude. Eventually they were forced to bow to world-wide pressure and bring in a hasty rule limiting the amount of time spent using Mexican facilities to train above sea level. This of course favoured nations like the Ethiopians and Kenyans who could train naturally at high altitudes. Numerous experiments were undertaken in an effort to nullify the effects of altitude, but there was found to be no substitute to training and living at a height of above 7,500ft, Mexico City level.

Just as Melbourne was overshadowed by the Hungarian uprising, so all eyes were on Czechoslovakia at the time of Mexico City. Vera Cavlaska, who married Czech athlete Josef Odlozil amid scenes of wild enthusiasm in the City's Catholic Cathedral, made Olympic history by winning four gold medals for gymnastics which she later presented to the instigators of Czechoslovakia's bid for independence: Dubcek, Cernik, Svoboda and Smrkovsky. She had won them against all odds, for she had gone into hiding when the Russian tanks advanced, and could only keep fit by humping bags of coal. She was the emblem of Czechoslovak freedom. Not surprisingly when Dubcek was ousted her bold actions in Mexico City were held against her: job after job was closed to her and her husband.

Because of the problems of altitude, athletics naturally attracted the general attention of the Games. The Americans dominated the explosive events such as sprints and jumps. They won gold medals in the 100 metres in which Jim Hines triumphed and in the 200 and 400 metres with Tommie Smith and Lee Evans. Another gold medal came in the 110 metres hurdles won by Willie Davenport. Although David Hemery of Great Britain was to win the gold in the 400 metres hurdles, the Americans continued their domination in the long jump, relays and the women's 100 metres and relay.

The Games were also a triumph in the athletics events for Kenya, who notched up three gold, four silver and a bronze, Kip Keino putting up a tremendous performance in the 1,500 metres to beat American Jim Ryan. This was better than any other country apart from the USSR, who also won three men's events but had no victories in the women's.

Mexico also witnessed the magnificent performances of the Americans in the swimming. The USA's swimmers won more medals than all the other countries put together, an astonishing total of twenty-three gold, fifteen silver, and twenty bronze. It was also a personal triumph for Debbie Meyer, the first girl swimmer to win three gold medals at a single Games.

The altitude was not the only controversial feature of the Mexican Olympics. During the victory ceremonies American Negro medal winners advertised their support for the Black Power campaign by bowing their heads and giving a clenched fist salute during the playing of the US national anthem.

Below At the 1968 Winter Olympics in Grenoble, Peggy Fleming of the US skates with an extraordinary lightness, to win a gold medal in the figure skating event.

Right One of the closest finishes of the Mexico Games. Colette Besson of France (left) robs Lillian Board of Great Britain of a gold medal in the 400 metres.

David Hemery's convincing superiority in the 400 metres hurdles is clearly shown in this photo-finish picture. The Briton's time of 48.1 seconds was a world record. Second man was not, surprisingly, John Sherwood, Great Britain (in foreground), who took the bronze medal, but the West German Gerhard Hennige in lane two.

Above A light-hearted Black Power salute by the winning US 4 x 400 metres relay squad.

Left Dick Fosbury of the US, whose 'flop' action, with his backwards leap, brought a new dimension to high jumping. Within a year, the 'Fosbury Flop' was being used by many of the world's leading high jump exponents—men and women.

Right The precise figures of the Russian Protopopovs, Oleg and Ludmilla, bring them yet another gold medal.

Overleaf Willie Davenport (US, centre) has a fractional lead over his colleague Erv Hall in their classic hurdles duel.

Naftali Temu of Kenya (centre) wins the 10,000 metres,
with Mamo Walde of Ethiopia (right) coming second. Kip
Keino (left) had been lapped in the race, although he won
the 1,500 metres and was second in the 5,000 metres.

Page 97—Top Tommie Smith (US) flings up his arms in
exultation even before he has snapped the thread marking
the finish of the 200 metres. John Carlos (US, left) was
third and Roger Bambuck (France, right) fifth.

Bottom This picture epitomizes the problems of perform-
ing at high altitudes: W. Perera (Ceylon) in agony after
finishing the Marathon at Mexico.

All eighteen stones of Eduard Gushchin (USSR) are behind the 16lb shot tucked neatly into his chin as he balances himself for a final throw. The Russian finished third behind two Americans.

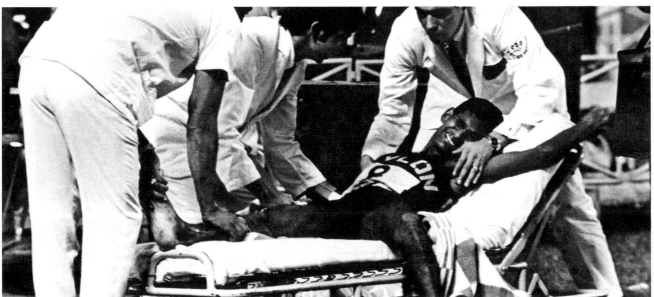

1972 Sapporo

Above Yukio Kasaya, winner of Japan's first ever Winter Games gold medal, who led a clean sweep in the 70 metres ski jump, is chaired by his colleagues.

Right The inherent danger of the luge event is belied by the apparent ease and smoothness with which Wolfgang Scheidel (East Germany) hurtles to victory.

There is unlikely to be another Winter Games quite like that at Sapporo–an event in which there were few heroes or heroines, only an anti-hero in Avery Brundage, the International Olympic Committee President, who waged an ideological war against the skiers with such effect that he, and he alone, manoeuvred the expulsion of the skier Karl Schranz of Austria from the Games. Yet Brundage had arrived in Sapporo with, he said, a list of the names of 40 skiers who were said to have broken the Olympic code because of alleged professionalism. The whole issue of the skiers and amateur-

ism attracted far more attention than the contests waged on the pistes, bob run, snow or ice.

Schranz was adjudged to be more guilty than, for example, Ard Schenk, the Dutch speed skater, or Galina Koulakova, the Russian cross-country skier, each a triple gold medallist, or Marie-Therese Nadig, Switzerland's surprise winner of the downhill and giant slalom. Yet Schenk had attracted as much attention as Schranz did, Koulakova was as 'subsidized' and Mademoiselle Nadig received as many free pairs of skis as Schranz.

Schranz's guilt was not that he was employed by a ski

manufacturer but that he stood for everything Brundage abhorred; a young man making a living out of his success in sport.

Schranz's absence definitely affected the chances of his team-mate Annemarie Proell, favourite in her ski disciplines as Schranz had been in his. Having to carry the weight of her country's hopes on her shoulders proved in the end too great a burden and it was her fate to finish second not once but twice to the 18-year-old Marie Therese Nadig. To be fair, the Austrian girl's defeat was due ·in no small part to the extremely thorough preparation of the Swiss, whose officials had gone to painstaking lengths to ensure the best prepared team – even to the extent of analysing the snow to decide the best possible wax for the skis. Indeed, Switzerland won altogether three gold, two silver and one bronze in the Alpine ski-ing events.

It was the ski-ing that provided the greatest surprise of the entire ten days' competititions when in the final event the completely unknown Francisco Fernandez Ochoa, from Navacherrada, gave Spain their first ever Winter Games medal – a gold in the men's slalom. It is true there were many absentees due to injury and other problems, but Schranz himself would have been the first to praise Ochoa for a victory described by Brundage as 'poetic justice': the win of the underdog over the heavily subsidized national teams of France, Italy, Austria and Switzerland. The Spanish team spent much of the summer training in Chile.

Ochoa showed the mark of a true champion by responding to the pressures that followed his fast first run, in which he led the highly favoured Jean-Noel Augert, of France, by four-tenths of a second. Both Augert and Henri Duvillard, the other French hope, failed to maintain the pace in the second run and Ochoa won in the final tally by more than a second over Gustavo Thoeni – a wide margin in a sport where success is counted in hundredths of a second.

If Ochoa's success was an occasion for Spanish rejoicing the French, in contrast, returned from Sapporo dragging their skis behind them, with their men medalless, complete disaster averted only by Danielle Debernard and Florence Steurer who finished second and third in the slalom behind the American girl Barbara Cochran from Richmond, Vermont. Inevitably an inquiry followed, but unlike many countries where heads would roll, France decided to pour more money into their skiers who in turn attract tourists (thus perhaps proving Brundage's adage that ski-ing is not a sport but a circus). Additionally M. Joseph Comité, Secretary of State for Sport, demanded greater discipline among French athletes.

Scandinavian and Alpine countries have traditionally dominated Winter Olympics, with the US and USSR usually strong. That trend was interrupted at Sapporo by two teams – Japan and East Germany. The Japanese hosts had a clean sweep in the 70-metres ski jump, due perhaps not so much to a general improvement in standards but more to intensive practice on the difficult, changeable conditions on the edge of the hill at Miyanomori. East Germany's imposing list of medals was perhaps predictable in a country where sport is looked on as a means of raising national prestige, and

where training, competition and technique are far more scientific than in most other nations. For these reasons they shone in the luge, winning eight out of nine medals, perhaps because it is an event where, unlike ski-ing, conditions are far more constant and less inspiration is needed, simply a dedication to the event in hand.

The Japanese spent an estimated £22,000,000 to stage these Games. While in the short term this is an extremely large sum, even taking into account the permanent infrastructure such as underground railways and new roads, in the long run it will establish Sapporo as the winter sports centre of Asia.

Right Ard Schenk of the Netherlands, winner of three gold medals in the speed skating, glides through the snowflakes in the 5,000 metres. His other victories were in the 1,500 metres and the 10,000 metres.

Below Francisco Fernandez Ochoa of Spain was the surprise champion of the slalom.

1972 Munich

When the privilege of staging the next Olympics in Munich was conferred on the Germans, there were instant misgivings that there would be a repeat of the 'Hitler Games' of 1936, when an exaggerated nationalism – then inspired by Fascism – prevailed, and international politics weighed heavily. Thirty-six years later, Munich and the Organizing Committee were determined that there would be no repetition of this. They would stage the greatest show on earth, to exceed all previous pageants of the glorification of man's physical prowess and joyful sporting rivalry, with the latest gadgets that computers could evolve, and the best possible facilities for the sportsmen. It would be an Olympic Games more of the twenty-first than the twentieth century. They built an underground railway system, ring roads, the futuristic Olympic Stadium with its acrylic spider's-web roof, a swimming pool in which competitors could perform faster than at any time in history, and they devised computers to provide the minutest detail about the most trivial Olympic fact.

Somehow in the midst of all this the Olympics became dehumanized. Instead of a sports meeting it became a synthesized public relations package, in which the individual became a statistic.

Perhaps 'München 1972' could have been crowned with success if all that had taken place was sport. The 599 gold, silver and bronze medals would have been won and we could have gone home looking forward to Montreal. The exploits of Mark Spitz, winner of seven gold medals in the swimming pool, were amazing. The double victory by Lasse Viren in the 5,000 and 10,000 metres was in its way unique. The vivacious little Russian gymnast, Olga Korbut, displayed such beauty and grace. The strength of the weightlifter, Vassili Alexeev, winner of the super-heavyweight class in weightlifting, was awesome. Yet as the tens of thousands of spectators and competitors packed for home, what did they feel they were leaving? 'A fairground in a graveyard' was how one commentator put it. The $1,971m (about £820m) so painstakingly spent by the Germans to stage their Games could not be measured against the lives of eleven Israeli sportsmen. The kidnapping halfway through the Games by the members of the Black September Movement of nine Israelis after having killed two of them was news which shocked the world into realizing that the Olympics was no longer the oasis of peace on a troubled planet that the International Olympic Committee and the whole Olympic movement had valiantly but vainly attempted to project.

Even before this, the very roots of the International Olympic Committee had been shaken by the debate on whether to expel the Rhodesian team which had come to Munich wearing the Union Jack on their blazers, had accepted the Queen as their head, had recognized the British national anthem and was multiracial. Rhodesia's offence was, of course, that its white minority enjoyed power in government. By the time the Supreme Council for Sport in Africa and the Organization for African Unity had made their threats of boycott, the IOC had no alternative but to take a vote, and the vote by a narrow margin was that the Rhodesians should leave – a decision which proved that the members of this committee were as susceptible to verbal blackmail as

Above Australia's 15-year-old Shane Gould powers to victory in the 400 metres freestyle final to capture her second gold medal in world record time – the second of her three wins.

Above Heide Rosendahl of West Germany was the favourite of the spectators, above all when she won the long jump medal for the host country with a superb world record of 6·78 metres (22ft 3in).

Above and left Russia's Olga Korbut, aged 17, is the darling of the gymnastic hall. Spectators keep up a storm of whistles and booing when the judges score her low after a couple of mistakes on the asymmetrical bars (which Olga mourns, left). But she won gold medals for her beam work and brilliant, coquettish floor exercises.

other mortals. They feared that if they voted to allow Rhodesia to compete, many countries, some no more than dots on the world atlas, but whose presence is felt in the sporting arena, might indeed carry through their threats and pack up and go home. Instead it had to be Rhodesia's athletes, black and white, that were obliged to go home.

International politics became altogether nasty when the Black September gang struck. Early on Tuesday September 5, the news broke to a shocked world that nine Israeli athletes were being held hostage in their second floor quarters in the Olympic village itself by a group of Arab terrorists demanding the release of some two hundred Palestinian guerrilla prisoners then held in Israel. It was known that in the initial skirmish two more Israelis had died. For a whole day – with the Games suspended from mid-afternoon – attempts at bargaining between German officials (guided by Herr Willy Brandt, the West German Chancellor, himself) continued. Then at 9 p.m., the nine hostages and eight captors were moved by helicopter to the neighbouring military airport at Fürstenfeldbruck, apparently with the object of their being flown out to Egypt. Five German police marksmen lay in wait. One was seen by a terrorist, and firing broke out prematurely. Four of the Israelis died when a terrorist detonated a grenade in one of the helicopters. In the shindig four Arabs and all nine Israelis died, and also a German policeman.

The next morning the stadium was given over to a packed and moving memorial service. In place of athletes, Munich's famous orchestra had assembled to perform the Funeral March from Beethoven's Eroica symphony. The Israeli remnant wept quietly in the stands. Avery Brundage, the 84-year-old retiring President of the IOC, spoke pointedly about the double intrusion of politics that had ended in such tragedy. As was said at the service, the 'joyful' Games were over. Joyful or not, they resumed in the afternoon.

The sport itself was marred by squabbles and bad sportsmanship. The IOC felt obliged to censure Vince Matthews and Wayne Collett for showing their contempt for their country by chatting and slouching on the rostrum during the playing of the Stars and Stripes for Matthews' victory in the 400 metres. (Collett, who was second, gave the Black Power salute on leaving the stadium.) Both were banned from the Olympics for life. Five individual competitors were disqualified for taking drugs, which affected three medals. In the 100 kilometres team road-cycling race, one of the Dutch cyclists, who retired with a puncture, was found to have taken a stimulant, and the whole team was disqualified and their bronze medals withdrawn. The unfortunate young American Rick DeMont was ordered to hand back the gold medal he won in the 400 metres freestyle swimming after tests had shown that nose drops he used for asthma contained ephedrine, a proscribed drug. On the other hand, fourteen out of fifty-nine competitors in the Modern Pentathlon who took a tranquillizer in the shooting stage were not disqualified, because of a mix-up in the rules. Perhaps the worst behaviour was that of the Pakistan team after they had lost their final match in the hockey to Germany. They grabbed their silver medals, stamped on them and stuck them in their

The American Wayne Collett, second in the 400 metres, was booed for his behaviour during the playing of his country's national anthem. Here, he gives the Black Power salute as he leaves the stadium. With Vince Matthews, who followed suit, he was to find himself banned from all future Olympics.

Below In the most explosive and narrow track finish of the Games, Dave Wottle (US) who, in the early stages of the 800 metres final, lagged last, separated by as much as 18 yards from the leader, pulls out his characteristic but invariably astonishing final sprint to win in the very last stride by ·03 of a second over Russia's Evgeni Arzhanov, who falls exhausted at the finish.

pockets as a protest against the refereeing. They were later disqualified from the Olympic movement for four years.

On the final day, in an amazing basketball final, the Russians were given the gold medal over the hitherto unbeaten United States. The hooter to sound the end of the match went, erroneously, when there were still three seconds to play. At that moment the Americans were one point ahead. After an intensely exciting game, rejoicing had spontaneously broken out. But the players were called back for the final three seconds. In those three seconds the Russians scored to put them one point ahead. Pandemonium ensued, with the Americans at first refusing to accept the silver medal.

The swimmer Mark Spitz's gold medals marked the greatest individual Olympic haul in one Games. The only comparable achievement has been that of Willes Lee, an obscure American rifleman, who won five golds, one silver and one bronze in the 1920 Games – but they were all in team events. To win his seven gold medals Spitz had to compete thirteen times in a space of eight days, and four events were individual – the 100 and 200 metres freestyle and the 100 and 200 metres butterfly. And if that was not enough, he set a world record in every one of his individual events, while the relay teams of which he was a member also improved the previous world record.

Shane Gould, the 15-year-old Australian, who had come to Munich with an astonishing list of records, swam for seven days, in thirteen races, and returned home, tearfully, with three golds, one silver and one bronze, to her father's comment that no young girl should be allowed to compete so often.

For the first time for several Olympics, the American team – with certain outstanding exceptions – failed to dominate in track and field events in the main stadium. The US girls, for example, were unable to win a single gold medal and only one silver and two bronzes. By

Above Valeriy Borzov (USSR) becomes one of only three Europeans to have won the 100 metres, after America's hopes for the event – Eddie Hart and Rey Robinson – literally missed the bus to the stadium at the second round.

Below The end of a great running career – Jim Ryun of the US, world mile record holder, trips and falls in the semi-finals of the 1,500 metres. The event was then won by Finland's Pekka Vasala, helping to restore little Finland's tradition of Olympic glory.

Above Kenya's Kip Keino pulls off a gamble by winning the 3,000 metres steeplechase (in less than perfect jumping style) after an athletics career in which he had dominated the 1,500 metres. Another Kenyan, Ben Jipcho, took the silver.

Below Lasse Viren, the Helsinki policeman, here leading Mariano Haro (Spain) and Dave Bedford (Britain) in the 10,000 metres, was the first man to pull off both the 10,000 and the 5,000 metres since Kuts 1956.

Above Yorihide Isogai of Japan cannot do much about it when Chris Taylor (US), over 30 stones, settles down on top of him in the freestyle wrestling; but Taylor later lost points for non-aggression and finished up with a bronze medal.

comparison, Britain's Mary Peters (Pentathlon winner), West Germany's Heide Rosendahl (long jump) and the outstanding British girls in the equestrian events – Ann Moore and Mary Gordon-Watson – and above all the little Russian gymnast Olga Korbut, won the spectators' hearts. The American joint world-record holders in the 100 metres, Eddie Hart and Rey Robinson, missed the call to the stadium for the second round of their event, which was run without them. So black supremacy in these events gave way to the Russian Valeriy Borzov, who became the first man since Bobby Morrow in 1956 to win both the 100 and 200 metres.

Not surprisingly, the East Germans, with their ever-increasing emphasis on sport and a budget which in comparison exceeded what most countries spend on armaments, had a most successful Games. With their superb competitors able to produce the best performances on the day, they finished third in the medals table, only lagging behind the Soviet Union and the United States, but well ahead of their neighbours, West Germany. Their women, especially, were awesome in their ability, albeit retaining a remarkable amount of femininity.

Finland, recalling those wonderful days when their ng-distance runners ruled the world (runners such as ι annes Kolehmainen, Paavo Nurmi, Ville Ritola, Volmari Iso-Hollo and Lauri Lehtinen), won the 1,500 metres, that most classic of Olympic events, with Pekka Vasala, and the 5,000 and 10,000 metres with Lasse Viren. Viren, who before the Games had set a world two miles record, broke Ron Clarke's world 10,000 metres record in a race which for Britain was the great disappointment – Dave Bedford, the European champion, finishing only sixth. After the Games, Viren showed his form when he took another of Clarke's records, the 5,000 metres.

Medal-winning had become a habit with some Olympic competitors, not only with Mark Spitz, the American, who could add to his seven Munich gold medals his two golds, one silver and one bronze he won in Mexico, but with West Germany's show jumper Hans Günter Winkler (who in the space of five Olympics won five gold medals – his last at Munich – and one bronze), and another durable cavalier, Piero d'Inzeo from Italy, aged forty-nine, who had been winning medals regularly since 1956, his last a team bronze at Munich. As for gamesmanship, the supreme gesture was surely that of Private John Williams, the master bowman from the USA, who chose to miss the target completely (it was said to be nerves and a strained back) and still finished a double Fédération Internationale de Tir de l'Arc round in a world record 2,528 points.

Many world records were broken. There were moments of high excitement. Yet the consensus was surely that the Olympics had become somehow too obsessive, too frenetic, too bitterly nationalistic. When it was all over, many respected voices were raised suggesting that in Olympic contests to come the number of events should be cut back, team games and aquatic sports held at different places and times in the four-year cycle, that national anthems and flag-raisings should be eliminated, and somehow the delight of competition for its own sake should replace the scramble for medals.

With the conclusion of the grimly shadowed Munich Games comes the simple ceremony at Lausanne (presided over by its mayor, centre) at which the gavel of office is handed over by the outgoing president of the International Olympic Committee, 84-year-old Avery Brundage (left) to the incoming president, Lord Killanin, from Ireland.

As the vast assembly of spectators were expectantly awaiting the arrival of the Marathon front runner, America's Frank Shorter, a young figure of surprising freshness emerged from beneath the tunnel running strongly round the stadium. Applause turned to dismay as spectators realized this was a hoax. Perhaps it was not a great joke. But if a sense of humour means a sense of proportion, perhaps it helped.

1976 Innsbruck

Innsbruck, a city of charm and beauty, where for once the Olympic Games displayed not extravagance and opulence, but modesty, efficiency and friendliness. Innsbruck had taken over the hosting of these Winter Games when Denver was forced to give up the candidature owing to local environmental and financial pressure groups, and had promised to stage them without the huge expense that accompanied the preparations of Tokyo, Sapporo, Munich and Montreal. And how successful they were. Although there was always tight security, there was never a military atmosphere, but one felt secure, as indeed one should, without overt signs.

Sportsmanship was at its height: even the final of the ice hockey between those two political and traditional rivals, the Soviet Union and Czechoslovakia, which could so easily have ended up as disastrously as that famous water polo match between Hungary and the Soviet Union in 1956, was a masterpiece of fair play. True there were troubles: a flu epidemic raged through the village, and this contributed indirectly to the disqualifications by the International Olympic Committee of various competitors.

Galina Kulakova, aged thirty-three, perhaps the most famous of all women cross-country skiers from a country with eight million skiers, finished third in the 5 kilometres but had her bronze medal taken away because the cold pills she had taken showed the minutest traces of ephedrine. These were too small, the IOC Medical Commission admitted, to affect her skiing, but nevertheless rules were rules and out she went. However, she was permitted to compete in the 4×5 kilometres relay and as a member of the victorious Soviet team collected her fourth Olympic gold medal, a very real achievement. And then when flu hit the Czech ice hockey team the doctor, Otto Trefny, unwisely gave Codeine pills to various members but did not report this to the IOC. As a result, when random tests were taken, the Czech team captain, the veteran Frantisek Pospisil, was found to have traces of the proscribed drug in his system. He was disqualified, but it had been his last Olympics anyway, and the doctor was banned for life from being connected with an Olympic team.

These upsets apart, there were some wonderful competitions, particularly in the luge and bob, so splendidly monopolized by the German Democratic Republic, who brought new techniques and a new look to an old sport. They took not simply bob or luge specialists but heavy athletes, a javelin thrower, Meinhard Nehmer, and a hurdler, Bernhard Germeshausen, each man with speed, strength, and sharp reactions, put them in a bob, pointed them at the bottom, and then coached them in the finer points.

Rosi Mittermaier of West Germany came near to winning all three Alpine ski events, but just missed the triple crown by .33 sec., coming second in the giant slalom to Kathy Kreiner of Canada.

The figure skaters followed a stereotyped pattern until along came the European champion, John Curry, eleventh in Sapporo four years earlier, whose Nureyev-style interpretation and bold choice of music made him the darling of the world's television viewers. How could ordinary skaters challenge this young man, who managed to overcome even the traditional East–West bias of the judges and bring to his coach, Carlo Fassi, the first of two gold medals, the second coming from the women's champion, the American Dorothy Hamill, who nevertheless could not show the same beauty, technical fluency and feeling that this Birmingham boy showed. This was only Britain's fifth gold medal since the Winter Games began, but it was one that will long be remembered for its bold, original execution and the controversy that followed when Curry admitted to his unorthodox mode of life.

The ski-ing was a dream for the Austrian hosts for whom at least one victory was essential for their vast winter sports industry which, besides tourism, includes the manufacture of skis, ski clothing, goggles, shoes and so on. Victory came from the man who managed to overcome the favourite's tag, Franz Klammer, who took a gamble at every possible point and just managed to pull off the vital gold medal in the downhill. It had not been easy for him, but he achieved it, and even when an article in an American sports magazine suggested that he received hundreds of thousands of dollars, nothing could tarnish his moment of glory. He had the gold medal and nothing would ever make him give it up.

On the women's side the young German girl, Rosi Mittermaier, decided to follow in the steps of Toni Sailer and Jean-Claude Killy, both of whom won all three Alpine ski events in previous Olympics. She won the downhill by more than half a second, and then the special slalom two days later by ·33 sec. This left her with the giant slalom, but alas she was robbed of the grand slam by the merest of fingernail thicknesses, ·12 sec, less than the time it takes to flick an eyelid, and even her victor, Kathy Kreiner of Canada, must have been a little sorrowful in her moment of joy to have robbed this girl of a unique achievement.

The American contingent also had its successes, chiefly in the speed skating, but of all the surprises the greatest came in the 30 kilometres cross-country skiing event, which has hitherto been reserved for Russians, Scandinavians and Finns. Three years previously, the American Bill Koch decided at the age of seventeen to devote himself simply to cross-country skiing, a strange sport, one might think, for an asthma sufferer, let alone a country boy from a Vermont farm. Yet in these Olympics he won a silver medal . . . which only goes to prove that anyone can win a medal if he tries hard enough; a motto most Olympians try to live up to, though few succeed.

Russia's powerful skater Tatiana Averina dominated the women's speed skating, with two gold – the 1,000 and 3,000 metres – and two bronze medals.

1976 Montreal

Destiny guaranteed that there was no way Montreal could survive an Olympics without major problems, especially following the initial statement by Mayor Jean Drapeau that the Olympics could no more have a deficit than a man have a baby. A combination of spiralling inflation, over-ambitious plans and repeated strikes ensured that almost up to the moment of the opening ceremony it was doubtful whether the Olympic buildings would be completed on time.

Mayor Drapeau promised the International Olympic Committee at their Amsterdam meeting in 1970 that the budget would be moderate, claiming that lotteries, the sales of coins and postage stamps, and sponsorship would raise $400 million, enabling the Games to be fully self-supporting. His avowed intention was to show that state intervention was not a prerequisite for the staging of a Games. Unfortunately, he had not done his groundwork sufficiently well.

One of Drapeau's major errors concerned the financial arrangement made with the French architect of the Olympic Park, Roger Taillibert, who stood to make more than $30 million in fees and royalties although the 1972 estimate for the entire Games was only $310 million. The final bill was nearer $1,000 million and that was without the mast on the controversial Olympic Stadium, making the tower only 51 metres high instead of 168 metres. This mast was anyway intended for use only during the winter so that the entire Stadium could be covered and sport could continue the year round.

It was inevitable that the constructional organization would finally be taken over from the hands of the City of Montreal where it seemed that graft and corruption were more important than the organization of an Olympic Games. Thus, in 1975 an Olympic Installations Board with representatives of federal and national governments took over the responsibility for those buildings which they decided would be essential if the Games were to be opened on time on July 17.

By January 1976 though, when the lowest temperatures for ten years caused 2,000 workers to be sent home, it was even suggested that the Olympics should be moved from Montreal–Los Angeles and Mexico were considered as alternatives. Fortunately, a mild spring enabled construction to proceed faster than at any time in the previous four years, but then came the worries about other influences. Among these were the security aspect following the killing of the Israeli competitors by terrorists in 1972, and whether a Supreme Council for Sport in Africa would force the issue over South Africa and Rhodesia.

When Palestinian guerrillas murdered eleven members of the Israeli team in Munich, it was inevitable that fears of another similar episode should arise, so the Canadians made sure from the outset that there would

Alberto Juantorena of Cuba, known as 'The Horse' in his own country because of his strength, was the first man in Olympic history to win the gold medal in both the 400 and 800 metres events. Here, he is seen in the latter, which he won in a world record time.

be no repetition. Unprecedented border controls and policing of the Olympic City were instituted. Unfortunately, the line between over-policing and complete security—a narrow one—was frequently surpassed and this led to repeated accusations of 'police state control' and, in the case of some journalists, 'police brutality'.

There was no doubt that there was poor co-ordination between CoJo (the organizing committee of the Olympic Games) and the police. Each was concerned with their own job and the result was that CoJo officials would allow photographers to stand in one place, yet two minutes later the police would come and rescind these decisions, moving the protesting photographers to places where they could not properly undertake their work.

When New Zealand announced that they would send a rugby team to South Africa this was immediately seized on by Black Africa as an opportunity to flex their muscles. And even if they did withdraw from the Games there is no doubt that ultimately Uganda, Kenya, Nigeria, Tanzania and the other African nations were the losers, not the Olympic movement. With hindsight it seems certain that the officials of the Supreme Council for Sport in Africa overplayed their hand and were pushed into a stand from which they could not withdraw without losing face. What had started out as a threat to withdraw from the Games if New Zealand were not expelled, ended up as a promise, and when the International Olympic Committee refused to bow to their demands they had no alternative but to withdraw. The idiocy of the situation was highlighted when New Zealand officials pointed out that there were competitors from many other countries, including Britain and West Germany, who had competed against South Africans whereas not one New Zealander had ever competed face to face with a Springbok.

The opening ceremony was a lottery as spectators eagerly sought out countries' banners to see who had withdrawn. By the time the Games were under way it was found that twenty-four nations had recalled their teams leaving a final total of ninety-three taking part. There was no disruption of the sports, only the boxing draw and the track and field programme being affected in any way. Fewer than 700 competitors and officials out of a total of 10,500 left the Olympic village—most of them, incidentally, bitterly upset at missing the opportunity of a lifetime to compete in the supreme sports festival of them all.

Long after the closing ceremony the echoes of the Games continued; within a matter of weeks it was announced by the Medical Commission that several competitors, specifically weightlifters, had traces of prohibited drugs in their systems. As three of these were medallists, two Bulgarians, Valentin Khristov, the

Finland's Lasse Viren, here seen leading the field with three laps to go in the 5,000 metres, set a remarkable record when he became the first man ever to win both the 5,000 and 10,000 metres in two successive Olympics.

heavyweight champion, and Blagoi Blagoev, light heavyweight silver medallist, and one Pole, the lightweight champion, Zbigniew Kaczmarek, the findings were extremely significant.

Although champions and other medallists have in the past been disqualified for various reasons, this was only the second time (the case of Galina Kulakova in the Winter Olympics being the first) anyone had lost a medal on medical grounds alone.

Above The undisputed queen of the Montreal Games was the young Rumanian gymnast Nadia Comaneci, who won three gold medals and one bronze, to the delight of the spectators. Time and again on the asymmetrical bars or the beam her perfect timing, daring and balance won her maximum points.
Right Nadia's closest rival was Russia's Nelli Kim, a gymnast with an incomparable sense of space and timing, who took the golds in the floor exercises and the horse vault.

At the other end of the scale hundreds of millions of spectators were enthralled by the beauty and grace of Nadia Comaneci who became the first gymnast in Olympic history to score the maximum 10 points. So high were her standards that she repeated this several times. Others too achieved this ultimate goal, creating problems for judges and coaches who believed that the degree of difficulty of some of the exercises was so hard that no competitor could ever be perfect.

The gymnastics almost overshadowed the major events, athletics and swimming. In the former, the absence of the Africans scarcely counted, as world records were broken time and again and Finland's Lasse Viren became the first man to retain in successive Games both his 5,000 metres and 10,000 metres titles. The Cubans, led by Alberto Juantorena, the first man to win the 400 metres and 800 metres in the same Olympics, showed that they are rapidly becoming one of the major nations in track and field events, while as usual the East German women showed remarkable depth, winning nine titles out of fourteen, although the top women's athlete was without any doubt the Pole, Irena Szewinska, who improved her own world record in the 400 metres and added to a long list of honours which started twelve years earlier when she was a teenager in the Tokyo Olympics.

In their Olympic swimming trials the women from the German Democratic Republic rewrote the existing record book and this was carried through by Kornelia Ender who became the 'Mark Spitz' of the 1976 Olympic Pool by winning four gold medals. A product of the meticulous system of her country, Miss Ender set fine individual records in the East German championships and thus her victories in Montreal justified her pre-Games form. As a tiny 13-year-old she had won one of East Germany's two silver medals in Munich four years earlier. By Montreal she had grown to 5ft 10in and was a well-built eleven stone with a technical proficiency far beyond that of most of her rivals.

East Germany's success in women's swimming was again a demonstration of what can be done when a country applies systematic and scientific coaching principles. From two silver medals in Munich they improved to eleven gold, seven silver and one bronze within the short space of four years.

In the boxing, Teofilo Stevenson of Cuba became the first heavyweight to retain his title and he demonstrated with some savage punching that given the chance he could become heavyweight champion of the world. But in the main the honours went to the United States with five gold medals of which the Spinks brothers, Michael and Leon, were responsible for two.

Ed Moses became the only member of the United States team to win a gold in the track events when he came first in the 400 metres hurdles, an event which he has since dominated.

1980

After the experiences of the seventies – terrorism, strikes, boycotts and walkouts – the first Olympics of the 1980s were approached with care and caution by the hosts, but with a certain amount of scepticism in many quarters.

However, there could be no criticism of the preparations for the Winter Olympics in Lake Placid. Months before the Games were due to start, the sites were prepared and the facilities tested. And such was the confidence of the organizers that banners proclaimed 'Welcome world, we're ready'.

A resort in the Adirondack Mountains in upstate New York, Lake Placid had hosted the third Winter Games forty-eight years earlier. Some of the old sites were renovated and new ones were built for the thirteenth celebration. The work was completed without any fuss, the trade unions concerned having guaranteed not to strike, although as ever there were potential scandals concerning escalating costs (the government had to step in at one time with a $60 million subsidy), financial irregularities, and faults in construction.

The 1932 ice rink, the Olympic Arena, was renovated and next to it was built the 8,500-seater Fieldhouse Arena – the dual complex catering for figure skating and ice hockey, with the outdoor speed circuit alongside. With the twin ski-jump towers only two miles away at Intervale, the Nordic racing and luge and bobsleigh runs seven miles away at Mount Van Hoevenberg, and the Alpine ski courses nine miles from Lake Placid on Whiteface Mountain, the sports sites are easily accessible from the centre.

The 1,000-metre luge toboggan run, the first to be built in North America, and the mile-long, reconstructed bobsleigh course are both refrigerated along their entire length. But the greatest trouble was taken over the construction of the athletes' village. So high is the cost now of meeting the IOC's stringent security conditions for the complex, which has to be enclosed by two twelve-foot-high wire-net fences, that the organizers decided to design it in such a way that after the Games it could be converted into a prison.

The thirty-eight events contested at Lake Placid from February 13 to 24 show an increase of one over the previous Games – a so-called 'sprint' individual biathlon (over 10 kilometres, in addition to the 20-kilometre event); this compares with the fourteen events held in 1932. And some forty countries are expected to send about 1,200 competitors to the 1980 Games.

The events themselves promise to be as spectacular and keenly contested as always. Much attention will be focused on the skating, in which Robin Cousins is favoured to keep the men's title in Britain and the world champion American pair Randy Gardner and Tai Babylonia will be fighting off the challenge of the Russian 'veteran' Irina Rodnina, who, having had a baby in the interim, will be back with her husband and going for her third title. Other American stars expected to shine at Lake Placid include the women's world champion figure skater Linda Fratianne and the brother and sister speed skaters Eric and Beth Heiden.

Moscow was a controversial choice for the celebration of the twenty-second Olympiad. There has to be a very large question-mark against the wisdom of allowing a country where freedom of movement and freedom of expression is so restricted to host such an international showpiece. It is difficult not to draw a parallel between the Nazi Olympics of 1936 and the 'Marxist' Olympics of 1980. And what conclusions could be drawn from Russia's decision late in 1979 to banish all schoolchildren between the ages of seven and fifteen from Moscow during the Games. Ostensibly this was to save foreign visitors from being pestered for such items as badges, ballpoint pens and chewing-gum and was part of a general plan to clear Moscow for the influx of visitors – anyone living outside Moscow would need special permission to visit the capital during the Games. But whether the plan was designed to shield the foreigners, or to shield the youngsters and others from 'ideological contamination' by foreigners, or to disguise the true situation behind the Iron Curtain is open to question. The defection to the West, at about the same time, of the Protopopovs – the great husband-and-wife team who dominated pairs skating in the 1960s – must have been a huge embarrassment to the Soviet authorities, for they had always been held up as a fine product of the Communist ideology.

However, right or wrong, the Games were scheduled to be held behind the Iron Curtain for the first time. And, like the Americans at Lake Placid, the Russians completed their preparations sufficiently in advance to allow them to stage a 'dress rehearsal' a year before the Games. This took the form of the seventh Spartakiad, the quadrennial national games that take place over a fortnight in summer. These games featured some 10,000 Soviet competitors plus, for the first time, 2,500 invited from abroad. Sure enough, there were countless minor snags and hitches and little misunderstandings, but this was the purpose of opening the games up to foreign athletes, officials and Press – to pinpoint the problems so that they could be worked out in time for the Olympics.

The Russians undertook nearly a hundred building projects, either new or major reconstructions, about threequarters of them in Moscow and the rest in Leningrad, Kiev, Tallinn and Minsk. They began over three years in advance, and despite some fearful weather and a no less formidable amount of red tape completed most of the work on schedule – thanks to the recruitment of volunteers from the Young Communist League and the redeployment of building squads from the Army.

Special attention was paid to designing new facilities that could be put to good use after the Games. The Olympic Village, for example, is a massive development in the south-west of Moscow, consisting of eighteen sixteen-story apartment blocks for housing some 12,000 competitors, coaches, and officials, with more than adequate training, medical and catering facilities and even a concert hall, library and cinemas.

The main sports centre, the 24-year-old Lenin Stadium, was completely renovated, and held over 100,000 spectators for the Spartakiad, including the 6,000 highly-trained card flashers who gave a remark-

Lake Placid and Moscow

able performance of precision picture-making, producing a vast ever-changing tableau of colour. A roofless ellipsoid of beautiful simplicity, the stadium has facilities for 1,350 journalists. And in the centre, mechanical aids to efficiency include a pole vault bar that can be raised electronically and contraptions for returning the throwing implements to competitors.

The other stadia include the 45,000-seater Olimpiisky Sports Centre, for games such as basketball. The largest covered arena in Europe, it can be used for a single event or adapted by means of a movable wall to accommodate two matches. The Velodrome Krylatskoe was the product of a nationwide architectural competition.

It has been estimated that two billion people—half the world's population—from over 140 countries will watch some part of the Olympics on television, including for the first time viewers in China. Japanese television is scheduled to show an average of sixteen hours a day. Two large hotels were designated to house the 7,500 reporters, commentators and technicians. This includes some 3,000 from television and radio to interpret the pictures produced by over 300 TV cameras and 50 video recorders, and use the hundred or so radio channels.

So the Spartakiad gave the world a preview of the Olympics organization, and it also gave a glimpse of two or three possible Olympic heroes. Certainly the 17-year-old Russian gymnast Natalia Shaposhnikova impressed, but perhaps the sensation of the games was the victory of British Modern Pentathlete Danny Nightingale over a field including forty-eight home competitors. And does freestyler Vladimer Salnikov's performances signal a Russian breakthrough in men's swimming?

Of the twenty-one sports (the same as at Montreal, although women's hockey would be making its first appearance at Moscow and other minor changes within sports include the return of the Star class in yachting), track and field athletics as always promise to provide the greatest dramas. Can Lasse Viren emerge once more from comparative mid-Olympics obscurity and prove himself the greatest distance runner of all time? Will the Cubans show that their Montreal triumphs were no flash in the pan? Can the Americans restore their declining prestige in track and field? The answer to the last question will lie not only in the hands of established champions and favourites such as 400 metres hurdler Ed Moses, who completely dominated his event between the Olympics, but also with the maturing talents of those such as Larry Myricks (whose 27ft 11½in long jump in the 1979 World Cup was the second best in history), high-hurdler Renaldo Nehemiah, and sprinter Evelyn Ashford, who inspires hopes of a return to the days of Wilma Rudolph, Wyomia Tyus and Edith McGuire, the American sprinters who dominated the Olympics of the 1960s.

Or will the dominance of the East German women at Montreal continue and perhaps spread to the men's events in Moscow? There seems less likelihood of the latter happening—at least not with such talent around as triple world-record breakers Henry Rono of Kenya and Sebastian Coe of Great Britain. Indeed, one of the most intriguing confrontations of the Games promises to be between team-mates and rivals Coe and Steve Ovett, who separately took apart most of the world's leading 800 and 1,500 metres runners in 1979 to the extent that many of them started to look for other events for Moscow.

Yet, sadly, there is still a political cloud hanging over these athletes, threatening at any time to build up into a storm. The question is whether the threatened Black African boycott will materialize, as happened at the last moment in Montreal, and whether Britain will find itself out in the cold? Again the root of the inter-Commonwealth squabbling is the problem of sporting contact with South Africa—first the controversial rugby tour of Britain by a (multiracial) South African side in 1979 and then the proposed tour by the British Lions of South Africa in Olympics year.

The Soviet hosts are committed to accepting all countries recognized by the IOC—and the IOC are not going to be blackmailed by the third-world bloc into expelling Britain. The Africans did their own noble cause little good by their walkout at Montreal. A repeat performance in Moscow would be senseless; but political brinkmanship is not always tempered with commonsense. The very fact that the Games are being held in the USSR negates most moral arguments. For who is to say, when it comes to the infringement of human rights, that the Soviet regime—or those of East Germany or Czechoslovakia or of some of the Black African states themselves—is any less oppressive than that of South Africa? Ultimately such questions must be left to the individual. One thing is certain—in these political struggles it is always the athletes who suffer. This has been highlighted by the case of Sydney Maree, a black South African middle-distance runner who has produced world-class times of 3 min 53 sec for the mile and 13 min 20 sec for the 5,000 metres. Because his fare to the United States to take up a university scholarship there had been paid by an organization that, unknown to him, was set up by the South African government, he has become a victim of discrimination himself—barred not only from international competition but even from many national and intervarsity meetings. He is not the only one to believe that the sporting isolation of South Africa has hurt black and coloured competitors more than whites.

At least one political problem has been resolved, however, with the reacceptance—at last—of the People's Republic of China into the Olympic movement. It will be intriguing to see how their sportsmen fare in top international competition after what has been in most sports a very long period of voluntary exile. And it will be fascinating to see also how their policy of 'friendship first' stands up in, of all places, Moscow.

Appendices

Progress of the Games

	Year	Place	Date	Competitors	Nations	Sports
I	1896	Athens	Apr 5–14	285	13	10
II	1900	Paris	May 14–Oct 20	1066	20	14
III	1904	St. Louis	Jul 11–Oct 29	496	11	13
IV	1908	London	May 6–Oct 29	2059	22	21
V	1912	Stockholm	Jun 29–Jul 22	2541	28	15
VI	1916	Berlin	Cancelled due to war			
VII	1920	Antwerp	Apr 20–Sep 21	2606	29	20
VIII	1924	Paris	May 3–Jul 27	3092	44	17
IX	1928	Amsterdam	Jul 28–Aug 12	3290	46	17
X	1932	Los Angeles	Jul 31–Aug 7	1429	40	14
XI	1936	Berlin	Aug 2–16	4793	49	22
XII	1940	Tokyo, then Helsinki–Cancelled due to war				
XIII	1944	London	Cancelled due to war			
XIV	1948	London	Jul 29–Aug 14	4106	59	19
XV	1952	Helsinki	Jul 19–Aug 3	4925	69	19
XVI	1956	Melbourne	Nov 22–Dec 8	3184	68	20
		(+164 in Equestrian events at Stockholm)				
XVII	1960	Rome	Aug 25–Sep 11	5337	84	18
XVIII	1964	Tokyo	Oct 10–24	5558	94	18
XIX	1968	Mex. City	Oct 12–27	6082	109	18
XX	1972	Munich	Aug 26–Sep 10	10,500	123	21
XXI	1976	Montreal	July 17–Aug 1	8500	92	21
XXII	1980	Moscow	Aug 10–24			

Winter Olympic Games

	Year	Place	Date	Competitors	Nations	Sports
I	1924	Chamonix	Jan 24–Feb 4	418	18	6
II	1928	St. Moritz	Feb 11–18	940	25	4
III	1932	Lake Placid	Feb 4–13	364	17	5
IV	1936	Garmisch-Partenkirchen	Feb 6–13	757	28	5
V	1948	St. Moritz	Jan 30–Feb 8	932	29	6
VI	1952	Oslo	Feb 14–25	880	30	5
VII	1956	Cortina d'Ampezzo	Jan 26–Feb 5	947	32	6
VIII	1960	Squaw Valley	Feb 18–28	900	30	6
IX	1964	Innsbruck	Jan 29–Feb 9	1186	36	6
X	1968	Grenoble	Feb 6–18	1560	37	6
XI	1972	Sapporo	Feb 3–13	1275	35	6
XII	1976	Innsbruck	Feb 4–15	1261	38	6
XIII	1980	Lake Placid	Feb 14–23			

Metric Guide

1 metre – 3ft. $3\frac{1}{2}$in.
100m. – 109yd. 1ft. 1in.
200m. – 218yd. 2ft. 2in.
400m. – 437yd. 1ft. 4in.
800m. – 874yd. 2ft. 8in.
1000m. – 1093yd. 1ft. 10in.
1500m. – 1640yd. 1ft. 3in.
    (1609·3m – 1 mile)
3000m. – 1 mile 1520yd. 2ft. 6in.
5000m. – 3 miles 188yd. 2·4in.
10,000m. – 6 miles 376yd. 4·8in.
42kms 195yd. – 26 miles 385yd. (marathon)
100kms – $62\frac{1}{2}$ miles (approx.)
194kms – 120 miles

Gold medal countries since 1896

Country	Gold	Silver	Bronze
United States of America	567	423	378
U.S.S.R.	260	213	205
Great Britain	138	178	154
Sweden	127	121	140
Italy	111	100	97
Germany (until 1964)	108	149	136
France	108	127	124
Hungary	103	95	113
Finland	88	72	70
Japan	74	74	61
East Germany (after 1964)	69	57	55
Australia	62	53	65
Switzerland	42	41	47
Czechoslovakia	40	43	36
Netherlands	36	40	48
Norway	36	29	30
Belgium	35	40	33
Poland	35	37	71
Denmark	30	47	50
West Germany (after 1964)	28	34	43
Canada	23	40	49
Turkey	23	12	7
Greece	22	38	33
Rumania	22	31	46
Bulgaria	19	34	22
South Africa	16	15	22
Austria	15	23	31
Cuba	15	17	8
Yugoslavia	14	18	12
New Zealand	14	3	11
Argentina	13	18	13
Mexico	7	9	11
India	7	3	3
U.A.R.	6	5	6
Iran	5	11	12
Kenya	5	7	6
Jamaica	4	7	3
Brazil	3	2	13
Ethiopia	3	1	2
Pakistan	2	3	2
North Korea	2	2	3
Uruguay	2	1	6
Spain	1	6	4
Tunisia	1	2	1
South Korea	1	1	4
Luxembourg	1	1	0
Venezuela	1	1	0
Uganda	1	0	0
Bahamas	1	0	0
Trinidad	1	0	0
Peru	1	0	0

Where Winter medals have gone

Country	Gold	Silver	Bronze
U.S.S.R.	51	32	35
Norway	50	51	43
U.S.A.	30	38	26
Finland	23	35	21
Austria	22	31	27
Sweden	22	21	25
Switzerland	15	17	16
Germany (until 1964)	14	11	10
East Germany (since 1964)	12	10	16
France	12	9	12
Canada	11	7	14
Italy	10	7	7
Netherlands	9	13	12
West Germany (since 1964)	7	7	7
Great Britain	5	2	6
Czechoslovakia	2	5	5
Japan	1	2	1
Poland	1	2	1
Belgium	1	1	2
Spain	1	0	0
Hungary	0	1	4
North Korea	0	1	0
Liechtenstein	0	0	2
Rumania	0	0	1

Results

These statistics are of events currently competed for in the Olympics with the exception of canoeing and rowing. Details of obsolete contests such as the 60 metres have been omitted. The absence of times in some early events is due to their not having been recorded.

ARCHERY (MEN)

1972 John Williams (USA) 2528	Gunnar Jarvil (Sweden) 2481	Kyoesti Laasonen (Finland) 2467
1976 Darrell Pace (USA) 2571	Hiroshi Michinaga (Japan) 2502	Carlo Ferrari (Italy) 2495
1980	....	....

ARCHERY (WOMEN)

1972 Dorren Wilber (USA) 2424	Irena Szydlowska (Poland) 2407	Emma Gaptchenko (USSR) 2403
1976 Luann Ryon (USA) 2499	Valentina Kovpan (USSR) 2460	Zebiniso Rustamova (USSR) 2407
1980	....	....

ATHLETICS (MEN)

100 METRES

1896 Thomas Burke (USA) 12.0s	Fritz Hofmann (Germany)	Alajos Szokolyi (Hungary)
1900 Frank Jarvis (USA) 11.0s	Walter Tewksbury (USA)	Stan Rowley (Australia)
1904 Archie Hahn (USA) 11.0s	Nathan Cartmell (USA)	William Hogensen (USA)
1908 Reginald Walker (S.Africa) 10.8s	James Rector (USA)	Robert Kerr (Canada)
1912 Ralph Craig (USA) 10.8s	Alvah Meyer (USA) 10.9s	Donald Lippincott (USA) 10.9s
1920 Charles Paddock (USA) 10.8s	Morris Kirksey (USA)	Harry Edward (GB)
1924 Harold Abrahams (GB) 10.6s	Jackson Scholz (USA)	Arthur Porritt (NZ)
1928 Percy Williams (Canada) 10.8s	Jack London (GB)	George Lammers (Germany)
1932 Eddie Tolan (USA) 10.3s	Ralph Metcalfe (USA) 10.3s	Arthur Jonath (Germany) 10.4s
1936 Jesse Owens (USA) 10.3s	Ralph Metcalfe (USA) 10.4s	Martinus Osendarp (Netherlands) 10.5s
1948 Harrison Dillard (USA) 10.3s	Barney Ewell (USA) 10.4s	Lloyd La Beach (Panama) 10.4s
1952 Lindy Remigino (USA) 10.4s	Herb McKenley (Jamaica) 10.4s	McDonald Bailey (GB) 10.4s
1956 Bobby Morrow (USA) 10.5s	Thane Baker (USA) 10.5	Hector Hogan (Australia) 10.6s
1960 Armin Hary (Germany) 10.2s	Dave Sime (USA) 10.2s	Peter Radford (GB) 10.3s
1964 Bob Hayes (USA) 10.0s	Enrique Figuerola (Cuba) 10.2s	Harry Jerome (Canada) 10.2s
1968 Jim Hines (USA) 9.9s	Lennox Miller (Jamaica) 10.0s	Charles Greene (USA) 10.0s
1972 Valeriy Borzov (USSR) 10.14s	Robert Taylor (USA) 10.24s	Lennox Miller (Jam) 10.33s
1976 Haseley Crawford (Trinidad) 10.06s	Donald Quarrie (Jamaica) 10.08s	Valeriy Borzov (USSR) 10.14s
1980	....	....

200 METRES

1900 Walter Tewksbury (USA) 22.2s	Norman Pritchard (India)	Stan Rowley (Australia)
1904 Archie Hahn (USA) 21.6s	Nathan Cartmell (USA)	William Hogenson (USA)
1908 Robert Kerr (Canada) 22.6s	Robert Cloughen (USA)	Nathan Cartmell (USA)
1912 Ralph Craig (USA) 21.7s	Donald Lippincott (USA) 21.8s	William Applegarth (GB) 22.0s
1920 Allen Woodring (USA) 22.0s	Charles Paddock (USA)	Harry Edward (GB)
1924 Jackson Scholz (USA) 21.6s	Charles Paddock (USA)	Eric Liddell (GB)
1928 Percy Williams (Canada) 21.8s	Walter Rangeley (GB)	Helmut Körnig (Germany)
1932 Eddie Tolan (USA) 21.2s	George Simpson (USA) 21.4s	Ralph Metcalfe (USA) 21.5s
1936 Jesse Owens (USA) 20.7s	Mack Robinson (USA) 21.1s	Martinus Osendarp (Netherlands) 21.3s
1948 Mel Patton (USA) 21.1s	Barney Ewell (USA) 21.1s	Lloyd La Beach (Panama) 21.2s
1952 Andy Stanfield (USA) 20.7s	Thane Baker (USA) 20.8s	James Gathers (USA) 20.8s
1956 Bobby Morrow (USA) 20.6s	Andy Stanfield (USA) 20.7s	Thane Baker (USA) 20.9s
1960 Livio Berutti (Italy) 20.5s	Les Carney (USA) 20.6s	Abdoulaye Seye (France) 20.7s
1964 Henry Carr (USA) 20.3s	Paul Drayton (USA) 20.5s	Ed Roberts (Trinidad) 20.6s
1968 Tommie Smith (USA) 19.8s	Peter Norman (Australia) 20.0s	John Carlos (USA) 20.0s

1972 Valeriy Borzov (USSR) 20.00s	Larry Black (USA) 20.19s	Pietro Mennea (Italy) 20.30s
1976 Donald Quarrie (Jamaica) 20.23s	Millard Hampton (USA) 20.29s	Dwayne Evans (USA) 20.43s
1980	....	....

400 METRES

1896 Thomas Burke (USA) 54.2s	Herbert Jamison (USA) 55.2s	Charles Gmelin (GB)
1900 Maxie Long (USA) 49.4s	William Holland (USA)	Ernst Schultz (Denmark)
1904 Harry Hillman (USA) 49.2s	Frank Waller (USA)	H. C. Groman (USA)
1908 Wyndham Halswelle (GB) 50.0s		
1912 Charles Reidpath (USA) 48.2s	Hanns Braun (Germany) 48.3s	Edward Lindberg (USA) 48.4s
1920 Bevil Rudd (S.Africa) 49.6s	Guy Butler (GB)	Nils Engdahl (Sweden)
1924 Eric Liddell (GB) 47.6s	Horatio Fitch (USA) 48.4s	Guy Butler (GB) 48.6s
1928 Raymond Barbuti (USA) 47.8s	James Ball (Canada) 48.0s	Joachim Büchner (Germany) 48.2s
1932 William Carr (USA) 46.2s	Benjamin Eastman (USA) 46.4s	Alex Wilson (Canada) 47.4s
1936 Archie Williams (USA) 46.5s	Godfrey Brown (GB) 46.7s	James LuValle (USA) 46.8s
1948 Arthur Wint (Jamaica) 46.2s	Herb McKenley (Jamaica) 46.4s	Mal Whitfield (USA) 46.9s
1952 George Rhoden (Jamaica) 45.9s	Herb McKenley (Jamaica) 45.9s	Ollie Matson (USA) 46.8s
1956 Charles Jenkins (USA) 46.7s	Karl-Friedrich Haas (Germany) 46.8s	Voitto Hellsten (Finland) 47.0s Ardalion Ignatyev (USSR) 47.0s
1960 Otis Davis (USA) 44.9s	Carl Kaufmann (Germany) 44.9s	Mal Spence (S.Africa) 45.5s
1964 Michael Larrabee (USA) 45.1s	Wendell Mottley (Trinidad) 45.2s	Andrzej Badenski (Poland) 45.6s
1968 Lee Evans (USA) 43.8s	Larry James (USA) 43.9s	Ron Freeman (USA) 44.4s
1972 Vince Matthews (USA) 44.66s	Wayne Collett (USA) 44.80s	Julius Sang (Kenya) 44.92s
1976 Alberto Juantorena (Cuba) 44.26s	Fred Newhouse (USA) 44.40s	Herman Frazier (USA) 44.95s
1980	....	....

800 METRES

1896 Edwin Flack (Australia) 2m 11.0s	Nándor Dáni (Hungary) 2m 11.8s	Demetrius Golemis (Greece)
1900 Alfred Tysoe (GB) 2m 01.2s	John Cregan (USA) 2m 3s	David Hall (USA)
1904 James Lightbody (USA) 1m 56.0s	Howard Valentine (USA)	Emil Breitkreutz (USA)
1908 Melvin Sheppard (USA) 1m 52.8s	Emilio Lunghi (Italy) 1m 54.2s	Hanns Braun (Germany) 1m 55.4s
1912 James Meredith (USA) 1m 51.9s	Melvin Sheppard (USA) 1m 52.0s	Ira Davenport (USA) 1m 52.0s
1920 Albert Hill (GB) 1m 53.4s	Earl Eby (USA) 1m 53.7s	Bevil Rudd (S.Africa) 1m 53.7s
1924 Douglas Lowe (GB) 1m 52.4s	Paul Martin (Switzerland) 1m 52.6s	Schuyler Enck (USA) 1m 53.0s
1928 Douglas Lowe (GB) 1m 51.8s	Erik Bylehn (Sweden) 1m 52.8s	Hermann Engelhardt (Germany) 1m 53.2s
1932 Thomas Hampson (GB) 1m 49.7s	Alex Wilson (Canada) 1m 49.9s	Philip Edwards (Canada) 1m 51.5s
1936 John Woodruff (USA) 1m 52.9s	Mario Lanzi (Italy) 1m 53.3s	Philip Edwards (Canada) 1m 53.6s
1948 Malvin Whitfield (USA) 1m 49.2s	Arthur Wint (Jamaica) 1m 49.5s	Marcel Hansenne (France) 1m 49.8s
1952 Malvin Whitfield (USA) 1m 49.2s	Arthur Wint (Jamaica) 1m 49.4s	Heinz Ulzheimer (Germany) 1m 49.7s
1956 Thomas Courtney (USA) 1m 47.7s	Derek Johnson (GB) 1m 47.8s	Audun Boysen (Norway) 1m 48.1s
1960 Peter Snell (NZ) 1m 46.3s	Roger Moens (Belgium) 1m 46.5s	George Kerr (Jamaica) 1m 47.1s
1964 Peter Snell (NZ) 1m 45.1s	Bill Crothers (Canada) 1m 45.6s	Wilson Kiprugut (Kenya) 1m 45.9s
1968 Ralph Doubell (Australia) 1m 44.3s	Wilson Kiprugut (Kenya) 1m 44.5s	Tom Farrell (USA) 1m 45.4s
1972 Dave Wottle (USA) 1m 45.9s	Evgeni Arzhanov (USSR) 1m 45.9s	Mike Boit (Kenya) 1m 46s
1976 Alberto Juantorena (Cuba) 1m 43.50s	Ivo Vandamme (Belgium) 1m 43.86s	Richard Wohlhuter (USA) 1m 44.12s
1980		

1,500 METRES

1896 Edwin Flack (Australia) 4m 33.2s	Arthur Blake (USA) 4m 35.4s	Albin Lermusiaux (France) 4m 37s
1900 Charles Bennett (GB) 4m 06.2s	Henri Deloge (France)	John Bray (USA)
1904 James Lightbody (USA) 4m 05.4s	Frank Verner (USA)	L. Hearn (USA)

1908	Melvin Sheppard (USA) 4m 03.4s	Harold Wilson (GB) 4m 03.6s	Norman Hallows (GB) 4m 0.40s
1912	Arnold Jackson (GB) 3m 56.8s	Abel Kiviat (USA) 3m 56.9s	Norman Taber (USA) 3m 56.9s
1920	Albert Hill (GB) 4m 01.8s	Philip Baker (GB) 4m 02.4s	Lawrence Shields (USA)
1924	Paavo Nurmi (Finland) 3m 53.6s	Willy Sherrer (Switzerland) 3m 55.0s	Henry Stallard (GB) 3m 55.6s
1928	Harri Larva (Finland) 3m 53.2s	Jules Ladoumègue (France) 3m 53.8s	Eino Purje (Finland) 3m 56.4s
1932	Luigi Beccali (Italy) 3m 51.2s	John Cornes (GB) 3m 52.6s	Philip Edwards (Canada) 3m 52.8s
1936	Jack Lovelock (NZ) 3m 47.8s	Glenn Cunningham (USA) 3m 48.4s	Luigi Beccali (Italy) 3m 49.2s
1948	Henry Eriksson (Sweden) 3m 49.8s	Lennart Strand (Sweden) 3m 50.4s	Willem Slykhuis (Netherlands) 3m 50.4s
1952	Jose Barthel (Luxemburg) 3m 45.1s	Robert McMillen (USA) 3m 45.2s	Werner Lueg (Germany) 3m 45.4s
1956	Ron Delany (Eire) 3m 41.2s	Klaus Richtzenhain (Germany) 3m 42.0s	John Landy (Australia) 3m 42.0s
1960	Herb Elliott (Australia) 3m 35.6s	Michel Jazy (France) 3m 38.4s	István Rozsavolgyi (Hungary) 3m 39.2s
1964	Peter Snell (NZ) 3m 38.1s	Josef Odlozil (Czech) 3m 39.6s	John Davies (NZ) 3m 39.6s
1968	Kipchoge Keino (Kenya) 3m 34.9s	Jim Ryun (USA) 3m 37.8s	Bodo Tummler (W.Germany) 3m 39.0s
1972	Pekka Vasala (Finland) 3m 36.3s	Kipchoge Keino (Kenya) 3m 36.8s	Rod Dixon (NZ) 3m 37.5s
1976	John Walker (NZ) 3m 39.17s	Ivo Vandamme (Belgium) 3m 39.27s	Paul Hein Wellman (W. Germany) 3m 39.33s
1980	....	....	....

5,000 METRES

1912	Hannes Kolehmainen (Finland) 14m 36.6s	Jean Bouin (France) 15m 36.7s	George Hutson (GB) 15m 07.6s
1920	Joseph Guillemot (France) 14m 55.6s	Paavo Nurmi (Finland) 15m 00.0s	Eric Backman (Sweden) 15m 13.0s
1924	Paavo Nurmi (Finland) 14m 31.2s	Ville Ritola (Finland) 14m 31.4s	Edvin Wide (Sweden) 15m 01.8s
1928	Ville Ritola (Finland) 14m 38.0s	Paavo Nurmi (Finland) 14m 40.0s	Edvin Wide (Sweden) 14m 41.2s
1932	Lauri Lehtinen (Finland) 14m 30.0s	Ralph Hill (USA) 14m 30.0s	Lauri Virtanen (Finland) 14m 44.0s
1936	Gunnar Höckert (Finland) 14m 22.2s	Lauri Lehtinen (Finland) 14m 25.8s	Henry Jonsson (Sweden) 14m 29.0s
1948	Gaston Rieff (Belgium) 14m 17.6s	Emil Zatopek (Czech) 14m 17.8s	Willem Slykhuis (Netherlands) 14m 26.8s
1952	Emil Zatopek (Czech) 14m 06.6s	Alain Mimoun (France) 14m 07.4s	Herbert Schade (Germany) 14m 08.6s
1956	Vladimir Kuts (USSR) 13m 39.6s	Gordon Pirie (GB) 13m 50.6s	Derek Ibbotson (GB) 13m 54.4s
1960	Murray Halberg (NZ) 13m 43.4s	Hans Grodotzki (Germany) 13m 44.6s	Kazimierz Zimny (Poland) 13m 44.8s
1964	Robert Schul (USA) 13m 48.8s	Harald Norpoth (Germany) 13m 49.6s	William Dellinger (USA) 13m 49.8s
1968	Mohamed Gammoudi (Tunisia) 14m 05.0s	Kipchoge Keino (Kenya) 14m 05.2s	Naftali Temu (Kenya) 14m 06.4s
1972	Lasse Viren (Finland) 13m 26.4s	Mohamed Gammoudi (Tunisia) 13m 27.4s	Ian Stewart (GB) 13m 27.6s
1976	Lasse Viren (Finland) 13m 24.76s	Dick Quax (NZ) 13m 25.16s	Klaus Peter Hildenbrand (W. Germany) 13m 25.38s
1980	....	....	....

10,000 METRES

1912	Hannes Kolemainen (Finland) 31m 20.8s	Lewis Tewanima (USA) 32m 06.6s	Albin Stenroos (Finland) 32m 21.8s
1920	Paavo Nurmi (Finland) 31m 45.8s	Joseph Guillemot (France) 31m 47.2s	James Wilson (GB) 31m 50.8s
1924	Ville Ritola (Finland) 30m 23.2s	Edvin Wide (Sweden) 30m 55.2s	Eero Berg (Finland) 31m 43.0s
1928	Paavo Nurmi (Finland) 30m 18.8s	Ville Ritola (Finland) 30m 19.4s	Edvin Wide (Sweden) 31m 00.8s
1932	Janusz Kusocinski (Poland) 30m 11.4s	Volmari Iso-Hollo (Finland) 30m 12.6s	Lauri Virtanen (Finland) 30m 35.0s
1936	Ilmari Salminen (Finland) 30m 15.4s	Arvo Askola (Finland) 30m 15.6s	Volmari Iso-Hollo (Finland) 30m 20.2s
1948	Emil Zatopek (Czech) 29m 59.6s	Alain Mimoun (France) 30m 47.4s	Bertil Albertsson (Sweden) 30m 53.6s
1952	Emil Zatopek (Czech) 29m 17.0s	Alain Mimoun (France) 29m 32.8s	Aleksandr Anufriayev (USSR) 29m 48.2s
1956	Vladimir Kuts (USSR) 28m 45.6s	Jozsef Kovacs (Hungary) 28m 52.4s	Allan Lawrence (Australia) 28m 53.6s
1960	Pyotr Bolotnikov (USSR) 28m 32.2s	Hans Grodotzki (Germany) 28m 37.0s	Dave Power (Australia) 28m 38.2s
1964	Billy Mills (USA) 28m 24.4s	Mohamed Gammoudi (Tunisia) 28m 24.8s	Ron Clarke (Australia) 28m 25.8s
1968	Naftali Temu (Kenya) 29m 27.4s	Mamo Wolde (Ethiopia) 29m 28.0s	Mohammed Gammoudi (Tunisia) 29m 34.2s
1972	Lasse Viren (Finland) 27m 38.4s	Emiel Puttemans (Belgium) 27m 39.6s	Merus Yifter (Ethiopia) 27m 41s
1976	Lasse Viren (Finland) 27m 40.38s	Carlos Lopez (Portugal) 27m 45.17s	Brendan Foster (GB) 27m 54.92s
1980	....	....	....

MARATHON

1896	Spiridon Louis (Greece) 2h 58m 50.0s	Haralambos Vasilakos (Greece) 3h 06m 03.0s	Gyula Kellner (Hungary) 3h 09m 35.0s
1900	Michel Théato (France) 2h 59m 45.0s	Emile Champion (France) 3h 04m 17.0s	Ernst Fast (Sweden) 3h 37m 14.0s
1904	Thomas Hicks (USA) 3h 28m 53.0s	Albert Corey (USA) 3h 34m 52.0s	Arthur Newton (USA) 3h 47m 33.0s
1908	John Hayes (USA) 2h 55m 18.4s	Charles Hefferon (USA) 2h 56m 06.0s	Joseph Forshaw (USA) 2h 57m 10.4s
1912	Kenneth McArthur (S.Africa) 2h 36m 54.8s	Christopher Gitsham (S.Africa) 2h 37m 52.0s	Gaston Strobino (USA) 2h 38m 42.4s
1920	Hannes Kolehmainen (Finland) 2h 32m 35.8s	Jüri Lossman (Estonia) 2h 32m 48.6s	Valerio Arri (Italy) 2h 36m 32.8s
1924	Albin Stenroos (Finland) 2h 41m 22.6s	Romeo Bertini (Italy) 2h 47m 19.6s	Clarence De Mar (USA) 2h 48m 14.0s
1928	El Ouafi (France) 2h 32m 57.0s	Miguel Plaza (Chile) 2h 33m 23.0s	Martti Marttelin (Finland) 2h 35m 02.0s
1932	Juan Zabala (Argentina) 2h 31m 36.0s	Sam Ferris (GB) 2h 31m 55.0s	Armas Toivonen (Finland) 2h 32m 12.0s
1936	Kitei Son (Japan) 2h 29m 19.2s	Ernest Harper (GB) 2h 31m 23.2s	Shoryu Nan (Japan) 2h 31m 42.0s
1948	Delfo Cabrera (Argentina) 2h 34m 51.6s	Thomas Richards (GB) 2h 35m 07.6s	Etienne Gailly (Belgium) 2h 35m 33.6s
1952	Emil Zatopek (Czech) 2h 23m 03.2s	Reinaldo Gorno (Argentina) 2h 25m 35.0s	Gustaf Jansson (Sweden) 2h 26m 07.0s
1956	Alain Mimoun (France) 2h 25m 00.0s	Franjo Mihalic (Yugos) 2h 26m 32.0s	Veikko Karvonen (Finland) 2h 27m 47.0s
1960	Abebe Bikila (Ethiopia) 2h 15m 16.2s	Rhadi (Morocco) 2h 15m 41.6s	Barry Magee (NZ) 2h 17m 18.2s
1964	Abebe Bikila (Ethiopia) 2h 12m 11.2s	Basil Heatley (GB) 2h 16m 19.2s	Kokichi Tsuburaya (Japan) 2h 16m 22.8s
1968	Mamo Wolde (Ethiopia) 2h 20m 26.4s	Kenji Kimihara (Japan) 2h 23m 31.0s	Mike Ryan (NZ) 2h 23m 45.0s
1972	Frank Shorter (USA) 2h 12m 19.7s	Karel Lismont (Belgium) 2h 14m 31.8s	Mamo Walde (Ethiopia) 2h 15m 8.4s
1976	Waldemar Cierpinski (E. Germany) 2h 09m 55s	Frank Shorter (USA) 2h 10m 45.8s	Karel Lismont (Belgium) 2h 11m 12.6s
1980	....	....	....

110 METRES HURDLES

1896	Thomas Curtis (USA) 17.6s	Grantley Goulding (GB) 18.0s	
1900	Alvin Kraenzlein (USA) 15.4s	John McLean (USA)	Fred Moloney (USA)
1904	Fred Schule (USA) 16.0s	Thaddeus Shideler (USA)	L. Ashburner (USA)
1908	Forrest Smithson (USA) 15.0s	John Garrets (USA)	Arthur Shaw (USA)
1912	Fred Kelly (USA) 15.1s	James Wendell (USA) 15.2s	Martin Hawkins (USA) 15.3s
1920	Earl Thomson (Canada) 14.8s	Harold Barron (USA)	Fred Murray (USA)
1924	Daniel Kinsey (USA) 15.0s	Sydney Atkinson (S.Africa)	Sten Pettersson (Sweden)
1928	Sydney Atkinson (S.Africa) 14.8s	Stephen Anderson (USA) 14.8s	John Collier (USA) 15.0s
1932	George Saling (USA) 14.6s	Percy Beard (USA) 14.7s	Donald Finlay (GB) 14.8s
1936	Forrest Towns (USA) 14.2s	Donald Finlay (GB) 14.4s	Fred Pollard (USA) 14.4s
1948	William Porter (USA) 13.9s	Clyde Scott (USA) 14.1s	Craig Dixon (USA) 14.1s
1952	Harrison Dillard (USA) 13.7s	Jack Davis (USA) 13.7s	Art Barnard (USA) 14.1s
1956	Lee Calhoun (USA) 13.5s	Jack Davis (USA) 13.5s	Joel Shankle (USA) 14.1s
1960	Lee Calhoun (USA) 13.8s	Willie May (USA) 13.8s	Hayes Jones (USA) 14.0s
1964	Hayes Jones (USA) 13.6s	Blaine Lindgren (USA) 13.7s	Anatol Mikhailov (USSR) 13.7s
1968	Willie Davenport (USA) 13.3s	Erv Hall (USA) 13.4s	Eddy Ottoz (Italy) 13.4s
1972	Rod Milburn (USA) 13.24s	Guy Drut (France) 13.34s	Tom Hill (USA) 13.48s
1976	Guy Drut (France) 13.30s	Alejandro Casanas (Cuba) 13.33s	Willie Davenport (USA) 13.38s
1980	....	....	....

400 METRES HURDLES

1900	Walter Tewksbury (USA) 57.6s	Henri Tauzin (France)	George Orton (USA)
1904	Harry Hillman (USA) 53.0s	Frank Waller (USA)	George Poage (USA)
1908	Charles Bacon (USA) 55.0s	Harry Hillman (USA)	Leonard Tremeer (USA)
1920	Frank Loomis (USA) 54.0s	John Norton (USA)	August Desch (USA)
1924	Morgan Taylor (USA) 52.6s	Erik Vilen (Finland) 53.8s	Ivan Riley (USA) 54.2s
1928	Lord Burghley (GB) 53.4s	Frank Cuhel (USA) 53.6s	Morgan Taylor (USA) 53.6s
1932	Robert Tisdall (Eire) 51.8s	Glenn Hardin (USA) 52.0s	Morgan Taylor (USA) 52.2s
1936	Glenn Hardin (USA) 52.4s	John Loaring (Canada) 52.7s	Miguel White (Philippines) 52.8s
1948	Roy Cochran (USA) 51.1s	Duncan White (Ceylon) 51.8s	Rune Larsson (Sweden) 52.2s
1952	Charles Moore (USA) 50.8s	Yuriy Lituyev (USSR) 51.3s	John Holland (NZ) 52.2s
1956	Glenn Davis (USA) 50.1s	Eddie Southern (USA) 50.8s	Josh Culbreath (USA) 51.6s

1960	Glenn Davis (USA) 49.3s	Cliff Cushman (USA) 49.6s	Richard Howard (USA) 49.7s
1964	Rex Cawley (USA) 49.6s	John Cooper (GB) 50.1s	Salvadore Morale (Italy) 50.1s
1968	David Hemery (GB) 48.1s	Gerhard Hennige (W.Germany) 49.0s	John Sherwood (GB) 49.0s
1972	John Akii-Bua (Uganda) 47.82s	Ralph Mann (USA) 48.51s	David Hemery (GB) 48.52s
1976	Edwin Moses (USA) 47.64s	Michael Shine (USA) 48.69s	Evgeniy Gavrilenko (USSR) 49.45s
1980			

3,000 METRES STEEPLECHASE

1920	Percy Hodge (GB) 10m 00.4s	Patrick Flynn (USA)	Ernesto Ambrosini (Italy)
1924	Ville Ritola (Finland) 9m 33.6s	Elias Katz (Finland) 9m 44.0s	Paul Bontemps (France) 9m 45.2s
1928	Toivo Loukola (Finland) 9m 21.8s	Paavo Nurmi (Finland) 9m 31.2s	Ove Andersen (Finland) 9m 35.6s
1932	Volmari Iso-Hollo (Finland) 10m 33.4s	Thomas Evenson (GB) 10m 46.0s	Joseph McCluskey (USA) 10m 46.2s
1936	Volmari Iso-Hollo (Finland) 9m 03.8s	Kaarlo Tuominen (Finland) 9m 06.8s	Alfred Dompert (Germany) 9m 07.2s
1948	Tore Sjöstrand (Sweden) 9m 04.6s	Erik Elmsäter (Sweden) 9m 08.2s	Göte Hagström (Sweden) 9m 11.8s
1952	Horace Ashenfelter (USA) 8m 45.4s	Vladimir Kazantsev (USSR) 8m 51.6s	John Disley (GB) 8m 51.8s
1956	Christopher Brasher (GB) 8m 41.2s	Sandor Rozsnyoi (Hungary) 8m 43.6s	Ernst Larsen (Norway) 8m 44.0s
1960	Zdzislaw Krzyszkowiak (Poland) 8m 34.2s	Nikolay Sokolov (USSR) 8m 36.4s	Semyon Rzhishchin (USSR) 8m 42.2s
1964	Gaston Roelants (Belgium) 8m 30.8s	Maurice Herriott (GB) 8m 32.4s	Ivan Belyayev (USSR) 8m 33.8s
1968	Amos Biwott (Kenya 8m 51.0s	Benjamin Kogo (Kenya) 8m 51.6s	George Young (USA) 8m 51.8s
1972	Kipchoge Keino (Kenya) 8m 23.6s	Ben Jipcho (Kenya) 8m 24.6s	Tapio Kantanen (Finland) 8m 24.8s
1976	Anders Garderud (Sweden) 8m 08.02s	Bronislaw Malinowski (Poland) 8m 09.11s	Frank Baumgartl (E. Germany) 8m 10.36s
1980			

4×100 METRES RELAY

1912	GB 42.4s	Sweden 42.6s	
1920	USA 42.2s	France 42.6s	Sweden
1924	USA 41.0s	GB 41.2s	Netherlands 41.8s
1928	USA 41.0s	Germany 41.2s	GB 41.8s
1932	USA 40.0s	Germany 40.9s	Italy 41.2s
1936	USA 39.8s	Italy 41.1s	Germany 41.2s
1948	USA 40.6s	GB 41.3s	Italy 41.5s
1952	USA 40.1s	USSR 40.3s	Hungary 40.5s
1956	USA 39.5s	USSR 39.8s	Germany 40.3s
1960	Germany 39.5s	USSR 40.1s	GB 40.2s
1964	USA 39.0s	Poland 39.3s	France 39.3s
1968	USA 38.2s	Cuba 38.3s	France 38.4s
1972	USA 38.19s	USSR 38.50s	W. Germany 38.79s
1976	USA 38.33s	E. Germany 38.66s	USSR 38.78s
1980			

4×400 METRES RELAY

1912	USA 3m 16.6s	France 3m 20.7s	GB 3m 23.2s
1920	GB 3m 22.2s	S.Africa	France
1924	USA 3m 16.0s	Sweden 3m 17.0s	GB 3m 17.4s
1928	USA 3m 14.2s	Germany 3m 14.8s	Canada 3m 15.4s
1932	USA 3m 08.2s	GB 3m 11.2s	Canada 3m 12.8s
1936	GB 3m 09.0s	USA 3m 11.0s	Germany 3m 11.8s
1948	USA 3m 10.4s	France 3m 14.8s	Sweden 3m 16.3s
1952	Jamaica 3m 03.9s	USA 3m 04.0s	Germany 3m 06.6s
1956	USA 3m 04.8s	Australia 3m 06.1s	GB 3m 07.2s
1960	USA 3m 02.2s	Germany 3m 02.7s	West Indies 3m 04.0s
1964	USA 3m 00.7s	GB 3m 01.6s	Trinidad 3m 1.7s
1968	USA 2m 56.1s	Kenya 2m 59.6s	W Germany 3m 00.5s
1972	Kenya 2m 59.8s	GB 3m 00.5s	France 3m 00.7s
1976	USA 2m 58.65s	Poland 3m 01.43s	W. Germany 3m 01.98s
1980			

20,000 METRES WALK

1956	Leonid Spirin (USSR) 1h 31m 27.4s	Antonas Mikenas (USSR) 1h 32m 03.0s	Bruno Junk (USSR) 1h 32m 12.0s
1960	Viktor Golubnichy (USSR) 1h 34m 07.2s	Noel Freeman (Australia) 1h 34m 16.4s	Stan Vickers (GB) 1h 34m 56.4s
1964	Ken Matthews (GB) 1h 29m 34.0s	Dieter Lindner (Germany) 1h 31m 13.2s	Viktor Golubnichy (USSR) 1h 31m 59.4s
1968	Viktor Golubnichy (USSR) 1h 33m 58.4s	Jose Pedraza (Mexico) 1h 34m 00s	Nikolai Smaga (USSR) 1h 34m 03.4s
1972	Peter Frenkel (E. Ger) 1h 26m 42.90s	Viktor Golubnichiy (USSR) 1h 26m 55.18s	Hans Reimann (E. Ger) 1h 27m 16.88s
1976	Daniel Bautista (Mexico) 1h 24m 40.6s	Hans Reimann (E. Ger) 1h 25m 13.8s	Peter Frenkel (E. Ger) 1h 25m 29.4s
1980			

50,000 METRES WALK

1932	Thomas Green (GB) 4h 50m 10.0s	Janis Dalinsh (Latvia) 4h 47m 20.0s	Ugo Frigerio (Italy) 4h 59m 06.0s
1936	Harold Whitlock (GB) 4h 30m 41.1s	Arthur Schwab (Switz) 4h 32m 09.2s	Adalberts Bubenko (Latvia) 4h 32m 42.2s
1948	John Ljunggren (Sweden) 4h 41m 52.0s	Gaston Godel (Switz) 4h 48m 17.0s	Terence Johnson (GB) 4h 48m 31.0s
1952	Giuseppe Dordoni (Italy) 4h 28m 07.8s	Josef Dolezal (Czech) 4h 30m 17.8s	Antal Roka (Hungary) 4h 31m 27.2s
1956	Norman Read (NZ) 4h 30m 42.8s	Yevgeniy Maskinskov (USSR) 4h 32m 57.0s	John Ljunggren (Sweden) 4h 35m 02.0s
1960	Don Thompson (GB) 4h 25m 30.0s	John Ljunggren (Sweden) 4h 25m 47.0s	Abdon Pamich (Italy) 4h 27m 55.4)
1964	Abdon Pamich (Italy) 4h 11m 12.4s	Paul Nihill (GB) 4h 11m 31.2s	Ingvar Pettersson (Sweden) 4h 14m 17.4s
1968	Christoph Hohne (E Ger) 4h 20m 13.6s	Antal Kiss (Hungary) 4h 30m 17.0s	Larry Young (USA) 4h 31m 55.4s
1972	Berndt Kannenberg (W. Ger) 3h 56m 11.6s	Veniamin Soldatenko (USSR) 3h 58m 24s	Larry Young (USA) 4h 00.46s
1976	Not held		
1980			

HIGH JUMP

1896	Ellery Clark (USA) 5'11¼" (1.81m)	James Connolly (USA) 5'7¾" (1.72)	Robert Garrett (USA) 5'7⅜" (1.71)
1900	Irving Baxter (USA) 6'2¾" (1.90)	Patrick Leahy (GB) 5'10⅛" (1.78)	Lajor Gönczy (Hungary) 5'8⅞" (1.75)
1904	Samuel Jones (USA) 5'11" (1.80)	G. P. Serviss (USA) 5'10" (1.76)	Paul Weinstein (Germany) 5'10" (1.76)
1908	Harry Porter (USA) 6'3" (1.90)	Patrick Leahy (GB) 6'2" (1.88)	Istvan Somodi (Hungary) Geo Andre (France) 6'2" (1.88)
1912	Alma Richards (USA) 6'4" (1.93)	Hans Liesche (Germany) 6'3¼" (1.91)	George Horine (USA) 6'2½" (1.89)
1920	Richmond Landon (USA) 6'4¼" (1.94)	Harold Muller (USA) 6'2¾" (1.90)	Bo Ekelund (Sweden) 6'2¾" (1.90)
1924	Harold Obsorn (USA) 6'6" (1.98)	Leroy Brown (USA) 6'4¾" (1.95)	Pierre Lewden (France) 6'3⅝" (1.92)
1928	Robert King (USA) 6'4⅜" (1.94)	Ben Hedges (USA) 6'3¼" (1.91)	Claude Menard (France) 6'3¼" (1.91)
1932	Duncan McNaughton (Canada) 6'5½" (1.97)	Robert Van Osdel (USA) 6'5½" (1.97)	Simeon Toribio (Phil) 6'5½" (1.97)
1936	Cornelius Johnson (USA) 6'7⅞" (2.03)	David Albritton (USA) 6'6¾" (2.00)	Delos Thurber (USA) 6'6¾" (2.00)
1948	John Winter (Australia) 6'6" (1.98)	Björn Paulsen (Norway) 6'4¾" (1.95)	George Stanich (USA) 6'4¾" (1.95)
1952	Walter Davis (USA) 6'8¾" (2.04)	Kenneth Wiesner (USA) 6'7⅞" (2.01)	Jose Tellesda (Brazil) 6'6" (1.98)
1956	Charles Dumas (USA) 6'11½" (2.12)	Charles Porter (Australia) 6'10¾" (2.10)	Igor Kashkarov (USA) 6'9⅞" (2.08)
1960	Robert Shavlakadze (USSR) 7'1" (2.16)	Valeriy Brumel (USSR) 7'1" (2.16)	John Thomas (USA) 7'0¼" (2.14)
1964	Valeriy Brumel (USSR) 7'1¾" (2.18)	John Thomas (USA) 7'1¾" (2.18)	John Rambo (USA) 7'1" (2.16)
1968	Richard Fosbury (USA) 7'4¼" (2.24)	Ed Caruthers (USA) 7'3½" (2.22)	Valentin Gavrilov (USSR) 7'2⅝" (2.20)
1972	Yuri Tarmak (USSR) 7'3¾" (2.23)	Stefan Junge (E. Germany) 7'3" (2.21)	Dwight Stones (USA) 7'3" (2.21)
1976	Jacek Wszola (Poland) 7'4½" (2.25)	Greg Joy (Canada) 7'3¾" (2.23)	Dwight Stones (USA) 7'3" (2.21)
1980			

LONG JUMP

1896	Ellery Clark (USA) 20'10" (6.35)	Robert Garrett (USA) 20'3¼" (6.18)	James Connolly (USA) 20'0½" (6.11)
1900	Alvin Kraenzlein (USA) 23'6⅞" (7.19)	Myer Prinstein (USA) 23'6½" (7.18)	Patrick Leahy (GB) 22'9½" (6.95)
1904	Myer Prinstein (USA) 24'1" (7.34)	Daniel Frank (USA) 22'7¼" (6.89)	R. Stangland (USA) 22'7" (6.88)
1908	Frank Irons (USA) 24'6½" (7.48)	Daniel Kelly (USA) 23'3¼" (7.09)	Calvin Bricker (Canada) 23'3" (7.08)
1912	Albert Gutterson (USA) 24'11¼" (7.60)	Calvin Bricker (Canada) 23'7¾" (7.21)	Georg Aberg (Sweden) 23'6¾" (7.18)
1920	William Pettersson (Sweden) 23'5½" (7.15)	Carl Johnson (USA) 23'3¼" (7.10)	Eric Abrahamsson (Sweden) 23'2¾" (7.08)
1924	William De Hart Hubbard (USA) 24'5" (7.445)	Edward Gourdin (USA) 23'10½" (7.28)	Sverre Hansen (Norway) 23'9¾" (7.26)
1928	Edward Hamm (USA) 25'4½" (7.73)	Silvio Cator (Haiti) 24'10½" (7.58)	Alfred Bates (USA) 24'3¼" (7.40)
1932	Edward Gordon (USA) 25'0¾" (7.64)	Lambert Redd (USA) 24'11¼" (7.60)	Chuhei Nambu (Japan) 24'5¼" (7.45)
1936	Jesse Owens (USA) 26'5¼" (8.06)	Luz Long (USA) 25'9¾" (7.87)	Naoto Tajima (Japan) 25'4¾" (7.74)
1948	Willie Steele (USA) 25'8" (7.83)	Thomas Bruce (Australia) 24'9¼" (7.56)	Herbert Douglas (USA) 24'9" (7.55)
1952	Jerome Biffle (USA) 24'10" (7.57)	Meredith Gourdine (USA) 24'8½" (7.53)	Odön Földessy (Hung) 23'11½" (7.30)
1956	Greg Bell (USA) 25'8¼" (7.83)	John Bennett (USA) 25'2¼" (7.68)	Jorma Valkama (Finland) 24'6½" (7.48)
1960	Ralph Boston (USA) 26'7½" (8.12)	Irvin Roberson (USA) 26'7¼" (8.11)	Igor Ter-Ovanesyan (USSR) 26'4½" (8.04)
1964	Lynn Davies (GB) 26'5¾" (8.07)	Ralph Boston (USA) 26'4" (8.03)	Igor Ter-Ovanesyan (USSR) 26'2½" (7.99)
1968	Robert Beamon (USA) 29'2½" (8.90)	Klaus Beer (E.Ger) 26'10½" (8.19)	Ralph Boston (USA) 26'9¼" (8.16)
1972	Randy Williams (USA) 27'0½" (8.24)	Hans Baumgartner (W. Ger) 26'10" (8.18)	Arnie Robinson (USA) 26'4¼" (8.03)
1976	Arnie Robinson (USA) 27'4¾" (8.35)	Randy Williams (USA) 26'7¼" (8.11)	Frank Wartenberg (E. Ger) 26'3¾" (8.02)
1980			

TRIPLE JUMP

1896	James Connolly (USA) 44'11¾" (13.71)	Alexandre Tuffère (France) 41'8" (12.70)	Joannis Persakis (Greece) 41'1" (12.52)
1900	Myer Prinstein (USA) 47'5¾" (14.47)	James Connolly (USA) 45'10" (13.97)	L. P. Sheldon (USA) 44'9" (13.64)
1904	Myer Prinstein (USA) 47'1" (14.35)	Fred Englehardt (USA) 45'7¼" (13.90)	R. Stangland (USA) 43'10¼" (13.36)
1908	Timothy Ahearne (GB) 48'11¼" (14.91)	Garfield MacDonald (Canada) 48'5¼" (14.76)	Edvard Larsen (Nor) 47'2¾" (14.39)
1912	Gustaf Lindblom (Sweden) 48'5" (14.76)	George Aberg (Sweden) 47'7¼" (14.51)	Erik Almlöf (Swed) 46'5¾" (14.17)
1920	Vilho Tuulos (Finland) 47'7" (14.51)	Folke Jansson (Sweden) 47'6" (14.48)	Erik Almlöf (Swed) 46'10" (14.27)
1924	Archie Winter (Aust) 50'11¼" (15.53)	Luis Brunetto (Arg) 50'7¼" (14.43)	Vilho Tuulos (Finland) 50'5" (15.37)
1928	Mikio Oda (Japan) 49'10¾" (15.21)	Levi Casey (USA) 49'9¼" (15.17)	Vilho Tuulos (Finland) 49'7" (15.11)
1932	Chuhei Nambu (Japan) 51'7" (15.72)	Erik Svensson (Sweden) 50'3¼" (15.32)	Kenkichi Oshima (Japan) 49'7¼" (15.12)
1936	Naoto Tajima (Japan) 52'6" (16m)	Masao Harada (Japan) 51'4½" (15.66)	Jack Metcalfe (Aust) 50'10¼" (15.50)
1948	Arne Ahman (Sweden) 50'6¼" (15.40)	George Avery (Australia) 50'5" (15.37)	Ruhi Sarialp (Turkey) 49'3½" (15.03)
1952	Adhemar Ferreira da Silva Brazil) 53'2½" (16.22)	Leonid Shcherbakov (USSR) 52'5¼" (15.98)	Arnoldo Devonish (Ven) 50'11" (15.52)
1956	Adhemar Ferreira da Silva (Brazil) 53'7¾" (16.35)	Vilhjalmur Einarsson (Iceland) 53'4¼" (16.26)	Vitold Kreyer (USSR) 52'6¾" (16.02)
1960	Josef Schmidt (Poland) 55'1¾" (16.81)	Vladimir Goryayev (USSR) 54'6½" (16.63)	Vitold Kreyer (USSR) 53'10¾" (16.43)
1964	Josef Schmidt (Poland) 55'3½" (16.85)	Olyeg Fyedoseyev (USSR) 54'4¾" (16.58)	Victor Kravchenko (USSR) 54'4¼" (16.57)
1968	Viktor Saneyev (USSR) 57'0¾" (17.39)	Nascimento Prudencio (Brazil) 56'8" (17.27)	Giuseppe Gentile (Italy) 56'6" (17.22)
1972	Viktor Saneyev (USSR) 56'11" (17.35)	Jorg Drehmel (E. Ger) 56'9¼" (17.31)	Nelson Prudencio (Brazil) 55'11¼" (17.05)
1976	Viktor Saneyev (USSR) 57'4¼" (17.59)	James Butts (USA) 56'4¼" (17.18)	João de Oliviera (Brazil) 55'5¼" (16.90)
1980			

POLE VAULT

1896	William Hoyt (USA) 10'10" (3.30)	Albert Tyler (USA) 10'8" (3.25)	Joannis Theodoropoulos (Greece) 9'4¼" (2.85)
1900	Irving Baxter (USA) 10'10" (3.30)	M. B. Colkett (USA) 10'8" (3.25)	Carl-Albert Andersen (Norway) 10'6" (3.20)
1904	Charles Dvorak (USA) 11'6" (3.50)	Leroy Samse (USA) 11'3" (3.43)	L. Wilkins (USA) 11'3" (3.43)
1908	Alfred Gilbert & Edward Cook (USA) 12'2" (3.71)		Ernest Archibald (Canada) 11'9" (3.58)
1912	Henry Babcock (USA) 12'11½" (3.95)	Frank Nelson & Marc Wright (USA) 12'7½" (3.85)	
1920	Frank Foss (USA) 13'5" (4.09)	Henry Petersen (Denmark) 12'1¾" (3.70)	Edwin Meyers (USA) 11'9¾" (3.60)
1924	Lee Barnes (USA) 12'11½" (3.95)	Glenn Graham (USA) 12'11½" (3.95)	James Brooker (USA) 12'9½" (3.90)
1928	Sabin Carr (USA) 13'9¼" (4.20)	William Droegemuller (USA) 13'5½" (4.10)	Charles McGinnis (USA) 12'11½" (3.95)
1932	William Miller (USA) 14'1⅞" (4.32)	Shuhei Nishida (Japan) 14'0" (4.27)	George Jefferson (USA) 13'9" (4.19)
1936	Earle Meadows (USA) 14'3¼" (4.35)	Shuhei Nishida (Japan) 13'11¼" (4.25)	Sueo Oe (Japan) 13'11¼" (4.25)
1948	Guinn Smith (USA) 14'1¼" (4.30)	Erkki Kataja (Finland) 13'9½" (4.20)	Robert Richards (USA) 13'9½" (4.20)
1952	Robert Richards (USA) 14'11¼" (4.55)	Donald Laz (USA) 14'9¼" (4.50)	Ragnar Lundberg (Sweden) 14'5¼" (4.40)
1956	Robert Richards (USA) 14'11½" (4.56)	Robert Gutowski (USA) 14'10¼" (4.53)	Georgios Roubanis (Greece) 14'9¼" (4.50)
1960	Don Bragg (USA) 15'5" (4.70)	Ron Morris (USA) 15'1¼" (4.60)	Eeles Landström (Finland) 14'11¼" (4.55)
1964	Fred Hansen (USA) 16'8¾" (5.10)	Wolfgang Reinhardt (Germany) 16'6¾" (5.05)	Klaus Lehnertz (Germany) 16'5" (5m)
1968	Robert Seagren (USA) 17'8½" (5.40)	Claus Schiprowski (W.Germany) 17'8½" (5.40)	Wolfgang Nordwig (E.Germany) 17'8½" (5.40)
1972	Wolfgang Nordwig (E. Ger) 18'0½" (5.50)	Robert Seagren (USA) 17'8½" (5.40)	Jan Johnson (USA) 17'6¾" (5.35)
1976	Tadeusz Slusarski (Poland) 18'0½" (5.50)	Antti Kalliomaki (Finland) 18'0½" (5.50)	David Roberts (USA) 18'0½" (5.50)
1980			

SHOT PUT

1896	Robert Garrett (USA) 36'9¾" (11.22)	Mitiades Gouscos (Greece) 36'9" (11.20)	Georgios Papasideris (Greece) 34'0" (10.36)
1900	Richard Sheldon (USA) 46'3" (14.10)	Josiah McCracken (USA) 42'2" (12.85)	Robert Garrett (USA) 40'7" (12.37)
1904	Ralph Rose (USA) 48'7" (14.81)	Wesley Coe (USA) 47'3" (14.40)	L. Feuerbach (USA) 43'10½" (13.37)
1908	Ralph Rose (USA) 46'7½" (14.21)	Dennis Horgan (GB) 44'8¼" (13.62)	John Garrels (USA) 43'3" (13.18)
1912	Patrick McDonald (USA) 50'4" (15.34)	Ralph Rose (USA) 50'0½" (15.25)	Lawrence Whitney (USA) 45'8½" (13.93)
1920	Ville Pörhölä (Finland) 48'7" (14.81)	Elmer Niklander (Finland) 46'5¼" (14.16)	Harry Liversedge (USA) 46'5" (14.15)
1924	Clarence Houser (USA) 49'2¼" (15m)	Glenn Hartranft (USA) 48'10½" (14.90)	Ralph Hills (USA) 48'0½" (14.64)
1928	John Kuck (USA) 52'0¾" (15.87)	Herman Brix (USA) 51'8" (15.75)	Emil Hirschfield (Ger) 51'7" (15.72)
1932	Leo Sexton (USA) 52'6" (16.01)	Harlow Rothert (USA) 51'5" (15.68)	Douda Frantisek (Czech) 51'2½" (15.61)
1936	Hans Wölke (Germany) 53'1¾" (16.20)	Sulo Bärlund (Finland) 52'10¾" (16.12)	Gerhard Stöck (Ger) 51'4½" (15.66)
1948	Wilbur Thompson (USA) 56'2" (17.12)	James Delaney (USA) 54'8¾" (16.68)	James Fuchs (USA) 53'10½" (16.42)
1952	Parry O'Brien (USA) 57'1½" (17.41)	Darrow Hooper (USA) 57'0¾" (17.39)	James Fuchs (USA) 55'11¾" (17.06)
1956	Parry O'Brien (USA) 60'11¼" (18.57)	Bill Nieder (USA) 59'7¾" (18.18)	Jiri Skobla (Czech) 57'11" (17.65)
1960	Bill Nieder (USA) 65'6¾" (19.68)	Parry O'Brien (USA) 62'8¼" (19.11)	Dallas Long (USA) 62'4¼" (19.01)
1964	Dallas Long (USA) 66'8½" (20.33)	Randy Matson (USA) 66'3¼" (20.20)	Vilmos Varju (Hung) 63'7½" (19.39)
1968	Randy Matson (USA) 67'4¾" (20.54)	George Woods (USA) 66'0¼" (20.12)	Eduard Gushchin (USSR) 65'11" (20.09)
1972	Wladyslaw Komar (Poland) 69'6" (21.18)	George Woods (USA) 69'5½" (21.17)	Hartmut Briesenick (E. Ger) 69'4¼" (21.14)
1976	Udo Beyer (E. Ger) 69'0¾" (21.05)	Evgeniy Mironov (USSR) 69' (21.03)	Alexandr Barisnikov (USSR) 68'10¼" (21.00)
1980			

DISCUS THROW

1896	Robert Garrett (USA) 95'7¼" (29.15)	P. Paraskevopoulos (Greece) 95'0" (28.96)	Sotirios Versis (Greece) 94'5" (28.78)
1900	Rudolf Bauer (Hungary) 118'3" (36.04)	Janda Frantisek (Boh) 115'7¾" (35.25)	Richard Sheldon (USA) 113'6" (34.50)
1904	Martin Sheridan (USA) 128'10½" (39.28)	Ralph Rose (USA) 128'10½" (39.28)	Nicolas Georgantos (Greece) 123'7½" (37.68)
1908	Martin Sheridan (USA) 134'2" (40.89)	M. H. Griffin (USA) 133'6½" (40.70)	Marquis Horr (USA) 129'5¼" (39.45)
1912	Armas Taipale (Finland) 148'4" (45.21)	Richard Byrd (USA) 138'10" (42.32)	James Duncan (USA) 138'8¼" (42.28)
1920	Elmer Niklander (Finland) 146'7½" (44.69)	Armas Taipale (Fin) 144'11½" (44.19)	Augustus Pope (USA) 138'2½" (42.13)
1924	Clarence Houser (USA) 151'5" (46.16)	Vilho Niittymaa (Finland) 147'5½" (44.95)	Thomas Lieb (USA) 147'1" (44.83)
1928	Clarence Houser (USA) 155'3" (47.32)	Antero Kivi (Fin) 154'11½" (47.23)	James Corson (USA) 154'6½" (47.10)
1932	John Anderson (USA) 162'4½" (49.49)	Henri Laborde (France) 159'0½" (48.47)	Paul Winter (France) 157'0" (47.85)
1936	Kenneth Carpenter (USA) 165'7½" (50.48)	Gordon Dunn (USA) 161'11" (49.36)	Giorgio Oberweger (Italy) 161'6" (49.23)
1948	Adolfo Consolini (Italy) 172'2" (52.78)	Giuseppe Tosi (Italy) 169'10½" (51.78)	Fortune Gordien (USA) 166'7" (50.77)
1952	Sim Iness (USA) 180'6½" (55.03)	Adolfo Consolini (Italy) 176'5" (53.78)	James Dillon (USA) 174'9½" (53.28)
1956	Al Oerter (USA) 184'11" (56.36)	Fortune Gordien (USA) 179'0" (54.81)	Desmond Koch (USA) 178'5½" (54.40)
1960	Al Oerter (USA) 194'1¾" (59.18)	Rink Babka (USA) 190'4¼" (58.02)	Richard Cochran (USA) 187'6¼" (57.16)
1964	Al Oerter (USA) 200'1½" (61m)	Ludvik Danek (Czech) 198'6½" (60.52)	David Weill (USA) 195'2" (59.49)
1968	Al Oerter (USA) 212'6½" (64.78)	Lothar Milde (E.Ger) 206'11½" (63.08)	Ludvik Danek (Czech) 206'5" (62.92)
1972	Ludvik Danek (Czech) 211'3½" (64.40)	Jay Silvester (USA) 208'4" (63.50)	Ricky Bruch (Sweden) 208' (63.40)
1976	Mac Wilkins (USA) 221'5½" (67.50)	Wolfgang Schmidt (E. Ger) 217'3" (66.22)	John Powell (USA) 215'6½" (65.70)
1980			

HAMMER THROW

1900	John Flanagan (USA) 163'2" (49.73)	Truxton Hare (USA) 161'2" (49.13)	Josiah McCracken (USA) 139'3½" (42.46)
1904	John Flanagan (USA) 168'1" (51.23)	John DeWitt (USA) 164'11" (50.27)	Ralph Rose (USA) 150'0½" (45.73)
1908	John Flanagan (USA) 170'4¼" (51.92)	Matthew McGrath (USA) 167'11" (51.18)	Con Walsh (USA) 159'1½" (48.50)
1912	Matthew McGrath (USA) 179'7" (54.74)	Duncan Gillis (Canada) 158'9" (48.39)	Clarence Childs (USA) 158'0½" (48.17)
1920	Patrick Ryan (USA) 173'5½" (52.88)	Carl Johan Lind (Swed) 158'10½" (48.43)	Basil Bennett (USA) 158'3½" (48.25)
1924	Fred Tootell (USA) 174'10" (53.30)	Matthew McGrath (USA) 166'9½" (50.84)	Malcolm Nokes (GB) 160'4" (48.48)
1928	Patrick O'Callaghan (Eire) 168'7" (51.39)	Ossian Skiöld (Sweden) 168'3" (51.29)	Edmund Black (USA) 160'10" (49.03)
1932	Patrick O'Callaghan (Eire) 176'11" (53.92)	Ville Pörhölä (Finland) 171'6" (52.27)	Peter Zaremba (USA) 165'1½" (50.33)
1936	Karl Hein (Germany) 185'4" (56.49)	Erwin Blask (Germany) 180'7" (55.04)	Fred Warngard (Sweden) 179'10½" (54.83)
1948	Imre Nemeth (Hung) 183'11½" (56.07)	Ivan Gubijan (Yugos) 178'0½" (54.27)	Robert Bennett (USA) 176'3½" (53.73)
1952	Joszef Csermak (Hung) 197'11½" (60.34)	Karl Storch (Germany) 193'1" (58.86)	Imre Nemeth (Hung) 189'5" (57.74)
1956	Hal Connolly (USA) 207'3½" (63.19)	Mikhail Krivonosov (USSR) 206'9½" (63.03)	Anatoliy Samotsvetov (USSR) 205'3" (62.56)
1960	Vasiliy Rudenkov (USSR) 220'1¾" (67.10)	Gyula Zsivotzky (Hung) 215'10" (65.79)	Tadeusz Rut (Pol) 215'4½" (65.64)
1964	Romuald Klim (USSR) 228'10½" (69.74)	Gyula Zsivotsky (Hungary) 226'8" (69.09)	Uwe Beyer (Ger) 223'4½" (68.09)
1968	Gyula Zsivotsky (Hungary) 240'8" (73.36)	Romuald Klim (USSR) 240'5" (73.28)	Lazar Lovasz (Hung) 228'11" (69.78)
1972	Anatoli Bondarchuk (USSR) 247'8½" (75.50)	Ottomar Sachse (E. Ger) 245'11" (74.96)	Vasili Khmelevski (USSR) 242'11" (74.04)
1976	Yuriy Sedyh (USSR) 254'4" (77.52)	Alexey Spiridinov (USSR) 249'7" (76.08)	Anatoli Bondarchuk (USSR) 247'7½" (75.48)
1980			

JAVELIN

1908	Erik Lemming (Swed) 179'10½" (54.83)	Arne Halse (Norway) 165'11" (50.57)	Otto Nilsson (Swed) 154'6¼" (47.10)
1912	Erik Lemming (Swed) 198'11½" (60.64)	Juho Saaristo (Finland) 192'5½" (58.66)	Mór Kóczán (Hung) 182'1" (55.50)
1920	Jonni Myyrä (Finland) 215'9½" (65.78)	Urko Peltonen (Finland) 208'4" (63.50)	Pekka Johansson (Finland) 207'0" (63.10)
1924	Jonni Myyrä (Finland) 206'6½" (62.96)	Gunnar Lindstrom (Swed) 199'10½" (60.92)	Eugene Oberst (USA) 191'5" (58.35)
1928	Erik Lundquist (Sweden) 218'6" (66.60)	Béla Szepes (Hungary) 214'1" (65.26)	Olav Sunde (Nor) 209'10½" (63.97)
1932	Matti Järvinen (Finland) 238'6½" (72.71)	Martti Sippala (Finland) 229'0" (69.80)	Eino Penttilä (Fin) 225'4½" (68.70)
1936	Gerhard Stöck (Ger) 235'8½" (71.84)	Yrjö Nikkanen (Finland) 232'2" (70.77)	Kalervo Toivonen (Finland) 232'0" (70.72)
1948	Tapio Rautavaara (Finland) 228'11" (69.77)	Steve Seymour (USA) 221'8" (67.56)	Joszef Varszegi (Hung) 219'11" (67.03)
1952	Cyrus Young (USA) 242'0½" (73.78)	William Miller (USA) 237'8½" (72.46)	Toivo Hyytiäinen (Fin) 235'10½" (71.89)
1956	Egil Danielsen (Norway) 281'2½" (85.71)	Janusz Sidlo (Poland) 262'4½" (79.98)	Viktor Tsibulenko (USSR) 260'10" (79.50)
1960	Viktor Tsibulenko (USSR) 277'8" (84.64)	Walter Krüger (Ger) 260'4½" (79.36)	Gergely Kulcsar (Hung) 257'9¼" (78.57)
1964	Pauli Nevala (Finland) 271'2" (82.66)	Gergely Kulcsar (Hung) 270'0½" (82.32)	Janis Lusis (USSR) 264'2" (80.57)
1968	Janis Lusis (USSR) 295'7" (90.10)	Jorma Kinnunen (Finland) 290'7½" (88.58)	Gergely Kulcsar (Hung) 285'7½" (87.06)
1972	Klaus Wolfermann (W. Ger) 296'10.8s (90.48)	Janis Lusis (USSR) 296'5½" (90.46)	Bill Schmidt (USA) 276'11½" (84.42)
1976	Miklos Nemeth (Hung) 310'3½" (94.58)	Hannu Siitonen (Fin) 288'5¼" (87.92)	Gheorghe Megelea (Rum) 285'11½" (87.16)
1980	....	....	....

DECATHLON

1912	Hugo Wieslander (Sweden) 7,724.495pts	Charles Lomberg (Sweden) 7,413.510	Gösta Holmer (Sweden) 7,347.855
1920	Helge Lovland (Norway) 6,804	Brutus Hamilton (USA) 6,770.86	Bertil Ohlson (Sweden) 6,579.80
1924	Harold Osborn (USA) 7,710.775	Emerson Norton (USA) 7,350.895	Aleksander Klumberg (Estonia) 7,329.36
1928	Paavo Yrjölä (Finland) 8,053.29	Akilles Järvinen (Finland) 7,931.50	Kenneth Doherty (USA) 7,706.65
1932	James Bausch (USA) 8,462.32	Akilles Järvinen (Finland) 8,292.48	Wolrad Eberle (Germany) 8,030.80
1936	Glenn Morris (USA) 7,900	Robert Clark (USA) 7,601	Jack Parker (USA) 7,275
1948	Bob Mathias (USA) 7,139	Ignace Heinrich (France) 6,974	Floyd Simmons (USA) 6,950
1952	Bob Mathias (USA) 7,887	Milton Campbell (USA) 6,975	Floyd Simmons (USA) 6,788
1956	Milton Campbell (USA) 7,937	Rafer Johnson (USA) 7,587	Vasiliy Kuznetsov (USSR) 7,465
1960	Rafer Johnson (USA) 8,392	Chuan-Kwang Yang (Taiwan) 8,334	Vasiliy Kuznetsov (USSR) 7,809
1964	Willi Holdorf (Germany) 7,887	Rein Aun (USSR) 7,842	Hans-Joachim Walde (Germany) 7,809
1968	Bill Toomey (USA) 8,193	Hans-Joachim Walde (W. Germany) 8,111	Kurt Bendlin (W. Germany) 8,064
1972	Nikolai Avilov (USSR) 8,454	Leonid Litvinenko (USSR) 8,035	Ryszard Katus (Hungary) 7,984
1976	Bruce Jenner (USA) 8,618	Guido Kratschmer (W. Germany) 8,411	Nicolai Avilov (USSR) 8,369
1980	....	....	....

ATHLETICS (WOMEN)

100 METRES

1928	Elizabeth Robinson (USA) 12.2s	Fanny Rosenfeld (Canada) 12.2s	Ethel Smith (Canada) 12.2s
1932	Stanislawa Walasiewicz (Poland) 11.9s	Hilda Strike (Canada) 11.9s	Wilhelmina von Bremen (USA) 12.0s
1936	Helen Stephens (USA) 11.5s	Stanislawa Walasiewicz (Poland) 11.7s	Kathe Krauss (Germany) 11.9s
1948	Fanny Blankers-Koen (Netherlands) 11.9s	Dorothy Manley (GB) 12.2s	Shirley Strickland (Australia) 12.2s
1952	Marjorie Jackson (Australia) 11.5s	Daphne Hasenjager (S.Africa) 11.8s	Shirley Strickland (Australia) 11.9s
1956	Betty Cuthbert (Australia) 11.5s	Christa Stubnick (Germany) 11.7s	Marlene Mathews (Australia) 11.7s
1960	Wilma Rudolph (USA) 11.0s	Dorothy Hyman (GB) 11.3s	Giuseppina Leone (Italy) 11.3s
1964	Wyomia Tyus (USA) 11.4s	Edith Maguire (USA) 11.6s	Ewa Klobukowska (Poland) 11.6s
1968	Wyomia Tyus (USA) 11.0s	Barbara Ferrell (USA) 11.1s	Irena Kirszenstein (Poland) 11.1s
1972	Renate Stecher (E. Germany) 11.07s	Raelene Boyle (Australia) 11.23s	Silvia Chivas (Cuba) 11.24s
1976	Annegret Richter (W. Germany) 11.08s	Renate Stecher (E. Germany) 11.13s	Inge Helten (W. Germany) 11.17s
1980	....	....	....

200 METRES

1948	Fanny Blankers-Koen (Netherlands) 24.4s	Audrey Williamson (GB) 25.1s	Audrey Patterson (USA) 25.2s
1952	Marjorie Jackson (Australia) 23.7s	Bertha Brouwer (Netherlands) 24.2s	Nadyezhda Khnykina (USSR) 24.2s
1956	Betty Cuthbert (Australia) 23.4s	Christa Stubnick (Germany) 23.7s	Marlene Mathews (Australia) 23.8s
1960	Wilma Rudolph (USA) 24.0s	Jutta Heine (Germany) 24.4s	Dorothy Hyman (GB) 24.7s
1964	Edith Maguire (USA) 23.0s	Irena Kirszenstein (Poland) 23.1s	Marilyn Black (Australia) 23.1s
1968	Irena Kirszenstein (Poland) 22.5s	Raelene Boyle (Australia) 22.7s	Jennifer Lamy (Australia) 22.8s
1972	Renate Stecher (E. Germany) 22.40s	Raelene Boyle (Australia) 22.45s	Irena Szewinska (Poland) 22.74s
1976	Baerbel Eckert (E. Germany) 22.37s	Annegret Richter (W. Germany) 22.39s	Renate Stecher (E. Germany) 22.47s
1980	....	....	....

400 METRES

1964	Betty Cuthbert (Australia) 52.0s	Ann Packer (GB) 52.2s	Judith Amoore (Australia) 53.4s
1968	Colette Besson (France) 52.0s	Lillian Board (GB) 52.1s	Natalia Pechenkina (USSR) 52.2s
1972	Monika Zehrt (E. Germany) 51.08s	Rita Wilden (W. Germany) 51.21s	Kathy Hammond (USA) 61.64s
1976	Irena Szewinska (Poland) 49.29s	Christina Brehmer (E. Germany) 50.51s	Ellen Streidt (E. Germany) 50.55s
1980	....	....	....

800 METRES

1928	Lina Radke (Germany) 2m 16.8s	Kinuye Hitomi (Japan) 2m 17.6s	Inga Gentzel (Sweden) 2m 17.6s
1960	Ludmila Shevtsova (USSR) 2m 04.3s	Brenda Jones (Australia) 2m 04.4s	Ursula Donath (Germany) 2m 05.6s
1964	Ann Packer (GB) 2m 01.1s	Maryvonne Dupureur (France) 2m 01.9s	Marise Chamberlain (NZ) 2m 02.8s
1968	Madeleine Manning (USA) 2m 00.9s	Irena Silai (Romania) 2m 02.5s	Maria Gommers (Netherlands) 2m 02.6s
1972	Monika Zehit (E. Germany) 51.08s	Rita Wilden (W. Germany) 51.21s	Kathy Hammond (USA) 51.64s
1976	Tatiana Kazankina (USSR) 1m 54.94s	Nikolina Chtereva (Bulgaria) 1m 55.42s	Elfi Zinn (E. Germany) 1m 55.60s
1980	....	....	....

1500 METRES

1972	Liudmila Bragina (USSR) 4m 1.4s	Gunhild Hoffmeister (E. Germany) 4m 2.8s	Paola Cacchi (Italy) 4m 2.9s
1976	Tatiana Kazankina (USSR) 4m 5.48s	Gunhild Hoffmeister (E. Germany) 4m 6.02s	Ulrike Klapezynski (E. Germany) 4m 6.09s
1980	....	....	....

80 METRES HURDLES

1932	Mildred Didrikson (USA) 11.7s	Evelyn Hall (USA) 11.7s	Marjorie Clark (S.Africa) 11.8s
1936	Trebisonda Valla (Italy) 11.7s	Anny Steuer (Germany) 11.7s	Elizabeth Taylor (Canada) 11.7s
1948	Fanny Blankers-Koen (Netherlands) 11.2s	Maureen Gardner (GB) 11.2s	Shirley Strickland (Australia) 11.4s
1952	Shirley Strickland (Australia) 10.9s	Maria Golubnichaya (USSR) 11.1s	Maria Sander (Germany) 11.1s
1956	Shirley Strickland (Australia) 10.7s	Gisela Kohler (Germany) 10.9s	Norma Thrower (Australia) 11.0s
1960	Irina Press (USSR) 10.8s	Carole Quinton (GB) 10.9s	Gisela Birkemeyer (Germany) 11.0s
1964	Karin Balzer (Germany) 10.5s	Teresa Ciepla (Poland) 10.5s	Pamela Kilborn (Australia) 10.5s
1968	Maureen Caird (Australia) 10.3s	Pamela Kilborn (Australia) 10.4s	Chi Cheng (Taiwan) 10.4s

100 METRES HURDLES

1972	Annelie Ehrhardt (E. Germany) 12.59s	Valeria Bufanu (Rumania) 12.84s	Karin Balzer (E. Germany) 12.90s
1976	Johanna Schaller (E. Germany) 12.77s	Tatiana Anisimova (USSR) 12.78s	Natalia Lebedeva (USSR) 12.80s
1980	....	....	....

4 × 100 METRES RELAY

1928	Canada 48.4s	USA 48.8s	Germany 49.0s
1932	USA 47.0s	Canada 47.0s	GB 47.6s
1936	USA 46.9s	GB 47.6s	Canada 47.8s
1948	Netherlands 47.5s	Australia 47.6s	Canada 47.8s
1952	USA 45.9s	Germany 45.9s	GB 46.2s
1956	Australia 44.5s	GB 44.7s	USA 44.9s
1960	USA 44.5s	Germany 44.8s	Poland 45.0s
1964	Poland 43.6s	USA 43.9s	GB 44.0s
1968	USA 42.8s	Cuba 43.3s	USSR 43.4s
1972	W. Germany 42.81s	E. Germany 42.95s	Cuba 43.36s
1976	E. Germany 42.55s	W. Germany 42.59s	USSR 43.09s
1980	....	....	....

4 × 400 METRES

1972	E. Germany 3m 23s	USA 3m 25.2s	W. Germany 3m 26.5s
1976	E. Germany 3m 19.23s	USA 3m 22.81s	USSR 3m 24.24s
1980	....		

PENTATHLON

1964	Irina Press (USSR) 5,246pts	Mary Rand (GB) 5,035	Galina Bystrova (USSR) 4,956
1968	Ingrid Becker (W. Germany) 5,098	Liese Prokop (Austria) 4,966	Anna Toth Kovacs (Hungary) 4,959

1972	Mary Peters (GB) 4,801	Heide Rosendahl (W. Germany) 4,791	Burglinde Pollak (E. Germany) 4,768
1976	Siegrun Siegl (E. Germany) 4,745	Christine Laser (E. Germany) 4,745	Burglinde Pollak (E. Germany) 4,740
1980			

HIGH JUMP

1928	Ethel Catherwood (Canada) 5'2¾" (1.59)	Carolina Gisolf (Neths) 5'1½" (1.56)	Mildred Wiley (USA) 5'1½" (1.56)
1932	Jean Shiley (USA) 5'5" (1.65)	Mildred Didrikson (USA) 5'5" (1.65)	Eva Dawes (Canada) 5'3" (1.60)
1936	Ibolya Csak (Hungary) 5'3" (1.60)	Dorothy Odam (GB) 5'3" (1.60)	Elfriede Kaun (Germany) 5'3" (1.60)
1948	Alice Coachman (USA) 5'6" (1.68)	Dorothy Tyler (GB) 5'6" (1.68)	Micheline Ostermeyer (France) 5'3¼" (1.61)
1952	Esther Brand (S.Africa) 5'5¾" (1.67)	Sheila Lerwill (GB) 5'5" (1.65)	Alexandra Chudina (USSR) 5'4" (1.63)
1956	Mildred McDaniel (USA) 5'9¼" (1.76)	Thelma Hopkins (GB) & Maria Pisaryeva (USSR) 5'5¾" (1.67)	
1960	Iolanda Balas (Rumania) 6'0¾" (1.85)	Jaroslawa Jozwiakowska (Poland) & Dorothy Shirley (GB) 5'7¼" (1.71)	
1964	Iolanda Balas (Rumania) 6'2¾" (1.90)	Michele Brown (Australia) 5'11" (1.80)	Taisia Chenchik (USSR) 5'10" (1.78)
1968	Miloslava Rezkova (Czech) 5'11¾" (1.82)	Antonina Okorokova (USSR) 5'10¾" (1.80)	Valentina Kozyr (USSR) 5'10¾" (1.80)
1972	Ulrike Meyfarth (W. Ger) 6'3¾" (1.92)	Yordanka Blagoeva (Bulgaria) 6'2" (1.88)	Ilona Gusenbauer (Austria) 6'2" (1.88)
1976	Rosemarie Ackermann (E. Ger) 6'4" (1.93)	Sara Simeoni (Italy) 6'3¼" (1.91)	Yordanka Blagoeva (Bulgaria) 6'3¼" (1.91)
1980			

LONG JUMP

1948	Olga Gyarmati (Hungary) 18'8¼" (5.70)	Simonetto de Portela (Argentina) 18'4½" (5.60)	Ann-Britt Leyman (Sweden) 18'3¼" (5.58)
1952	Yvette Williams (NZ) 20'5½" (6.24)	Alexandra Chudina (USSR) 20'1¾" (6.14)	Shirley Cawley (GB) 19'5" (5.92)
1956	Elzbieta Krzesinska (Poland) 20'10" (6.35)	Willye White (USA) 19'11¾" (6.09)	Nadyezhda Dvalishvili (USSR) 19'11" (6.07)
1960	Vyera Krepkina (USSR) 20'10¾" (6.37)	Elzbieta Krzesinska (Poland) 20'6¾" (6.27)	Hildrun Claus (Ger) 20'4½" (6.21)
1964	Mary Rand (GB) 22'2¼" (6.76)	Irena Kirszenstein (Poland) 21'7¾" (6.60)	Tatyana Schelkanova (USSR) 21'0¾" (6.42)
1968	Viorica Viscopoleanu (Rumania) 22'4½" (6.82)	Sheila Sherwood (GB) 21'11" (6.68)	Tatyana Talycheva (USSR) 21'10¼" (6.66)
1972	Heide Rosendahl (W. Ger) 22'3" (6.78)	Diana Yorgova (Bulgaria) 22'2½" (6.77)	Eva Suranova (Czech) 21'10½" (6.67)
1976	Angela Voigt (E. Ger) 22'0½" (6.72)	Kathy McMillan (USA) 21'10¼" (6.66)	Lidiya Alfeeva (USSR) 21'7¾" (6.60)
1980			

SHOT PUT

1948	Micheline Ostermeyer (France) 45'1½" (13.75)	Amelia Piccinini (Italy) 42'11¼" (13.10)	Ina Schäffer (Austria) 42'10¾" (13.08)
1952	Galina Zybina (USSR) 50'1½" (15.28)	Marianne Werner (Germany) 47'9½" (14.57)	Klavdia Tochenova (USSR) 47'6¾" (14.50)
1956	Tamara Tyshkyevich (USSR) 54'5" (16.59)	Galina Zybina (USSR) 54'2¾" (16.53)	Marianne Werner (Ger) 51'2½" (15.61)
1960	Tamara Press (USSR) 56'10" (17.32)	Johanna Lüttge (Germany) 54'6" (16.61)	Earlene Brown (USA) 53'10½" (16.42)
1964	Tamara Press (USSR) 59'6" (18.14)	Renate Garisch (Germany) 57'9¼" (17.61)	Galina Zybina (USSR) 57'3" (17.45)
1968	Margitta Gummel (E.Ger) 64'4" (19.61)	Marita Lange (E. Ger) 61'7½" (18.78)	Nina Chizhova (USSR) 59'7¾" (18.19)
1972	Nina Chizhova (USSR) 69' (21.03)	Margitta Gummel (E. Ger) 66'4" (20.22)	Ivanka Khristova (Bulgaria) 63'5¾" (19.35)
1976	Ivanka Khristova (Bulgaria) 69'5" (21.16)	Nina Chizhova (USSR) 68'9¼" (20.96)	Helena Fibingerova (Czech) 67'9¾" (20.67)
1980			

DISCUS THROW

1928	Halina Konopacka (Pol) 129'11¾" (39.62)	Lilian Copeland (USA) 121'7¾" (37.08)	Ruth Svedberg (Sweden) 117'10¼" (35.92)
1932	Lilian Copeland (USA) 133'1¾" (40.58)	Ruth Osburn (USA) 131'7½" (40.12)	Jadwiga Wajsowna (Pol) 127'1¼" (38.74)
1936	Gisela Mauermayer (Ger) 156'3¼" (47.36)	Jadwiga Wajsowna (Poland) 151'7¾" (46.22)	Paula Mollenhauer (Ger) 130'6¾" (39.80)
1948	Micheline Ostermeyer (France) 137'6" (41.92)	Edera Gentile (Italy) 135'0¾" (41.17)	Jacqueline Mazeas (Fr) 132'7¼" (40.47)
1952	Nina Romashkova (USSR) 168'8½" (51.42)	Yelizaveta Bagryantseva (USSR) 154'5½" (47.08)	Nina Dumbadze (USSR) 151'10¾" (46.29)
1956	Olga Fikotova (Czech) 176'1½" (53.69)	Irina Beglyakova (USSR) 172'4½" (52.54)	Nina Ponomaryeva (USSR) 170'8" (52.02)
1960	Nina Ponomaryeva (USSR) 180'9¼" (55.10)	Tamara Press (USSR) 172'6½" (52.59)	Lia Manoliu (Rum) 171'9½" (52.36)
1964	Tamara Press (USSR) 187'10½" (52.27)	Ingrid Lotz (Ger) 187'8½" (57.21)	Lia Manoliu (Rum) 186'11" (56.97)
1968	Lia Manoliu (Rum) 191'2½" (58.28)	Liesel Westermann (W.Ger) 189'6" (57.76)	Jolan Kleiber (Hung) 180'1½" (54.90)
1972	Faina Mulnik (USSR) 218'7" (66.62)	Argentina Menis (Rum) 213'5½" (65.06)	Vassilka Stoyeva (Bulg) 211'1" (64.34)
1976	Evelin Schlaak (E. Ger) 226'4½" (69.00)	Maria Vergova (Bulg) 220'9½" (67.30)	Gabriele Hinzmann (E. Ger) 219'3½" (66.84)
1980			

JAVELIN THROW

1932	Mildred Didrikson (USA) 143'4" (43.68)	Ellen Braumüller (Ger) 142'8¾" (43.49)	Tilly Fleischer (Ger) 141'6⅞" (43m)
1936	Tilly Fleischer (Ger) 148'2¾" (45.18)	Luise Krüger (Ger) 142'0¼" (43.29)	Janina Kwasniewska (Pol) 137'1¼" (41.80)
1948	Hermine Bauma (Austria) 149'6" (45.57)	Kaisa Parviäinen (Finland) 143'8" (43.79)	Lilly Carlstedt (Den) 140'5" (42.08)
1952	Dana Zatopkova (Czech) 165'7" (50.47)	Alexandra Chudina (USSR) 164'0⅞" (50.01)	Yelena Gorchakova (USSR) 163'3" (49.76)
1956	Inese Jaunzeme (USSR) 176'8½" (53.86)	Marlene Ahrens (Chile) 165'3½" (50.38)	Nadyezhda Konyayeva (USSR) 164'11½" (50.28)
1960	Elvira Ozolina (USSR) 183'8" (55.98)	Dana Zatopkova (Czech) 176'5¼" (53.78)	Birute Kalediene (USSR) 175'4½" (53.45)
1964	Michaela Penes (Rum) 198'7½" (60.54)	Marta Rudasne (Hungary) 191'2" (58.27)	Yelena Gorchakova (USSR) 187'2½" (57.06)
1968	Angela Nemeth (Hung) 198'0½" (60.36)	Michaela Penes (Rumania) 196'7" (59.92)	Eva Janko (Austria) 190'5" (58.04)
1972	Ruth Fuchs (E. Ger) 209'7" (63.88)	Jacqueline Todten (E. Ger) 205'2" (62.54)	Kathy Schmidt (USA) 196'8" (59.94)
1976	Ruth Fuchs (E. Ger) 216'4" (65.94)	Marion Becker (W. Ger) 212'5¼" (64.70)	Kathy Schmidt (USA) 209'10" (63.96)
1980			

BASKETBALL

1936	USA	Canada	Mexico
1948	USA	France	Brazil
1952	USA	USSR	Uruguay
1956	USA	USSR	Uruguay
1960	USA	USSR	Brazil
1964	USA	USSR	Brazil
1968	USA	Yugoslavia	USSR
1972	USSR	USA	Cuba
1976	USA	Yugoslavia	USSR
1980			

BASKETBALL (WOMEN)

1976	USSR	USA	Bulgaria
1980			

BOXING

LIGHT FLYWEIGHT

1968	Francisco Rodriguez (Venezuela)	Yung-Ju Jee (S.Korea)	Harlan Marbley (USA) Hubert Skrzypczak (Poland)
1972	Gyoergy Gedo (Hungary)	Gil Kim (North Korea)	Ralph Evans (GB) Enrique Rodriguez (Spa)
1976	Jorge Hernandez (Cuba)	Uk Byong Li (North Korea)	Payao Pooltarat (Thai) Orlando Maldonado (Puerto Rico)
1980			

FLYWEIGHT

1904	George Finnegan (USA)	Miles Burke (USA)	
1920	Frank De Genaro (USA)	Anders Petersen (Denmark)	Bill Cuthbertson (GB)
1924	Fidel La Barba (USA)	James McKenzie (GB)	Raymond Fee (USA)
1928	Antal Kocsis (Hungrary)	Armand Apell (France)	Carlo Cavagnoli (Italy)
1932	Istvan Enekes (Hungary)	Francisco Cabanas (Mexico)	Louis Salica (USA)
1936	Willi Kaiser (Germany)	Gavino Matta (Italy)	Louis Laurie (USA)
1948	Pascual Perez (Argentina)	Spartaco Bandinelli (Italy)	Soo Ann Han (Korea)
1952	Nathan Brooks (USA)	Edgar Basel (Germany)	Anatoliy Bulakov (USSR) Willie Toweel (S.Africa)
1956	Terry Spinks (GB)	Mircea Dobrescu (Rumania)	John Caldwell (Eire) Rene Libeer (France)
1960	Gyula Török (Hungary)	Sergey Sivko (USSR)	Kiyoshi Tanabe (Japan) Abdelmoneim Elguindi (UAR)
1964	Fernando Atzori (Italy)	Artur Olech (Poland)	Stanislav Sorokin (USSR) Robert Carmody (USA)
1968	Ricardo Delgado (Mexico)	Artur Olech (Poland)	Servilio de Oliveira (Brazil) Leo Rwabogo (Uganda)
1972	Gheorghi Kostadinov (Bulgaria)	Leo Rwarwogo (Uganda)	Leszek Blazynski (Pol) Douglas Rodruigiez (Cuba)
1976	Leo Randolph (USA)	Ramon Duvalon (Cuba)	David Torosyan (USSR) Leszek Blazynski (Pol)
1980			

BANTAMWEIGHT

1904	O. L. Kirk (USA)	George Finnegan (USA)	

1908	H. Thomas (GB)	J. Condon (GB)	W. Webb (GB)
1920	Clarence Walker (S.Africa)	C. Graham (Canada)	James McKenzie (GB)
1924	William Smith (S.Africa)	Salvatore Tripoli (USA)	Jean Ces (France)
1928	Vittorio Tamagnini (Italy)	John Daley (USA)	Harry Isaacs (S.Africa)
1932	Horace Gwynne (Canada)	Hans Ziglarski (Germany)	Jose Villanueva (Philippines)
1936	Ulderico Sergo (Italy)	Jack Wilson (USA)	Fidel Ortiz (Mexico)
1948	Tibor Csik (Hungary)	Giovanni Zuddas (Italy)	Juan Venegas (Puerto Rico)
1952	Pentti Hämäläinen (Finland)	John McNally (Eire)	Gennadiy Garbuzov (USSR) / Joon Kang (Korea)
1956	Wolfgang Behrendt (Germany)	Soon Song Chung (Korea)	Freddie Gilroy (Eire) / Claudio Barrientos (Chile)
1960	Olyeg Grigoryev (USSR)	Primo Zamparini (Italy)	Oliver Taylor (Aust) / Bruno Bendig (Poland)
1964	Takao Sakurai (Japan)	Shin Cho Chung (S.Korea)	Juan Fabila (Mexico) / Washington Rodriguez (Uruguay)
1968	Valery Sokolov (USSR)	Eridadi Mukwanga (Uganda)	Eiji Morioka (Japan) / Soon Kill Chang (S.Korea)
1972	Orlando Martinez (Cuba)	Alfonso Zamora (Mexico)	George Turpin (GB) / Ricardo Carreras (USA)
1976	Yong Jo Gu (N. Korea)	Charles Mooney (USA)	Pat Cowdell (GB) / Victor Rybakov (USSR)
1980	....	....	....

FEATHERWEIGHT

1904	O. L. Kirk (USA)	Frank Haller (USA)	
1908	Richard Gunn (GB)	C. Morris (GB)	Hugh Roddin (GB)
1920	Paul Fritsch (France)	Jean Gachet (France)	Edoardo Garzena (Italy)
1924	John Fields (USA)	Joseph Salas (USA)	Pedro Quartucci (Argentina)
1928	Bep van Klaveren (Netherlands)	Victor Peralta (Argentina)	Harold Devine (USA)
1932	Carmelo Robledo (Argentina)	Josef Schleinkofer (Germany)	Carl Carlsson (Sweden)
1936	Oscar Casanova (Argentina)	Charles Catterall (S.Africa)	Josef Miner (Germany)
1948	Ernesto Formenti (Italy)	Denis Shepherd (S.Africa)	Aleksey Antkiewicz (Poland)
1952	Jan Zachara (Czechoslovakia)	Sergio Caprari (Italy)	Leonard Leisching (S.Africa) / Joseph Ventaja (France)
1956	Vladimir Safronov (USSR)	Tommy Nicholls (GB)	Henryk Niedzwiedzk (Poland) / Pentti Hämäläinen (Fin)
1960	Francesco Musso (Italy)	Jerzy Adamski (Poland)	William Meyers (S.Afr) / Jorma Limmonen (Fin)
1964	Stanislav Stepashkin (USSR)	Antony Villanueva (Philippines)	Charles Brown (USA) / Heinz Schultz (Ger)
1968	Antonio Roldan (Mexico)	Albert Robinson (USA)	Philip Waruingi (Kenya) / Ivan Michailov (Bulg)
1972	Boris Kousnetsov (USSR)	Philip Waruinge (Kenya)	Clemente Rojas (Col) / Andras Botos (Hun)
1976	Angel Herrera (Cuba)	Richard Nowakowski (E. Germany)	Leszek Kosedowski (Pol) / Davey Armstrong (USA)
1980	....	....	....

LIGHTWEIGHT

1904	H. J. Spanger (USA)	James Eagan (USA)	R. Van Horn (USA)
1908	Fred Grace (GB)	F. Spiller (GB)	H. Johnson (GB)
1920	Samuel Mosberg (USA)	Gotfred Johanssen (Denmark)	John Newton (Canada)
1924	Hans Nielsen (Denmark)	Alfredo Copello (Argentina)	Frederick Boylston (USA)
1928	Carlo Orlandi (Italy)	Stephen Halaiko (USA)	Gunnar Berggren (Sweden)
1932	Lawrence Stevens (S.Africa)	Thure Alhquist (Sweden)	Nathan Bor (USA)
1936	Imre Harangi (Hungary)	Nikolai Stepulov (Estonia)	Erik Agren (Sweden)
1948	Gerald Dreyer (S.Africa)	Joseph Vissers (Belgium)	Svend Wad (Denmark)
1952	Aureliano Bolognesi (Italy)	Aleksey Antkiewicz (Poland)	Gheorghe Fiat (Rum) / Erkki Pakkanen (Fin)
1956	Dick McTaggart (GB)	Harry Kurschat (Germany)	Anthony Byrne (Eire) / Anatoliy Laguetko (USSR)
1960	Kazimierz Pazdizior (Poland)	Sandro Lopopolo (Italy)	Dick McTaggart (GB) / Alberto Laudiono (Arg)
1964	Jozef Grudzien (Poland)	Vellikton Barannikov (USSR)	Ronnie Harris (USA) / James McCourt (Eire)
1968	Ronnie Harris (USA)	Jozef Grudzien (Poland)	Calistrast Cutov (Rum) / Zvonimir Vujin (Yugos)
1972	Jan Szczepanski (Poland)	Laszlo Orban (Hungary)	Samuel Mbugua (Ken) / Alfonso Perez (Col)
1976	Howard Davis (USA)	Simion Cutov (Rumania)	Vasiliy Solomin (USSR) / Tzvetan Tzvetkov (Bul)
1980	....	....	....

LIGHT-WELTERWEIGHT

1952	Charles Adkins (USA)	Viktor Mednov (USSR)	Erkki Malenius (Finland) / Bruno Visintin (Italy)
1956	Vladimir Jengibarian (USSR)	Franco Nenci (Italy)	Henry Loubscher (S.Afr) / Constantin Dumitrescu (Rumania)
1960	Bohumil Nemecek (Czechoslovakia)	Clement Quartey (Ghana)	Quincy Daniels (USA) / Marian Kasprzyk (Pol)
1964	Jerzy Kulej (Poland)	Evgeniy Frolov (USSR)	Eddie Blay (Ghana) / Habib Galhia (Tunisia)
1968	Jerzy Kulej (Poland)	Enrique Regueiferos (Cuba)	Arto Nilsson (Finland) / James Wallington (USA)
1972	Ray Seales (USA)	Anghel Anghelov (Bulgaria)	Zvonimir Vujiv (Yug) / Isaaka Daborg (Nig)
1976	Ray Leonard (USA)	Andreas Aldama (Cuba)	Vladimir Kolev (Bulg) / Kazimierz Szczerba (Pol)
1980	....	....	....

WELTERWEIGHT

1904	Albert Young (USA)	H. Spanger (USA)	Joseph Lydon (USA)
1920	Tony Schneider (Canada)	A. Ireland (GB)	Frederick Colberg (USA)
1924	Jean Delarge (Belgium)	Hector Mendez (Argentina)	Douglas Lewis (Canada)
1928	Edward Morgan (New Zealand)	Paul Landini (Argentina)	Raymond Smillie (Canada)
1932	Edward Flynn (USA)	Erich Campe (Germany)	Bruno Ahlberg (Finland)
1936	Sten Suvio (Finland)	Michael Murach (Germany)	Gerhard Petersen (Denmark)
1948	Julius Torma (Czechoslovakia)	Horace Herring (USA)	Alessandro d'Ottavio (Italy)
1952	Zygmunt Chychla (Poland)	Sergey Shcherbakov (USSR)	Victor Jörgensen (Den) / Gunther Heidmann (Ger)
1956	Necolae Linca (Rumania)	Frederick Tiedt (Eire)	Kevin Hogarth (Aust) / Nicholas Gargano (GB)
1960	Giovanni Benvenuti (Italy)	Yuriy Radnoyak (USSR)	Leszek Drogosz (Pol) / James Lloyd (GB)
1964	Marian Kasprzyk (Poland)	Richardas Tamulis (USSR)	Pertti Purhonen (Fin) / Silvano Bertini (Italy)
1968	Manfred Wolke (E.Germany)	Joseph Bessala (Cameroons)	Vladimir Masalimov (USSR) / Mario Guilloti (Arg)
1972	Emilio Correa (Cuba)	Janos Kadji (Hungary)	Dick Murunga (Ken) / Jesse Valdez (USA)
1976	Jochen Bachfeld (E. Germany)	Pedro Gamarro (Venezuela)	Reinhard Skricek (W. Germany) / Victor Zilberman (Rum)
1980	....	....	....

LIGHT-MIDDLEWEIGHT

1952	Laszlo Papp (Hungary)	Theunis Van Schalkwyk (S.Africa)	Boris Tishin (USSR) / Eladio Herrera (Arg)
1956	Laszlo Papp (Hungary)	Jose Torres (USA)	John McCormack (GB) / Zbigniew Pietrzykowski (Poland)
1960	Wilbert McClure (USA)	Carmelo Bossi (Italy)	Boris Lagutin (USSR) / William Fisher (GB)
1964	Boris Lagutin (USSR)	Jo Gonzales (France)	Nojim Maiyegun (Nig) / Jozef Grzesiak (Poland)
1968	Boris Lagutin (USSR)	Rolando Garbey (Cuba)	John Baldwin (USA) / Gunther Meyer (W.Ger)
1972	Dieter Kottysch (E. Germany)	Wieslaw Rudkowski (Poland)	Alan Minter (GB) / Peter Tiepold (W. Ger)
1976	Jerzy Rybicki (Poland)	Tadija Kacar (Yugoslavia)	Victor Savchenko (USSR) / Rolando Garbey (Cuba)
1980	....	....	....

MIDDLEWEIGHT

1904	Charles Mayer (USA)	Benjamin Spradley (USA)	
1908	John Douglas (GB)	Reginald Baker (Australia)	W. Philo (GB)
1920	Harry Mallin (GB)	Jean Prudhomme (Canada)	Henri Herzowitch (Canada)
1924	Harry Mallin (GB)	John Elliott (GB)	Joseph Beecken (Belgium)
1928	Pietro Toscani (Italy)	Jan Hermanek (Czechoslovakia)	Leonard Steyaert (Belgium)
1932	Carmen Barth (USA)	Amado Azar (Argentine)	Ernest Pierce (S.Africa)
1936	Jean Despeaux (France)	Henry Tiller (Norway)	Raul Villareal (Argentina)
1948	Laszlo Papp (Hungary)	John Wright (GB)	Ivano Fontana (Italy)
1952	Floyd Patterson (USA)	Vasile Tita (Rumania)	Boris Georgiev (Bulg) / Karl Sjölin (Sweden)
1956	Genadiy Schatkov (USSR)	Ramon Tapia (Chile)	Gilbert Chapron (Fr) / Victor Zalazar (Arg)

1960	Edward Crook (USA)	Tadeusz Walasek (Poland)	Ion Monea (Rumania) Evgeniv Feofanov (USSR)
1964	Valeriy Popenchenko (USSR)	Emil Schulz (Germany)	Franco Valla (Italy) Tadeusz Walasek (Pol)
1968	Chris Finnegan (GB)	Aleksey Kiselyov (USSR)	Agustin Zaragoza (Mex) Alfred Jones (USA)
1972	Viatsechiav Lemechev (USSR)	Reima Virtanen (Finland)	Prince Amartey (Gha) Jack Johnson (USA)
1976	Michael Spinks (USA)	Rufat Riskiev (USSR)	Luis Martinez (Cuba) Alec Nastac (Rumania)
1980	....	....	....

LIGHT-HEAVYWEIGHT

1920	Edward Eagan (USA)	Sverre Sörsdal (Norway)	H. Franks (GB)
1924	Harry Mitchell (GB)	Thyge Petersen (Denmark)	Sverre Sörsdal (Norway)
1928	Victorio Avendano (Argentine)	Ernst Pistulla (Germany)	Karel Miljon (Netherlands)
1932	David Carstens (S.Africa)	Gino Rossi (Italy)	Peter Jörgensen (Denmark)
1936	Roger Michelot (France)	Richard Voigt (Germany)	Francisco Risiglione (Argentina)
1948	George Hunter (S.Africa)	Donald Scott (GB)	M. Cia (Argentina)
1952	Norvel Lee (USA)	Antonio Pacenza (Argentina)	Anatoliy Perov (USSR) Harry Siljander (Finland)
1956	James Boyd (USA)	Gheorghe Negrea (Rumania)	Carlos Lucas (Chile) Romualdas Morauskas (USSR)
1960	Cassius Clay (USA)	Zbigniew Pietrzykowski (Poland)	Anthony Madigan (Aust) Giulio Saraudi (Italy)
1964	Cosimo Pinto (Italy)	Aleksey Kiselyov (USSR)	Alexander Nicolov (Bulgaria) Zbigniew Pietrzykowski (Poland)
1968	Dan Pozniak (USSR)	Ion Monea (Rumania)	Gueorgui Stankov (Bulgaria) Stanislaw Dragan (Pol)
1972	Mate Parlov (Yugoslavia)	Gilberto Carillo (Cuba)	Isaac Ikhouria (Nig) Janusz Gortat (Pol)
1976	Leon Spinks (USA)	Sixto Soria (Cuba)	Costica Dafinoiu (Rum) Janusz Gortat (Poland)
1980	....	....	....

HEAVYWEIGHT

1904	Samuel Berger (USA)	Charles Mayer (USA)	
1908	A. L. Oldman (GB)	S. Evans (GB)	F. Parks (GB)
1920	Ronald Rawson (GB)	Sören Petersen (Den)	Albert Eluere (France)
1924	Otto von Porat (Norway)	Sören Petersen (Den)	Alfredo Porzio (Arg)
1928	Arturo Jurado (Argentina)	Nils Ramm (Sweden)	Michael Michaelsen (Denmark)
1932	Santiago Lovell (Arg)	Luigi Rovati (Italy)	Frederick Feary (USA)
1936	Herbert Runge (Germany)	Guillermo Lovell (Arg)	Erling Nilsen (Norway)
1948	Rafael Iglesias (Arg)	Gunnar Nilsson (Sweden)	John Arthur (S.Africa)
1952	Edward Sanders (USA)	Andries Nieman (S.Africa)	Ikka Koski (Finland)
1956	Pete Rademacher (USA)	Lev Mukhin (USSR)	Daniel Bekker (S.Africa) Giacomo Bozzano (Italy)
1960	Franco de Piccoli (Italy)	Daniel Bekker (S.Africa)	Josef Nemec (Czech) Günter Siegmund (Ger)
1964	Joe Frazier (USA)	Hans Huber (Germany)	Guiseppe Ros (Italy) Vadim Yemelyanov (USSR)
1968	George Foreman (USA)	Iones Chepulis (USSR)	Giorgio Bambini (Italy) Joaquin Rocha (Mex)
1972	Teofilo Stevenson (Cuba)	Ion Alexe (Rumania)	Peter Hussing (W. Ger) Hasse Thomsen (Swe)
1976	Teofilo Stevenson (Cuba)	Mircea Simon (Rumania)	Clarence Hill (Bermuda) Johnny Tate (USA)
1980	....	....	....

CYCLING

1,000 METRES SPRINT

1900	G. Taillandier (France) 2m 16.0s	F. Vasserot (France)	F. Sanz (France)
1920	Mauritius Peeters (Netherlands) 1m 38.3s	Thomas Johnson (GB)	Harry Ryan (GB)
1924	Lucien Michard (France)	Jacob Meijer (Neths)	Jean Cugnot (France)
1928	Roger Beaufrand (France)	Antoine Mazairac (Netherlands)	Willy Falck-Hansen (Denmark)
1932	Jacobus van Egmond (Netherlands)	Louis Chaillot (France)	Bruno Pellizzari (Italy)
1936	Toni Merkens (Germany)	Arie van Vliet (Netherlands)	Louis Chaillot (France)
1948	Mario Ghella (Italy)	Reg Harris (GB)	Axel Schandorff (Denmark)
1952	Enzo Sacchi (Italy)	Lionel Cox (Australia)	Werner Potzernheim (Germany)
1956	Michel Rousseau (France)	Guglielmo Pesenti (Italy)	Richard Ploog (Australia)
1960	Sante Gaiardoni (Italy)	Leo Sterckx (Belgium)	Valentino Gasparella (Italy)
1964	Giovanni Pettenella (Italy)	Sergio Bianchetto (Italy)	Daniel Morelon (France)
1968	Daniel Morelon (France)	Giordano Turrini (Italy)	Pierre Trentin (France)

1972	Daniel Morelon (France)	John Nicholson (Australia)	Omari Phakadze (USSR)
1976	Anton Tkac (Czechoslovakia)	Daniel Morelon (France)	Hans Jurgen Geschke (E. Germany)
1980	....	....	....

1,000 METRES TIME TRIAL

1928	Willy Falck-Hansen (Denmark) 1m 14.4s	Gerard van Drakenstein (Netherlands) 1m 15.2s	Edgar Gray (Australia) 1m 15.6s
1932	Edgar Gray (Australia) 1m 13.0s	Jacobus van Egmond (Netherlands) 1m 13.3s	Charles Rampelberg (France) 1m 13.4s
1936	Arie van Vliet (Netherlands) 1m 12.0s	Pierre Georget (France) 1m 12.8s	Rudolph Karsch (Germany) 1m 13.2s
1948	Jacques Dupont (France) 1m 13.5s	Pierre Nihant (Belgium) 1m 14.5s	Thomas Godwin (GB) 1m 15.0s
1952	Russell Mockridge (Australia) 1m 11.1s	Marino Morettini (Italy) 1m 12.7s	Raymond Robinson (S.Africa) 1m 13.0s
1956	Leandro Faggin (Italy) 1m 09.8s	Ladislav Foucek (Czech) 1m 11.4s	Alfred Swift (S.Africa) 1m 11.6s
1960	Sante Gaiardoni (Italy) 1m 07.27s	Dieter Gieseler (Germany) 1m 08.75s	Rostislav Vargashkin (USSR) 1m 08.86s
1964	Patrick Sercu (Belgium) 1m 09.59s	Giovanni Pettenella (Italy) 1m 10.09s	Pierre Trentin (France) 1m 10.42s
1968	Pierre Trentin (France) 1m 03.91s	Niels Fredborg (Denmark) 1m 04.61s	Janusz Kierzkowski (Poland) 1m 04.63s
1972	Niels Fredborg (Denmark) 1m 06.44s	Daniel Clark (Australia) 1m 06.87s	Jurgen Schutze (E. Germany) 1m 07.02s
1976	Klaus Jurgen Grunke (E. Germany) 1m 5.927s	Michel Vaarten (Belgium) 1m 7.516s	Niels Fredborg (Denmark) 1m 7.617s
1980	....	....	....

2,000 METRES TANDEM

1908	France 3m 07.6s	GB	GB
1920	GB 2m 49.4s	S.Africa	Netherlands
1924	France 2m 40.0s	Denmark	Netherlands
1928	Netherlands	GB	Germany
1932	France	GB	Denmark
1936	Germany	Netherlands	France
1948	Italy	GB	France
1952	Australia	S.Africa	Italy
1956	Australia	Czechoslovakia	Italy
1960	Italy	Germany	USSR
1964	Italy	USSR	Germany
1968	France	Netherlands	Belgium
1972	USSR	E. Germany	Poland

4,000 METRES INDIVIDUAL PURSUIT

1964	Jiri Daler (Czech) 5m 04.75s	Giorgio Ursi (Italy) 5m 05.96s	Preben Isaksson (Denmark) 5m 01.90s
1968	Daniel Rebillard (France) 4m 41.71s	Mogens Frey (Denmark) 4m 42.43s	Xavier Kurmann (Switzerland) 4m 39.42s
1972	Knut Knudson (Norway) 4m 45.74s	Xaver Kurmann (Switz) 4m 51.96s	Hans Lutz (W. Germany) 4m 50.80
1976	Gregor Braun (W. Germany) 4m 47.61s	Herman Ponsteen (Netherlands) 4m 49.72s	Thomas Huschke (E. Germany) 4m 52.71s
1980	....	....	....

4,000 METRES TEAM PURSUIT

1920	Italy 5m 20.0s	GB	S.Africa
1924	Italy 5m 12.0s	Poland	Belgium
1928	Italy 5m 1.8s	Netherlands 5m 6.2s	GB 5m 2.4s
1932	Italy 4m 52.9s	France 4m 55.7s	GB 4m 56.0s
1936	France 4m 45.0s	Italy 4m 51.0s	GB 4m 53.6s
1948	France 4m 57.8s	Italy 5m 36.7s	GB 5m 55.8s
1952	Italy 4m 46.1s	S.Africa 4m 53.6s	GB 4m 51.5s
1956	Italy 4m 37.4s	France 4m 39.4s	GB 4m 42.2s
1960	Italy 4m 30.90s	Germany 4m 35.78s	USSR 4m 34.05s
1964	Germany 4m 35.67s	Italy 4m 35.74s	Netherlands 4m 38.99s
1968	Denmark 4m 22.44s	W.Germany 4m 18.35s	Italy 4m 18.35s
1972	W. Germany 4m 22.14s	E. Germany 4m 25.25s	Great Britain 4m 28.78s
1976	West Germany	USSR	Great Britain
1980	....	....	....

ROAD-RACE

1896	A. Konstantinidis (Greece) 3h 22m 31.0s	August Goedrich (Germany) 3h 42m 18.0s	F. Battel (GB)
1912	Rudolph Lewis (S.Africa) 10h 42m 39.0s	Frederick Grubb (GB) 10h 51m 24.2s	Carl Schutte (USA) 10h 52m 38.8s
Teams:	Sweden 44h 35m 33.6s	GB 44h 44m 39.2s	USA 44h 47m 55.5s
1920	Harry Stenqvist (Sweden) 4h 40m 01.8s	Henry Kaltenbrun (S.Africa) 4h 41m 26.6s	Francois Canteloube (France) 4h.42m 54.4s
Teams:	France 19h 16m 43.2s	Sweden 19h 23m 10.0s	Belgium 19h 28m 44.4s
1924	Armand Blanchonnet (France) 6h 20m 48.0s	Henry Hoevenaers (Belgium) 6h 30m 27.0s	Rene Hamel (France) 6h 30m 51.6s
Teams:	France 19h 30m 13.4s	Belgium 19h 46m 55.4s	Sweden 19h 59m 41.4
1928	Henry Hansen (Denmark) 4h 47m 18.0s	Frank Southall (GB) 4h 55m 6s	Gösta Carlsson (Sweden) 5h 00m 17s
Teams:	Denmark 15h 09m 14.0s	GB 15h 14m 49.0s	Sweden 15h 27m 22.0s
1932	Attilio Pavesi (Italy) 2h 28m 05.6s	Guglielmo Segato (Italy) 2h 29m 21.4s	Bernhard Britz (Sweden) 2h 29m 45.2s
Teams:	Italy 7h 27m 15.2s	Denmark 7h 38m 50.2s	Sweden 7h 39m 12.6s
1936	Robert Charpentier (France) 2h 33m 05.0s	Guy Lapebie (France) 2h 33m 05.2s	Ernst Nievergelt (Switz) 2h 33m 05.8s
Teams:	France 7h 39m 16.2s	Switz 7h 39m 20.4s	Belgium 7h 39m 21.2s

1948 Jose Beyaert (France) 5h 18m 12.6s / Petrus.Voorting (Neths) 5h 18m 16.2s / Lode Wouters (Belgium) 5h 18m 16.2s
Teams: Belgium 15h 58m 17.4s / GB 16h 03m 31.6s / France 16h 08m 19.4s
1952 Andre Noyelle (Belgium) 5h 06m 03.4s / Robert Grondelaers (Belgium) 5h 06m 51.2s / Edi Ziegler (Germany) 5h 07m 47.5s
Teams: Belgium 15h 20m 46.6s / Italy 15h 33m 27.3s / France 15h 38m 58.1s
1956 Ercole Baldini (Italy) 5h 21m 17.0s / Arnaud Geyre (France) 5h 23m 16.0s / Alan Jackson (GB) 5h 23m 16.0s
Teams: France 22pts / GB 23 / Germany 27
1960 Viktor Kapitanov (USSR) 4h 20m 37.0s / Livio Trape (Italy) 4h 20m 37.0s / Willy van den Berghen (Belgium) 4h 20m 57.0s
Teams: Italy 2h 14m 33.53s / Germany 2h 16m 56.31s / USSR 2h 18m 41.67s
1964 Mario Zanin (Italy) 4h 39m 51.63s / Kjell Rodian (Denmark) 4h 39m 51.65s / Walter Godefroot (Belg) 4h 39m 51.74s
Teams: Netherlands 2h 26m 31.19s / Italy 2h 26m 55.39s / Sweden 2h 27m 11.52s
1968 Franco Vianelli (Italy) 4h 41m 25.24s / Leif Mortensen (Denmark) 4h 42m 49.71s / Gosta Pettersson (Swed) 4h 43m 15.24s
Teams: Netherlands 2h 07m 49.06s / Sweden 2h 09m 26.60s / Italy 2h 10m 18.74s
1972 Hennie Kuiper (Neth) 4h 14m 37.0s / Kevin Sefton (Australia) 4h 15m 4s / Jaime Huelamo (Spain) 4h 15m 4s
Teams: USSR / Poland / Belgium
1976 Bernt Johansson (Sweden) 4h 46m 52s / Giuseppe Martinelli (Italy) 4h 47m 23s / Mieszysl Mowicki (Poland) 4h 47m 23s
1980

100 KMS TEAM TIME TRIAL
1976 USSR 2h 8m 53s / Poland 2h 9m 13s / Denmark 2h 12m 20s
1980

EQUESTRIAN SPORTS
GRAND PRIX (JUMPING)
1912 Jean Carion (France) 186pts / von Kröcher (Germany) 186 / Emanuel de Soye (Belgium) 185
Teams: Sweden 545pts / France 538 / Germany 530
1920 Tommaso di Lequio (Italy) no faults / Alessandro Valerio (Italy) 3 / Gustaf Lewenhaupt (Sweden) 4
Teams: Sweden 14 faults / Belgium 16.25 / Italy 18.75
1924 Alphonse-Gemusens (Switzerland) 6pts / Tommaso di Lequio (Italy) 8.75 / Adam Krolikiewicz (Poland) 10
Teams: Sweden 42.5pts / Switzerland 50 / Portugal 53
1928 Frantisek Ventura (Czech) no faults / Bertrand de Balandra (France) 2 / Chasimir Kuhn (Switzerland) 4
Teams: Spain 4 faults / Poland 8 / Sweden 10
1932 Takeichi Nishi (Japan) 8pts / Harry Chamberlin (USA) 12 / Clarence von Rosen (Sweden) 16
1936 Kurt Hasse (Germany) 4pts / Henri Rang (Rumania) 4 / Jozsef Platthy (Hungary) 8
Teams: Germany 44pts / Netherlands 51.5 / Portugal 56
1948 Humberto Mariles (Mexico) 6.25pts / Ruben Uriza (Mexico) 8 / Jeann d'Orgeix (France) 8
Teams: Mexico 34.25pts / Spain 56.5 / GB 67
1952 Pierre d'Oriola (France) no faults / Oscar Cristi (Chile) 4 / Fritz Thiedemann (Germany)
Teams: GB 40.75 faults / Chile 45.75 / USA 52.25
1956 Hans Winkler (Germany) 4 faults / Raimondo d'Inzeo (Italy) 8 / Piero d'Inzeo (Italy) 11
Teams: Germany 40 / Italy 66 / GB 69
1960 Raimondo d'Inzeo (Italy) 12 faults / Piero d'Inzeo (Italy) 16 / David Broome (GB) 23
Teams: Germany 46.5 / USA 66 / Italy 80.5
1964 Pierre d'Oriola (France) 9 faults / Herman Schridde (Germany) 13.75 / Peter Robeson (GB) 16
Teams: Germany 68.50 / France 77.75 / Italy 88.50
1968 Bill Steinkraus (USA) 4 faults / Marion Coakes (GB) 8 / David Broome (GB) 12
Teams: Canada 102.75 faults / France 110.50 / W.Germany 117.25
1972 Graziano Mancinelli (Italy) 0 faults / Ann Moore (GB) 3 / Neal Shapiro (USA) 8
Teams: W. Germany 32 faults / USA 32.25 / Italy 48
1976 Alwin Schockemoehle (W. Germany) 0 faults / Michel Vaillancourt (Canada) 12 / François Mathy (Canada) 12
Teams: France 40 faults / W. Germany 44 / Belgium 63
1980

GRAND PRIX (DRESSAGE)
1900 Aime Haegemann (Belgium) / Georges van de Poele (Belgium) / de Champsavin (France)
1912 Carl Bonde (Sweden) 15pts / Gustav Boltenstern (Sweden) 21 / Hans von Blixen-Finecke (Sweden) 32
1920 Janne Lundblad (Sweden) 27,937pts / Bertil Sandström (Sweden) 26,312 / Hans von Rosen (Sweden) 25,125
1924 Ernst Linder (Sweden) 276.4pts / Bertil Sandström (Sweden) 275.8 / François Lesage (France) 268.5
1928 Carl von Langen (Germany) 237.42pts / Charles Marion (France) 231.00 / Ragnar Olsson (Sweden) 229.78
Teams: Germany 669.72pts / Sweden 650.86 / Netherlands 642.96
1932 Francois Lesage (France) 1,031.25pts / Charles Marion (France) 916.25 / Hiram Tuttle (USA) 901.50
Teams: France 2,818.75pts / Sweden 2,678.00 / USA 2,576.75
1936 Heinz Pollay (Germany) 1,760.00pts / Friedrich Gerhard (Germany) 1,745.5 / Alois Podhajsky (Austria) 1,721.5
Teams: Germany 5,074pts / France 4,845 / Sweden 4,660.5

1948 Hans Moser (Switz) 492.5pts / André Jousseaume (France) 480.0 / Gustav Boltenstern (Sweden) 477.5
Teams: France 1,269pts / USA 1,256 / Portugal 1,182
1952 Henri St. Cyr (Sweden) 561.0pts / Lis Hartel (Denmark) 541.5 / André Jousseaume (France) 541.0
Teams: Sweden 1,597.5pts / Switzerland 1,579.0 / Germany 1,501.0
1956 Henri St. Cyr (Sweden) 860pts / Lis Hartel (Denmark) 850 / Liselott Linsenhoff (Germany) 832
Teams: Sweden 2,475pts / Germany 2,346 / Switzerland 2,346
1960 Sergey Filatov (USSR) 2,144pts / Gustav Fischer (Switzerland) 2,087 / Josef Neckermann (Germany) 2,082
1964 Henri Chammartin (Switzerland) 1,504pts / Harry Boldt (Germany) 1,503 / Sergey Filatov (USSR) 1,486
Teams: Germany 2,558pts / Switzerland 2,526 / USSR 2,311
1968 Ivan Kizimov (USSR) 1,572pts / Josef Neckermann (W.Germany) 1,546 / Reiner Klimke (W.Germany) 1,537
Teams: W.Germany 2,699pts / USSR 2,657 / Switzerland 2,547
1972 Liselott Linsenhoff (W. Germany) 1,763pts / Elena Petushkova (USSR) 1,747 / Josef Neckermann (W. Germany) 1,706
Teams: USSR 5,095pts / W. Germany 5,083 / Sweden 4,849
1976 Christina Stueckelberger (Switzerland) 1,486pts / Harry Boldt (W. Germany) 1,435 / Reiner Klimke (W. Germany) 1,395
Teams: W. Germany 5,155pts / Switzerland 4,684 / USA 4,647
1980

THREE-DAY EVENT
1912 Axel Nordlander (Sweden) 46.59pts / von Rochow (Germany) 46.42 / Jean Cariou (France) 46.32
Teams: Sweden 545pts / France 538 / Germany 530
1920 Helmer Mörner (Sweden) 1,775pts / Age Lundström (Sweden) 1,738.75 / Ettore Caffaratti (Italy) 1,733.75
Teams: Sweden 5,057.5pts / Italy 4,735 / Belgium 4,660
1924 Adolph van Zijp (Neths) 1,976pts / Fröde Kirkebjerg (Denmark) 1,873.5 / Sloan Doak (USA) 1,845.5
Teams: Neths 5,294.5pts / Sweden 4,743.5 / Italy 4,512
1928 Charles de Mortanges (Neths) 1,969.82pts / Gerard de Kruyff (Neths) 1,967.26 / Bruno Neumann (Germany) 1,944.42
Teams: Neths 5,865.68pts / Norway 5,395.68 / Poland 5,067.92
1932 Charles de Mortanges (Neths) 1,813.83pts / Earl Thomson (USA) 1,811 / Clarence von Rosen (Sweden) 1,809.42
Teams: USA 5,038.08pts / Neths 4,689.08
1936 Ludwig Stubbendorff (Germany) 362.30 faults / Earl Thomson (USA) 300.10 / Hans Lunding (Denmark) 297.80
Teams: Germany 676.65pts / Poland 991.70 / GB 9,195.50
1948 Bernard Chevallier (France) plus 4pts / Frank Henry (USA) 21 faults / Johan Selfelt (Sweden) 25 faults
Teams: USA 161.50 faults / Sweden 165.00 / Mexico 305.25
1952 Hans von Blixen-Finecke (Sweden) 28.33 faults / Guy Lefrant (France) 54.50 / Wilhelm Büsing (Germany) 55.50
Teams: Sweden 221.94 / Germany 235.49 / USA 587.16
1956 Petrus Kastenman (Sweden) 66.53 faults / August Lütke-Westhues (Germany) 84.87 / Frank Weldon (GB) 85.48
Teams: GB 355.48 / Germany 475.91 / Canada 572.72
1960 Lawrence Morgan (Australia) plus 7.5pts / Neale Lavis (Australia) 16.59 faults / Anton Bühler (Switz) 51.21 faults
Teams: Australia 128.18pts / Switzerland 386.02 / France 515.71
1964 Mauro Checcoli (Italy) 64.40pts / Carlos Moratorio (Argentina) 56.40 / Fritz Ligges (Germany) 49.20
Teams: Italy 85.80pts / USA 65.86 / Germany 56.73
1968 Jean Guyon (France) 38.86 faults / Derek Allhusen (GB) 41.61 / Michael Page (USA) 52.31
Teams: GB 175.93 faults / USA 246.87 / Australia 331.26
1972 Richard Meade (GB) 57.73pts / Alessa Argenton (Italy) 43.33 / Jan Jonsson (Sweden) 39.67
Teams: GB 95.53 / USA 10.81 / W. Germany 18.00
1976 Edmund Coffin (USA) 114.59pts / John Plumb (USA) 125.85 / Karl Schulz (W. Germany) 129.45
Teams: USA 441 / W. Germany 584.6 / Australia 599.54
1980

FENCING (MEN)
FOIL (INDIVIDUAL)
1896 E. Gravelotte (France) 4 wins / Henri Callott (France) 3 / Perikles Pierrakos (Greece) 2
1900 C. Coste (France) 6 wins / Henri Masson (France) 5 / Marcel Boulanger (France) 4
1904 Ramon Fonst (Cuba) / Albertson Post (Cuba) / Charles Tatham (Cuba)
1912 Nedo Nadi (Italy) 7 wins / Pietro Speciale (Italy) 5 / Richard Verderber (Austria) 4
1920 Nedo Nadi (Italy) 10 wins / Philippe Cattiau (France) 9 / Roger Ducret (France) 9
1924 Roger Ducret (France) 6 wins / Philippe Cattiau (France) 5 / Maurice van Damme (Belgium) 4
1928 Lucien Gaudin (France) 9 wins / Erwin Casmir (Germany) 9 / Giulio Gaudini (Italy) 9
1932 Gustavo Marzi (Italy) 9 wins / Joseph Levis (USA) 6 / Guilo Gaudini (Italy) 5
1936 Guilo Gaudini (Italy) 7 wins / Edouard Gardère (France) 6 / Giorgio Bocchino (Italy) 4
1948 Jean Buhan (France) 7 wins / Christian d'Oriola (France) 5 / Lajos Maszlay (Hungary) 4

Year	Gold	Silver	Bronze
1952	Christian d'Oriola (France) 8 wins	Edoardo Mangiarotti (Italy) 6	Manlio di Rosa (Italy) 5
1956	Christian d'Oriola (France) 6 wins	Giancarlo Bergamini (Italy) 5	Antonio Spallino (Italy) 5
1960	Viktor Zhdanovich (USSR) 7 wins	Yuriy Sisikin (USSR) 4	Albert Axelrod (USA) 3
1964	Egon Franke (Poland) 3 wins	Jean Magnan (France) 2	Daniel Revenu (France) 1
1968	Ion Drimba (Rumania) 4 wins	Jeno Kamuti (Hungary) 3	Daniel Revenu (France) 3
1972	Witold Woyda (Poland) 5 wins	Jeno Kamuti (Hungary) 4	Christian Noel (France) 2
1976	Fabio dal Zotto (Italy) 4 wins	Alexandr Romankov (USSR) 4	Bernard Talvet (France) 3
1980			

FOIL (TEAM)

Year	Gold	Silver	Bronze
1920	Italy	France	USA
1924	France	Belgium	Hungary
1928	Italy	France	Argentina
1932	France	Italy	USA
1936	Italy	France	Germany
1948	France	Italy	Belgium
1952	France	Italy	Hungary
1956	Italy	France	Hungary
1960	USSR	Italy	Germany
1964	USSR	Poland	France
1968	France	USSR	Poland
1972	Poland	USSR	France
1976	W. Germany	Italy	France
1980			

EPEE (INDIVIDUAL)

Year	Gold	Silver	Bronze
1900	Ramon Fonst (Cuba)	Louis Perée (France)	Léon Sée (France)
1904	Ramon Fonst (Cuba)	Charles Tatham (Cuba)	Albertson Post (Cuba)
1908	Gaston Alibert (France) 5 wins	Alexandre Lippmann (France) 4	Eugene Olivier (France) 4
1912	Paul Anspach (Belgium) 6 wins	Ivan Osiier (Denmark) 5	Philippe de Beaulieu (Belgium) 4
1920	Armand Massard (France)	Alexandre Lippmann (France)	Gustave Buchard (France)
1924	Charles Delporte (Belgium)	Roger Ducret (France)	Nils Hellsten (Sweden)
1928	Lucien Gaudin (France) 8 wins	Georges Buchard (France) 7	George Calnan (USA) 6
1932	Giancarlo Medici (Italy) 9 wins	Georges Buchard (France) 7	Carlo Agostini (Italy) 7
1936	Franco Riccardi (Italy) 13pts	Saverio Ragno (Italy) 12	Giancarlo Medici (Italy) 12
1948	Gino Cantone (Italy) 7 wins	Oswald Zappelli (Switzerland) 5	Edoardo Mangiarotti (Italy) 5
1952	Edoardo Mangiarotti (Italy) 7 wins	Dario Mangiarotti (Italy) 6	Oswald Zappelli (Switzerland) 6
1956	Carlo Pavesi (Italy) 5 wins	Giuseppe Delfino (Italy) 5	Edoardo Mangiarotti (Italy) 5
1960	Giuseppe Delfino (Italy) 5 wins	Allan Jay (GB) 5	Bruno Khabarov (USSR) 4
1964	Grigory Kriss (USSR)	Bill Hoskyns (GB)	Guram Kostava (USSR)
1968	Gyözö Kulcsar (Hungary) 4(14)	Grigory Kriss (USSR) 4(19)	Gianluigi Saccaro (Italy) 4(19)
1972	Csaba Fenyvesi (Hungary) 4 wins	Jacques la Degaillerie (France) 3(19-23)	Gyözö Kulcsar (Hungary) 3(19-20)
1976	Alexander Pusch (W. Germany) 3 wins	Jurgen Hehn (W. Germany) 3	Gyözö Kulcsar (Hungary) 3
1980			

EPEE (TEAM)

Year	Gold	Silver	Bronze
1908	France	GB	Belgium
1912	Belgium	GB	Netherlands
1920	Italy	Belgium	France
1924	France	Belgium	Italy
1928	Italy	France	Portugal
1932	France	Italy	USA
1936	Italy	Sweden	France
1948	France	Italy	Sweden
1952	Italy	Sweden	Switzerland
1956	Italy	Hungary	France
1960	Italy	GB	USSR
1964	Hungary	Italy	France
1968	Hungary	USSR	Poland
1972	Hungary	Switzerland	USSR
1976	Sweden	W. Germany	Switzerland
1980			

SABRE (INDIVIDUAL)

Year	Gold	Silver	Bronze
1896	Jean Georgiadis (Greece) 4 wins	Telemachos Karakalos (Greece) 3	Holger Nielsen (Denmark) 2
1900	Georges de la Falaise (France)	Leon Thiebaut (France)	Fritz Flesch (Austria)
1904	Manuel Diaz (Cuba)	William Grebe (USA)	Albertson Post (Cuba)
1908	Jenö Fuchs (Hungary) 6 wins	Bela Zulavsky (Hungary) 6	Vilhelm de Lobsdorf (Bohemia) 4
1912	Jenö Fuchs (Hungary) 6 wins	Bela Bekessy (Hungary) 5	Ervin Meszaros (Hungary) 5
1920	Nedo Nadi (Italy)	Aldo Nadi (Italy)	Adrian de Jong (Netherlands)
1924	Sandor Posta (Hungary) 5 wins	Roger Ducret (France) 5	Janos Garai (Hungary) 5
1928	Odön Tersztyanszky (Hungary) 9 wins	Attila Petschauer (Hungary) 9	Bino Bini (Italy) 8
1932	György Piller (Hungary) 8 wins	Guilio Gaudini (Italy) 7	Endre Kabos (Hungary) 5
1936	Endre Kabos (Hungary) 7 wins	Gustavo Marzi (Italy) 6	Aladar Gerevich (Hungary) 6
1948	Aladar Gerevich (Hungary) 7 wins	Vincenzo Pinton (Italy) 5	Pal Kovacs (Hungary) 5
1952	Pal Kovacs (Hungary) 8 wins	Aladar Gerevich (Hungary) 7	Tibor Berczelly (Hungary) 5
1956	Rudolf Karpati (Hungary) 6 wins	Jerzy Pawlowski (Poland) 5	Lav Kuznyetsov (USSR) 4
1960	Rudolf Karpati (Hungary) 5 wins	Zoltan Horvath (Hungary) 4	Wladimiro Calarese (Italy) 4
1964	Tibor Pezsa (Hungary)	Claude Arabo (France)	Umar Mavlikhanov (USSR)
1968	Jerzy Pawlowski (Poland) 4(18)	Mark Rakita (USSR) 4(16)	Tibor Pezsa (Hungary) 3(16)
1972	Viktor Sidiak (USSR) 4 wins	Peter Maroth (Hungary) 3(20)	Vladimir Nazylmov (USSR) 3(21)
1976	Viktor Krovonouskov (USSR) 5 wins	Vladimir Nazlymov (USSR) 4	Viktor Sidiak (USSR) 3
1980			

SABRE (TEAM)

Year	Gold	Silver	Bronze
1908	Hungary	Italy	Bohemia
1912	Hungary	Austria	Netherlands
1920	Italy	France	Netherlands
1924	Italy	Hungary	Netherlands
1928	Hungary	Italy	Poland
1932	Hungary	Italy	Poland
1936	Hungary	Italy	Germany
1948	Hungary	Italy	USA
1952	Hungary	Italy	France
1956	Hungary	Poland	USSR
1960	Hungary	Poland	Italy
1964	USSR	Italy	Poland
1968	USSR	Italy	Hungary
1972	Italy	USSR	Hungary
1976	USSR	Italy	Rumania
1980			

FENCING (WOMEN)
FOIL (INDIVIDUAL)

Year	Gold	Silver	Bronze
1924	Ellen Osiier (Denmark) 5 wins	Gladys Davis (GB) 4	Grete Heckschner (Denmark)
1928	Helene Mayer (Germany) 7 wins	Muriel Freeman (GB) 6	Olga Oelkers (Germany) 4
1932	Ellen Preis (Austria) 9 wins	Heather Guiness (GB) 8	Ena Bogen (Hungary) 7
1936	Ilona Elek (Hungary) 7 wins	Helene Mayer (Germany) 5	Ellen Preis (Austria) 5
1948	Ilona Elek (Hungary) 6 wins	Karen Lachmann (Denmark)	Ellen Preis (Austria) 5
1952	Irene Camber (Italy) 5 wins	Ilona Elek (Hungary) 5	Karen Lachmann (Denmark) 4
1956	Gillian Sheen (GB) 6 wins	Olga Orban (Rumania) 6	Renee Gariihe (France) 5
1960	Heidi Schmid (Germany) 6 wins	Valentina Rastvorova (USSR) 5	Maria Vicol (Rumania) 4
1964	Ildiko Rejtö (Hungary)	Helga Mees (Germany)	Antonella Ragno (Italy)
1968	Elena Novikova (USSR) 4 wins	Pilar Roldan (Mexico) 3	Ildiko Rejtö (Hungary) 3
1972	Antonella Ragno (Italy) 4 wins	Ildiko Bobis (Hungary) 3(14-17)	Galina Gorokhova (USSR) 3(14-16)
1976	Ildiko Schwarczenbereer (Hungary) 8 wins	Maria Collino (Italy) 8	Elena Belova (USSR) 6
1980			

FOIL TEAM

Year	Gold	Silver	Bronze
1960	USSR	Hungary	Italy
1964	Hungary	USSR	Germany
1968	USSR	Hungary	Rumania
1972	USSR	Hungary	Rumania
1976	USSR	France	Hungary
1980			

GYMNASTICS (MEN)
COMBINED EXERCISES (INDIVIDUAL)

Year	Gold	Silver	Bronze
1900	S. Sandras (France)	J. Bas (France)	G. Demanet (France)
1904	Adolf Spinnler (Germany) 43.49pts	Wilhelm Weber (Germany) 41.60	Hugo Peitsch (Germany) 41.56
1908	Alberto Braglia (Italy) 317pts	S. W. Tysal (GB) 312	Louis Segura (France) 297

Year	Gold	Silver	Bronze
1912	Alberto Braglia (Italy) 135pts	Louis Segura (France) 132.5	Adolfo Tunesi (Italy) 131.5
1920	Giorgio Zampori (Italy) 88.35pts	Marcel Torres (France) 87.62	Jean Gounot (France) 87.45
1924	Leon Stukelj (Yugoslavia) 110.34pts	Robert Prazak (Czech) 110.323	Bedrich Supcik (Czech) 106.930
1928	Georges Miez (Switz) 247.500pts	Hermann Hänggi (Switz) 246.625	Leon Stukelj (Yugoslavia) 244.875
1932	Romeo Neri (Italy) 140.625pts	Istvan Pelle (Hungary) 134.925	Heikki Savolainen (Finland) 134.575
1936	Karl Schwarzmann (Germany) 113.100pts	Eugen Mack (Switz) 112.234	Konrad Frey (Germany) 111.532
1948	Veikko Huhtanen (Finland) 229.7pts	Walter Lehmann (Switz) 229.0	Paavo Aaltonen (Finland) 228.8
1952	Viktor Chukarin (USSR) 115.70pts	Grant Shaginyan (USSR) 114.95	Josef Stalder (Switz) 114.75
1956	Viktor Chukarin (USSR) 114.25pts	Takashi Ono (Japan) 114.20	Yuriy Titov (USSR) 113.80
1960	Boris Shakhlin (USSR) 115.95pts	Takashi Ono (Japan) 115.90	Yuriy Titov (USSR) 115.60
1964	Yukio Endo (Japan)	Shuji Tsurumi (Japan) Boris Shakhlin (USSR) Victor Libitsky (USSR) 115.40	
1968	Sawao Kato (Japan) 115.90pts	Mickail Voronin (USSR) 115.85	Akinori Nakayama (Japan) 115.65
1972	Sawao Kato (Japan) 114.650pts	Eizo Kenmotsu (Japan) 114.575	Akinori Nakayama (Japan) 114.325
1976	Nikolai Andrianov (USSR) 116.650pts	Sawao Kato (Japan) 115.650	Mitsuo Tsukahara (Japan) 115.575
1980			

COMBINED EXERCISES (TEAM)

Year	Gold	Silver	Bronze
1924	Italy 839.058pts	France 820.528	Switzerland 816.661
1928	Switzerland 1,718.625pts	Czechoslovakia 1,712.25	Yugoslavia 1,648.75
1932	Italy 541.850pts	USA 522.275	Finland 509.995
1936	Germany 657.430pts	Switzerland 654.802	Finland 638.468
1948	Finland 1,358.3pts	Switzerland 1,356.7	Hungary 1,330.35
1952	USSR 574.4pts	Switzerland 567.5	Finland 564.2
1956	USSR 568.25pts	Japan 566.40	Finland 555.95
1960	Japan 575.20pts	USSR 572.70	Italy 559.05
1964	Japan 577.95pts	USSR 575.45	Germany 565.10
1968	Japan 575.90pts	USSR 571.10	E. Germany 557.15
1972	Japan 571.25pts	USSR 564.05	E. Germany 559.70
1976	Japan 576.85pts	USSR 576.45	E. Germany 564.65
1980			

FLOOR EXERCISES

Year	Gold	Silver	Bronze
1932	Istvan Pelle (Hungary) 28.8pts	Georges Miez (Switzerland) 28.4	Mario Lertora (Italy) 27.7
1936	Georges Miez (Switzerland) 18.666pts	Josef Walter (Switzerland) 18.5	Konrad Frey (Germany) Eugene Mack (Switzerland) 18.466
1948	Ferenc Pataki (Hungary) 38.7pts	Janos Mogyorosi (Hungary) 38.4	Zdenek Ruzicka (Czechoslovakia) 38.1
1952	Karl Thoresson (Sweden) 19.25pts	Tado Uesako (Japan) Jerzy Jokiel (Poland) 19.15	
1956	Valentin Muratov	Nobuyuki Aihara (Japan) William Thoresson (Sweden) Viktor Chukarin (USSR) 19.10	
1960	Nobuyuki Aihara (Japan) 19.45pts	Yuriy Titov (USSR) 19.325	Franco Menichelli (Italy) 19.275
1964	Franco Menichelli (Italy) 19.45pts	Victor Lisitsky (USSR) 19.35	Yukio Endo (Japan) 19.35
1968	Sawao Kato (Japan) 19.475pts	Akinori Nakayama (Japan) 19.400	Takeshi Kato (Japan) 19.275
1972	Nikolai Andrianov (USSR) 19.175pts	Akinori Nakayama (Japan) 19.125	Shigeru Kasamatsu (Japan) 19.025
1976	Nikolai Andrianov (USSR) 19.450pts	Vladimir Marchenko (USSR) 19.425	Peter Kormann (USA) 19.300
1980			

HORIZONTAL BAR

Year	Gold	Silver	Bronze
1896	Hermann Weingärtner (Germany)	Alfred Flatow (Germany)	Petmesas (Greece)
1904	Anton Heida (USA) Eduard Hennig (USA) 40pts		George Eyser 39
1924	Leon Stukelj (Yugoslavia) 19.73pts	Jean Gutwenniger (Switzerland) 19.236	Andre Higelin (France) 19.163
1928	Georges Miez (Switzerland) 19.17pts	Romeo Neri (Italy) 19.00	Eugen Mack (Switzerland) 18.92
1932	Dallas Bixler (USA) 18.33pts	Heikki Savolainen (Finland) 18.07	Einari Terasvirta (Finland) 18.07
1936	Aleksanteri Saarvala (Finland) 19.467pts	Konrad Frey (Germany) 19.267	Karl Schwarzmann (Germany) 19.233
1948	Josef Stalder (Switz) 39.7pts	Walter Lehmann (Switz) 39.4	Veikko Huhtanen (Finland) 39.2
1952	Jack Günthard (Switz) 19.55pts	Josef Stalder (Switzerland) & Karl Schwarzmann (Switzerland) 19.50	
1956	Takashi Ono (Japan) 19.60pts	Yuriy Titov (USSR) 19.40	Masao Takemoto (Japan) 19.30
1960	Takashi Ono (Japan) 19.60pts	Masao Takemoto (Japan) 19.52	Boris Shakhlin (USSR) 19.475
1964	Boris Shakhlin (USSR) 19.625pts	Yuriy Titov (USSR) 19.55	Miroslav Cerar (Yugoslavia) 19.50
1968	Mickail Voronin (USSR) Akinori Nakayama (Japan) 19.550pts		Eizo Kenmotsu (Japan) 19.375

Year	Gold	Silver	Bronze
1972	Mitsuo Tsukahara (Japan) 19.725pts	Sawao Kato (Japan) 19.525	Shigeru Kasamatsu (Japan) 19.450
1976	Mitsuo Tsukahara (Japan) 19.675pts	Eizo Kenmotsu (Japan) 19.500	Eberhard Gienger (W. Germany) 19.475 Henri Boerio (France) 19.475
1980			

PARALLEL BARS

Year	Gold	Silver	Bronze
1896	Alfred Flatow (Germany)	Louis Zutter (Switzerland)	Hermann Weingärtner (Germany)
1904	George Eyser (USA) 44pts	Anton Heida (USA) 43	John Duha (USA) 40
1924	August Güttinger (Switz) 21.63pts	Robert Prazak (Czech) 21.61	Giorgio Zampori (Italy) 21.45
1928	Ladislav Vacha (Czech) 18.83pts	Josip Primozic (Yugoslavia) 18.50	Hermann Hänggi (Switz) 18.08
1932	Romeo Neri (Italy) 18.97pts	Istvan Pelle (Hungary) 18.60	Heikki Savolainen (Finland) 18.27
1936	Konrad Frey (Germany) 19.067pts	Michael Reusch (Switzerland) 19.034	Karl Schwarzmann (Germany) 18.967
1948	Michael Reusch (Switz) 39.5pts	Veikko Huhtanen (Finland) 39.3	Christian Kipfer (Switz) Josef Stalder (Switz) 39.1
1952	Hans Eugster (Switz) 19.65pts	Viktor Chukarin (USSR) 19.60	Josef Stalder (Switz) 19.50
1956	Viktor Chukarin (USSR) 19.20pts	Masami Kubota (Japan) 19.15	Takashi Ono (Japan) Masao Takemoto (Japan) 19.10
1960	Boris Shakhlin (USSR) 19.40pts	Giovanni Carminucci (Italy) 19.375	Takashi Ono (Japan) 19.35
1964	Yukio Endo (Japan) 19.675pts	Shuji Tsurumi (Japan) 19.45	Franco Menichelli (Italy) 19.35
1968	Akinori Nakayama (Japan) 19.475pts	Michail Voronin (USSR) 19.425	Vladimir Klimenko (USSR) 19.225
1972	Sawao Kato (Japan) 19.475pts	Shigeru Kasamatsu (Japan) 19.375	Eizo Kenmotsu (Japan) 19.250
1976	Sawao Kato (Japan) 19.675pts	Nikolai Andrianov (USSR) 19.500	Mitsuo Tsukahara (Japan) 19.475
1980			

POMMELLED HORSE

Year	Gold	Silver	Bronze
1896	Louis Zutter (Switzerland)	Hermann Wingärtner (Germany)	Gyula Kokas (Hungary)
1904	Anton Heida (USA) 42pts	George Eyser (USA) 33	William Merz (USA) 29
1924	Josef Wilhelm (Switzerland) 21.23pts	Jean Gutwenniger (Switzerland) 21.13	Antoine Rebetez (Switzerland) 20.73
1928	Hermann Hänggi (Germany) 19.75pts	Georges Miez (Switzerland) 19.25	Heikki Savolainen (Finland) 18.83
1932	Istvan Pelle (Hungary) 19.07pts	Omero Bonoli (Italy) 18.87	Frank Haubold (USA) 18.57
1936	Konrad Frey (Germany) 19.333pts	Eugen Mack (Switzerland) 19.167	Albert Bachmann (Switzerland) 19.067
1948	Paavo Aaltonen, Veikko Huhtanen & Heikki Savolainen (Finland) 38.7pts		
1952	Viktor Chukarin (USSR) 19.50pts	Yevgeniy Korolkov (USSR) Grant Shaginjian (USSR) 19.40	
1956	Boris Shakhlin (USSR) 19.25pts	Takashi Ono (Japan) 19.20	Viktor Chukarin (USSR) 19.10
1960	Eugen Ekman (Finland) Boris Shakhlin (USSR) 19.375		Shuji Tsurumi (Japan) 19.15
1964	Miroslav Cerar (Yugoslavia) 19.525pts	Shuji Tsurumi (Japan) 19.325	Yury Tsapenko (USSR) 19.20
1968	Miroslav Cerar (Yugoslavia) 19.325pts	Olli Laiho (Finland) 19.225	Michail Voronin (USSR) 19.200
1972	Viktor Klimenko (USSR) 19.125pts	Sawao Kato (Japan) 19.0000	Eizo Kenmotsu (Japan) 18.950
1976	Zoltan Magyar (Hungary) 19.700pts	Eizo Kenmotsu (Japan) 19.575	Nikolai Andrianov (USSR) 19.525
1980			

HORSE VAULT

Year	Gold	Silver	Bronze
1896	Karl Schumann (Germany)	Louis Zutter (Switzerland)	
1904	Anton Heida (USA) George Eyser (USA) 36pts		William Merz (USA) 31
1924	Frank Kriz (USA) 9.98pts	Jan Koutny (Czechoslovakia) 9.97	Bohumil Morkovsky (Czechoslovakia) 9.93
1928	Eugen Mack (Switzerland) 9.58pts	Emanuel Löffler (Czechoslovakia) 9.50	Stane Drganc (Yugoslavia) 9.46
1932	Savino Guglielmetti (Italy) 18.03pts	Alfred Jochim (Germany) 17.77	Edward Carmichael (USA) 17.53
1936	Karl Schwarzmann (Germany) 19.20pts	Eugen Mack (Switzerland) 18.967	Matthias Volz (Germany) 18.467
1948	Paavo Aaltonen (Finland) 39.1pts	Olavi Rove (Finland) 39.0	Janos Mogyorosi (Hung) Ferenc Pataki (Hung) & Leos Sotornik (Czechoslovakia) 38.5
1952	Viktor Chukarin (USSR) 19.20pts	Masao Takemoto (Japan) 19.15	Tadao Uesako (Japan) & Takashi Ono (Japan) 19.10
1956	Helmuth Bantz (Germany) & Valentin Muratov (USSR) 18.85pts		Yuriy Titov (USSR) 18.75
1960	Takashi Ono (Japan) & Boris Shakhlin (USSR) 19.35pts		Vladimir Portnoi (USSR) 19.225

1964	Haruhiro Yamashita (Japan) 19.660pts	Victor Lisitsky (USSR) 19.325	Hannu Rantakari (Finland) 19.30
1968	Michail Voronin (USSR) 19.000pts	Yukio Endo (Japan) 18.950	Sergei Diomidov (USSR) 18.925
1972	Klaus Koeste (E. Germany) 18.850pts	Viktor Klimenko (USSR) 18.825	Nikolai Andrianov (USSR) 18.800
1976	Nikolai Andrianov (USSR) 19.450pts	Mitsuo Tsukahara (Japan) 19.375	Hiroshi Kajiyama (Japan) 19.275
1980			

RINGS

1896	Jean Mitropoulos (Greece)	Peter Persakis (Greece)	Hermann Weingartner (Germany)
1904	Hermann Glass (USA) 45pts	William Merz (USA) 35	Ed Voight (USA) 32
1924	Francesco Martino (Italy) 21.553pts	Robert Prazak (Czechoslovakia) 21.483	Ladislav Vacha (Czechoslovakia) 21.43
1928	Leon Stukelj (Yugoslavia) 19.25pts	Ladislav Vacha (Czechoslovakia) 19.17	Emanuel Löffler (Czechoslovakia) 18.83
1932	George Gulack (USA) 18.97pts	William Denton 18.60	Giovanni Lattuada (Italy) 18.50
1936	Alois Hudec (Czech) 19.433pts	Leon Stukelj (Yugoslavia) 18.87	Matthias Volz (Germany) 18.67
1948	Karl Frei (Switzerland) 39.6pts	Michael Reusch (Switzerland) 39.1	Zdenek Ruzicka (Czechoslovakia) 38.5
1952	Grant Shaginyan (USSR) 19.75pts	Viktor Chukarin (USSR) 19.55	Hans Eugster (Switz) & Dimitriy Leonkin (USSR) 19.40
1956	Albert Azaryan (USSR) 19.35pts	Valentin Muratov (USSR) 19.15	Masao Takemoto (Japan) & Masami Kubota (Japan) 19.10
1960	Albert Azaryan (USSR) 19.72pts	Boris Shakhlin (USSR) 19.50	Velik Kapsazov (Bulgaria) & Takashi Ono (Japan) 19.42
1964	Takuji Hayata (Japan) 19.475pts	Franco Menichelli (Italy) 19.425	Boris Shakhlin (USSR) 19.40
1968	Akinori Nakayama (Japan) 19.450pts	Michail Voronin (USSR) 19.325	Sawao Kato (Japan) 19.225
1972	Akinori Nakayama (Japan) 19.350pts	Michail Voronin (USSR) 19.275	Mitsuo Tsukahara (Japan) 19.225
1976	Nikolai Andrianov (USSR) 19.650pts	Alexandr Ditiatin (USSR) 19.550	Danut Grecu (Rumania) 19.200
1980			

GYMNASTICS (WOMEN)
COMBINED EXERCISES (INDIVIDUAL)

1952	Maria Gorokhovskaya (USSR) 76.78pts	Nina Bocharyova (USSR) 75.94	Margit Korondi (Hungary) 75.82
1956	Larissa Latynina (USSR) 74.933pts	Agnes Keleti (Hungary) 74.633	Sofia Muratova (USSR) 74.466
1960	Larissa Latynina (USSR) 77.031pts	Sofia Muratova (USSR) 76.696	Polina Astakhova (USSR) 76.164
1964	Vera Caslavska (Czech) 77.564pts	Larissa Latynina (USSR) 76.998	Polina Astakhova (USSR) 76.965
1968	Vera Caslavska (Czech) 78.25pts	Zinaida Voronina (USSR) 76.85	Natalia Kuchinskaya (USSR) 76.75
1972	Liudmila Tourischeva (USSR) 77.025pts	Karin Janz (E. Germany) 76.875	Tamara Lazakovitch (USSR) 76.850
1976	Nadia Comaneci (Rumania) 79.275pts	Nelli Kim (USSR) 78.675	Liudmila Tourischeva (USSR) 78.625
1980			

COMBINED EXERCISES (TEAM)

1928	Netherlands 316.75pts	Italy 289.00	GB 258.25
1936	Germany 506.50pts	Czechoslovakia 503.50	Hungary 499.00
1948	Czechoslovakia 445.45pts	Hungary 440.55	USA 422.63
1952	USSR 527.03pts	Hungary 520.96	Czechoslovakia 503.32
1956	USSR 444.80pts	Hungary 443.50	Rumania 438.20
1960	USSR 382.32pts	Czechoslovakia 373.32	Rumania 372.05
1964	USSR 380.890pts	Czechoslovakia 379.989	Japan 377.889
1968	USSR 382.85pts	Czechoslovakia 382.20	E Germany 379.10
1972	USSR 380.50pts	E. Germany 376.55	Hungary 368.25
1976	USSR 390.35pts	Rumania 387.15	E. Germany 385.10
1980			

BEAM

1952	Nina Bocharyova (USSR) 19.22pts	Maria Gorokhovskaya (USSR) 19.13	Margit Korondi (Hungary) 19.02
1956	Agnes Keleti (Hungary) 18.80pts	Eva Bosakova (Czechoslovakia) and Tamara Manina (USSR) 18.633	
1960	Eva Bosakova (Czech) 19.283pts	Larissa Latynina (USSR) 19.233	Sofia Muratova (USSR) 19.232
1964	Vera Caslavska (Czech) 19.449pts	Tamara Manina (USSR) 19.399	Larissa Latynina (USSR) 19.382
1968	Natalia Kuchinskaya (USSR) 19.650pts	Vera Caslavska (Czechoslovakia) 19.575	Larissa Petrik (USSR) 19.250
1972	Olga Korbut (USSR) 19.575pts	Liudmila Tourischeva (USSR) 19.550	Tamara Lazakovitch (USSR) 19.450
1976	Nadia Comaneci (Rumania) 19.950pts	Olga Korbut (USSR) 19.725	Teodora Ungureanu (Rumania) 19.700
1980			

ASYMMETRICAL BARS

1952	Margit Korondi (Hungary) 19.40pts	Maria Gorokhovskaya (USSR) 19.26	Agnes Keleti (Hungary) 19.16

1956	Agnes Keleti (Hungary) 18.96pts	Larissa Latynina (USSR) 18.83	Sofia Muratova (USSR) 18.80
1960	Polina Astakhova (USSR) 19.61pts	Larissa Latynina (USSR) 19.41	Tamara Lyukhina (USSR) 19.39
1964	Polina Astakhova (USSR) 19.332pts	Katalin Makray (Hungary) 19.216	Larissa Latynina (USSR) 19.199
1968	Vera Caslavska (Czech) 19.650pts	Karin Janz (W.Germany) 19.500	Zinaida Voronina (USSR) 19.425
1972	Karin Janz (E. Germany) 19.675pts	Olga Korbut (USSR) 19.450	Erika Zuchold (E. Germany) 19.450
1976	Nadia Comaneci (Rumania) 20.000pts	Teodora Ungureanu (Rumania) 19.800	Marta Egervari (Hungary) 19.775
1980			

HORSE VAULT

1952	Yekaterina Kalinchuk (USSR) 19.20pts	Maria Gorokhovskaya (USSR) 19.19	Galina Minaycheva (USSR) 19.16
1956	Larissa Latynina (USSR) 18.83pts	Tamara Manina (USSR) 18.80	Ann-Sofi Colling (Sweden) & Olga Tass (Hungary) 18.73
1960	Margarita Nikolayeva (USSR) 19.31pts	Sofia Muratova (USSR) 19.04	Larissa Latynina (USSR) 19.01
1964	Vera Caslavska (Czech) 19.483pts	Larissa Latynina (USSR) 19.283	Birgit Radochla (Germany) 19.283
1968	Vera Caslavska (Czech) 19.775pts	Erika Zuchold (W Germany) 19.625	Zinaida Voronina (USSR) 19.500
1972	Karin Janz (E. Germany) 19.525pts	Erika Zuchold (E. Germany) 19.275	Liudmila Tourischeva (USSR) 19.250
1976	Nelli Kim (USSR) 19.800pts	Liudmila Tourischeva (USSR) 19.650	Carola Dombeck (E. Germany) 19.650
1980			

FLOOR EXERCISES

1952	Agnes Keleti (Hungary) 19.36pts	Maria Gorokhovskaya (USSR) 19.20	Margit Korondi (Hungary) 19.00
1956	Larissa Latynina (USSR) & Agnes Keleti (Hungary) 18.733pts		Elena Leusteanu (Rumania) 18.70
1960	Larissa Latynina (USSR) 19.583pts	Polina Astakhova (USSR) 19.532	Tamara Lyukhina (USSR) 19.449
1964	Larissa Latynina (USSR) 19.599pts	Polina Astakhova (USSR) 19.50	Aniko Janosi (Hungary) 19.30
1968	Vera Caslavska (Czechoslovakia) & Larissa Petrik (USSR) 19.675pts		Natalia Kuchinskaya (USSR) 19.650
1972	Olga Korbut (USSR) 19.575pts	Liudmila Tourischeva (USSR) 19.550	Tamara Lazakovitch (USSR) 19.450
1976	Nelli Kim (USSR) 19.850pts	Liudmila Tourischeva (USSR) 19.825	Nadia Comaneci (Rumania) 19.750
1980			

HANDBALL (MEN)

1972	Yugoslavia	Czechoslovakia	Rumania
1976	USSR	Rumania	Poland
1980			

HANDBALL (WOMEN)

1976	USSR	E. Germany	Hungary
1980			

HOCKEY (MEN)

1908	England	Ireland	Scotland/Wales
1920	GB	Denmark	Belgium
1928	India	Netherlands	Germany
1932	India	Japan	USA
1936	India	Germany	Netherlands
1948	India	GB	Netherlands
1952	India	Netherlands	GB
1956	India	Pakistan	Germany
1960	Pakistan	India	Spain
1964	India	Pakistan	Australia
1968	Pakistan	Australia	India
1972	W. Germany	Pakistan	Netherlands
1976	New Zealand	Australia	Netherlands
1980			

HOCKEY (WOMEN)

1980			

JUDO
OPEN

1972	Wim Ruska (Netherlands)	Vitali Kusnezov (USSR)	Angelo Parisi (GB) Jean Brondani (France)
1976	Haruki Uemura (Japan)	Keith Remfrey (GB)	Shota Chochoshvili (USSR) Jeaki Cho (S. Korea)
1980			

UNDER 60 KILOS

1980			

UNDER 65 KILOS

1980			

UNDER 71 KILOS
1980 ....

UNDER 78 KILOS
1980 ....

UNDER 86 KILOS
1980 ....

UNDER 95 KILOS
1980 ....

OVER 95 KILOS
1980 ....

MODERN PENTATHLON

1912	Gustav Lilliehöök (Sweden) 27pts	Gösta Asbrink (Sweden) 28	Georg de Laval (Sweden) 30
1920	Gustaf Dyrssen (Sweden) 18pts	Erik de Laval (Sweden) 23	Gösta Runö (Sweden) 27
1924	Bo Lindman (Sweden) 18pts	Gustaf Dyrssen (Sweden) 39	Bertil Uggla (Sweden) 45
1928	Sven Thofelt (Sweden) 47pts	Bo Lindman (Sweden) 50	Helmuth Kahl (Germany) 52
1932	Johan Oxenstierna (Sweden) 32pts	Bo Lindman (Sweden) 35.5	Richard Mayo (USA) 38.5
1936	Gotthardt Handrick (Germany) 31.5pts	Charles Leonard (USA) 39.5	Silvano Abba (Italy) 45.5
1948	William Grut (Sweden) 16pts	George Moore (USA) 47	Gösta Gärdin (Sweden) 49
1952	Lars Hall (Sweden) 32pts	Gabor Benedek (Hungary) 32	Istvan Szondi (Hungary) 41
Teams:	Hungary 166pts	Sweden 182	Finland 213
1956	Lars Hall (Sweden) 4,833pts	Olavi Mannonen (Finland) 4,774.5	Väinö Korhonen (Finland) 4,750
Teams:	USSR 13,690.5pts	USA 13,482	Finland 13,185.5
1960	Ferenc Nemeth (Hungary) 5,024pts	Imre Nagy (Hungary) 4,988	Robert Beck (USA) 4,981
Teams:	Hungary 14,863pts	USSR 14,309	USA 14,192
1964	Ferenc Török (Hungary) 5,116pts	Igor Novikov (USSR) 5,067	Albert Mokeyev (USSR) 5,039
Teams:	USSR 14,961pts	USA 14,189	Hungary 14,173
1968	Björn Ferm (Sweden) 4,964pts	Andras Balczo (Hungary) 4,953	Pavel Lednev (USSR) 4,795
Teams:	Hungary 14,325pts	USSR 14,248	France 13,289
1972	Andras Balczo (Hungary) 5,412pts	Boris Onischenko (USSR) 5,335	Pavel Lednev (USSR) 5,328
Teams:	USSR 15,968pts	Hungary 15,348	Finland 14,812
1976	Janusz Pyciak-Peciak (Poland) 5,520pts	Pavel Lednev (USSR) 5,485	Jan Bartu (Czechoslovakia) 5,466
Teams:	GB	Czechoslovakia	Hungary
1980	....	....	....

SHOOTING

FREE PISTOL (RANGE 50 METRES)

1900	Karl Röderer (Switzerland) 503pts	Konrad Staeheli (Switzerland) 453	Louis Richardet (Switzerland) 448
1908	Paul van Asbroeck (Belgium) 490pts	Reginald Storms (Belgium) 487	J. Gorman (USA) 485
1912	Alfred Lane (USA) 499pts	Peter Dolfen (USA) 474	G. Stewart (GB) 470
1920	Carl Frederick (USA) 496pts	Afranio da Costa (Brazil) 489	Alfred Lane (US) 481
1932	Renzo Morigi (Italy) 42pts	Heinrich Hax (Germany) 40	Domenico Matteucci (Italy) 39
1936	Torsten Ullman (Sweden) 559pts	Erich Krempel (Germany) 544	Charles des Jammonières (France) 540
1948	Cam Vasquez (Peru) 545pts	Rudolf Schnyder (Switzerland) 539	Torsten Ullmann (Sweden) 539
1952	Huelet Benner (USA) 553pts	Angel Leon (Spain) 550	Ambrus Balogh (Hungary) 549
1956	Pentti Linnosvuo (Finland) 556pts	Makhmoud Oumarov (USSR) 556	Offutt Pinion (USA) 551
1960	Aleksey Gustchin (USSR) 560pts	Mahmoud Oumarov (USSR) 552	Yoshihisa Yoshikawa (Japan) 552
1964	Väinö Markkanen (Finland) 560pts	Franklin Green (USA) 557	Yoshihisa Yoshikawa (Japan) 554
1968	Gregory Kosykh (USSR) 562pts	Heinz Mertel (W.Germany) 562	Harald Vollmar (E.Germany) 560
1972	Ragnar Skanakar (Sweden) 567pts	Dan Iuga (Rumania) 562	Rudolf Dollinger (Austria) 560
1976	Uwe Potteck (E. Germany) 573pts	Harald Vollmer (E. Germany) 567	Rudolf Dollinger (Austria) 562
1980	....	....	....

RAPID FIRE PISTOL (RANGE 25 METRES)

1896	Jean Phrangudis (Greece) 344pts	George Orphanidis (Greece)	
1924	Paul Bailey (US) 18pts	Vilhelm Carlberg (Sweden) 18	Lennart Hannelius (Finland) 18
1936	Cornelius van Oyen (Germany) 36pts	Heinrich Han (Germany) 35	Thorsten Ullman (Sweden) 34
1948	Karoly Takacs (Hungary) 580pts	Enrique Valiente (Argentina) 571	Sven Lundquist (Sweden) 569

1952	Karoly Takacs (Hungary) 579pts	Szilard Kun (Hungary) 578	Gheorghe Lichiardopol (Rumania) 578
1956	Stefan Petrescu (Rumania) 587pts	Evgeniy Tcherkassov (USSR) 585	Gheorghe Lichiardopol (Rumania) 581
1960	William McMillan (USA) 587pts	Pentti Linnosvuo (Finland) 587	Aleksandr Zabelin (USSR) 587
1964	Pentti Linnosvuo (Finland) 592pts	Ion Tripsa (Rumania) 591	Lubomir Nacovsky (Czech) 590
1968	Jozef Zapedzki (Poland) 593pts	Marcel Rosca (Rumania) 591	Renart Suleimanov (USSR) 591
1972	Jozef Zapedzki (Poland) 595pts	Ladislav Faita (Czech) 594	Victor Torshin (USSR) 593
1976	Norbert Glaar (E. Germany) 597pts	Jurgen Wiefel (E. Germany) 596	Roberto Ferraris (Italy) 595
1980	....	....	....

SMALL-BORE RIFLE—PRONE

1900	A. Carnell (GB)		
1908	A. Carnell (GB) 387pts	Harry Humby (GB) 386	G. Barnes (GB) 385
1912	Frederick Hird (USA) 194pts	W. Milne (GB) 193	H. Burt (GB) 192
1920	Lawrence Nuesslein (USA) 391pts	Arthur Rothrock (USA) 386	Dennis Fenton (USA) 385
1924	Charles de Lisle (France) 398pts	Marcus Dinwiddie (USA) 396	Josias Hartmann (Switz) 394
1932	Bertil Rönnmark (Sweden) 294pts	Gustavo Huet (Mexico) 294	Zoltan Sóos (Hungary) 293
1936	Willy Rögeberg (Norway) 300pts	Ralph Berzsenyi (Hungary) 296	Wladyslaw Karas (Poland) 296
1948	Arthur Cook (USA) 599pts	Walter Tomsen (USA) 599	Jonas Jonsson (Sweden) 597
1952	Josif Sarbu (Rumania) 400pts	Boris Andreyev (USSR) 400	Arthur Jackson (USA) 399
1956	Gerald Quellette (Canada) 600pts	Vasiliy Borisov (USSR) 599	Gilmour Boa (Canada) 598
1960	Peter Kohnke (Germany) 590pts	James Hill (USA) 589	Enrico Forcella (Venezuela) 587
1964	Laszlo Hammerl (Hungary) 597pts	Lones Wigger (USA) 597	Tommy Pool (USA) 596
1968	Jan Kurka (Czech) 598pts	Laszlo Hammerl (Hungary) 598	Ian Ballinger (NZ) 597
1972	Ho Jun Li (N. Korea) 599pts	Victor Auer (USA) 598	Nicolae Rotaru (Rumania) 598
1976	Karl Smieszek (W. Germany) 599pts	Ulrich Lind (W. Germany) 597	Gennady Luschikov (USSR) 595
1980	....	....	....

SMALL-BORE RIFLE—THREE POSITIONS

1952	Erling Konsghaug (Norway) 1,164pts	Vilho Ylönen (Finland) 1,164	Boris Andreyev (USSR) 1,163
1956	Anatoliy Bogdanov (USSR) 1,172pts	Otto Horinek (Czech) 1,172	Nils Sundverg (Sweden) 1,167
1960	Viktor Shamburkin (USSR) 1,149pts	Marat Nyesov (USSR) 1,145	Klaus Zähringer (Germany) 1,139
1964	Lones Wigger (USA) 1,164pts	Velitchko Hustov (Bulgaria) 1,152	Laszlo Hammerl (Hungary) 1,151
1968	Bernd Klingner (W.Germany) 1,157pts	John Writer (USA) 1,156	Vitaly Parkhimovich (USSR) 1,154
1972	John Writer (USA) 1,166pts	Lanny Massham (USA) 1,157	Werner Lippoldt (E. Germany) 1,153
1976	Lanny Massham (USA) 1,162pts	Margaret Murdoch (USA) 1,162	Werner Seibold (W. Germany) 1,160
1980	....	....	....

OLYMPIC TRAP

1908	W. Ewing (Canada) 72pts	G. Beattie (Canada) 60	Alexander Maunder (GB) & Anastassios Metaxas (Greece) 57
1912	James Graham (USA) 96pts	Alfred Bronikowen (Germany) 94	Harry Blau (Russia) 91
1920	Mark Arie (USA) 95pts	Frank Troeh (USA) 93	Frank Wright (USA) 87
1924	Gyula Halasy (Hungary) 98pts	Konrad Huber (Finland) 98	Frank Hughes (USA) 97
1952	Georges Genereux (Canada) 192pts	Knut Holmqvist (Sweden) 191	Hans Liljedahl (Sweden) 190
1956	Galliano Rossini (Italy) 195pts	Adam Smelczysnki (Poland) 190	Alessandro Ciceri (Italy) 188
1960	Ion Dumitrescu (Rumania) 192pts	Galliano Rossini (Italy) 191	Sergei Kalinin (USSR) 190
1964	Ennio Mattarelli (Italy) 198pts	Pavel Senichev (USSR) 194	William Morris (USA) 194
1968	Bob Braithwaite (GB) 198pts	Tom Garrigus (USA) 196	Kurt Czekalla (E.Germany) 196
1972	Angelo Scalzone (Italy) 199pts	Michel Carrega (France) 198	Silvano Basagni (Italy) 195
1976	Donald Haldeman (USA) 190pts	Armando Marques (Portugal) 189	Ubaldesc Baldi (Italy) 189
1980	....	....	....

OLYMPIC SKEET

1968	Evgeny Petrov (USSR) 198 (25)pts	Romano Garagnani (Italy) 198 (24–25)	Konrad Wirnhier (W.Ger) 198 (24–23)

1972	Konrad Wirnhier (W. Germany) 195pts	Evgeni Petrov (USSR) 195	Michael Buccheim (E. Germany) 195
1976	Josef Panacek (Czechoslovakia) 198pts	Eric Swindels (Netherlands) 198	Wieslaw Gawlikowski (Poland) 196
1980			

MOVING TARGET

1900	Louis Debray (France) 20	P. Nivet (France) 20	de Lambert (France) 20
1972	Lakov Zhelzniak (USSR) 569	Helmut Bellingrodt (Colombia) 565	John Kynoch (GB) 562
1976	Alexandr Gazov (USSR) 579	Alexandr Keydarov (USSR) 576	Jerzy Greszkiewicz (Poland) 571
1980			

SOCCER

1908	GB	Denmark	Neths
1912	GB	Denmark	Neths
1920	Belgium	Spain	Neths
1924	Uruguay	Switz	Sweden
1928	Uruguay	Argentina	Italy
1936	Italy	Austria	Norway
1948	Sweden	Yugoslavia	Denmark
1952	Hungary	Yugoslavia	Sweden
1956	USSR	Yugoslavia	Bulgaria
1960	Yugoslavia	Denmark	Hungary
1964	Hungary	Czech	Germany
1968	Hungary	Bulgaria	Japan
1972	Poland	Hungary	East Germany USSR
1976	E. Germany	Poland	USSR
1980			

SWIMMING AND DIVING

100 METRES FREESTYLE

1896	Alfred Hajos (Hungary) 1m 22.2s	Gardrez Williams (USA) 1m 23.0s	Otto Herschmann (Austria)
1904*	Zoltan Halmay (Hungary) 1m 02.8s	Charles Daniels (USA)	Scott Leary (USA)
1908	Charles Daniels (USA) 1m 05.6s	Zoltan Halmay (Hungary) 1m 06.2s	Harald Julin (Sweden) 1m 08.8s
1912	Duke Kahanamoku (USA) 1m 03.4s	Cecil Healy (Australia) 1m 04.6s	Kenneth Huszagh (USA) 1m 05.6s
1920	Duke Kahanamoku (USA) 1m 00.4s	Pua Kealoha (USA) 1m 02.2s	William Harris (USA) 1m 03.2s
1924	Johnny Weissmuller (USA) 59.0s	Duke Kahanamoku (USA) 1m 01.4s	Sammy Kahanamoku (USA) 1m 01.8s
1928	Johnny Weissmuller (USA) 58.6s	Istvan Barany (Hungary) 59.8s	Katsuo Takaishi (Japan) 1m 00.0s
1932	Yasuji Miyazaki (Japan) 58.2s	Tatsugo Kawaishi (Japan) 58.6s	Albert Schwartz (USA) 58.8s
1936	Ferenc Csik (Hungary) 57.6s	Masanori Yusa (Japan) 57 9s	Shigeo Arai (Japan) 58.0s
1948	Walter Ris (USA) 57.3s	Alan Ford (USA) 57.8s	Geza Kadas (Hungary) 58.1s
1952	Clarke Scholes (USA) 57.4s	Hiroshi Suzuki (Japan) 57.4s	Goran Larsson (Sweden) 58.2s
1956	Jon Henricks (Australia) 55.4s	John Devitt (Australia) 55.8s	Gary Chapman (Australia) 56.7s
1960	John Devitt (Australia) 55.2s	Lance Larson (USA) 55.2s	Manoel dos Santos (Brazil) 55.4s
1964	Donald Schollander (USA) 53.4s	Robert McGregor (GB) 53.5s	Hans-Joachim Klein (Germany) 54.0s
1968	Michael Wenden (Australia) 52.2s	Kenneth Walsh (USA) 52.8s	Mark Spitz (USA) 53.0s
1972	Mark Spitz (USA) 51.22s	Jerry Heidenreich (USA) 51.65s	Vladimir Bure (USSR) 51.77
1976	Jim Montgomery (USA) 49.99s	Jack Babashoff (USA) 50.81s	Peter Nocke (W. Germany) 51.31s
1980			

* 100 yards

200 METRES FREESTYLE

1900	Frederick Lane (Australia) 2m 25.2s	Zoltan Halmay (Hungary) 2m 31.0s	Karl Ruberl (Austria) 2m 32.0s
1904*	Charles Daniels (USA) 2m 44.2s	Francis Gailey (USA) 2m 46.0s	Emil Rausch (Germany) 2m 56.0s
1968	Michael Wenden (Australia) 1m 55.2s	Donald Schollander (USA) 1m 55.8s	John Nelson (USA) 1m 58.1s
1972	Mark Spitz (USA) 1m 52.76s	Steven Genter (USA) 1m 53.73s	Werner Lampe (W. Germany) 1m 53.99s
1976	Bruce Furniss (USA) 1m 50.29s	John Naber (USA) 1m 50.50s	Jim Montgomery (USA) 1m 50.58s
1980			

* 220 yards

400 METRES FREESTYLE

1904*	Charles Daniels (USA) 6m 16.2s	Francis Gailey (USA) 6m 22.0s	Otto Wahle (Austria) 6m 39.0s
1908	Henry Taylor (GB) 5m 36.8s	Frank Beaurepaire (Australia) 5m 44.2s	Otto Scheff (Austria) 5m 46.0s
1912	George Hodgson (Canada) 5m 24.4s	Jack Hatfield (GB) 5m 25.8s	Harold Hardwick (Australia) 5m 31.2s
1920	Norman Ross (USA) 5m 26.8s	Ludy Langer (USA) 5m 29.2s	George Vernot (Canada) 5m 29.8s
1924	Johnny Weissmuller (USA) 5m 04.2s	Arne Borg (Sweden) 5m 05.6s	Andrew Charlton (Australia) 5m 06.6s
1928	Alberto Zorilla (Argentina) 5m 01.6s	Andrew Charlton (Australia) 5m 03.6s	Arne Borg (Sweden) 5m 04.6s
1932	Clarence Crabbe (USA) 4m 48.4s	Jean Taris (France) 4m 48.5s	Tsutoma Oyokota (Japan) 4m 52.3s
1936	Jack Medica (USA) 4m 44.5s	Shumpei Uto (Japan) 4m 45.6s	Shozo Makino (Japan) 4m 48.1s
1948	William Smith (USA) 4m 41.0s	James McLane (USA) 4m 43.4s	John Marshall (Australia) 4m 47.7s
1952	Jean Boiteux (France) 4m 30.7s	Ford Konno (USA) 4m 31.3s	Per-Olof Ostrand (Sweden) 4m 35.2s
1956	Murray Rose (Australia) 4m 27.3s	Tsuyoshi Yamanaka (Japan) 4m 30.4s	George Breen (USA) 4m 32.5s
1960	Murray Rose (Australia) 4m 18.3s	Tsuyoshi Yamanaka (Japan) 4m 21.4s	John Konrads (Australia) 4m 21.8s
1964	Donald Schollander (USA) 4m 12.2s	Frank Wiegand (Germany) 4m 14.9s	Allan Wood (Australia) 4m 15.1s
1968	Michael Burton (USA) 4m 09.0s	Ralph Hutton (Canada) 4m 11.7s	Alain Mosconi (France) 4m 13.3s
1972	Bradford Cooper (Australia) 4m 00.27s	Steven Genter (USA) 4m 01.94s	Tom McBreen (USA) 4m 02.64s
1976	Brian Goodell (USA) 3m 51.93s	Tim Shaw (USA) 3m 52.54s	Vladimir Raskatov (USSR) 3m 55.76s
1980			

*440 yards

1,500 METRES FREESTYLE

1904*	Emil Rausch (Germany) 27m 18.2s	Geza Kiss (Hungary) 28m 28.2s	Francis Gailey (USA) 28m 54.0s
1908	Henry Taylor (GB) 22m 48.4s	Sydney Battersby (GB) 22m 51.2s	Frank Beaurepaire (Australia) 22m 56.2s
1912	George Hodgson (Canada) 22m 00.0s	Jack Hatfield (GB) 22m 39.0s	Harold Hardwick (Australia) 23m 15.4s
1920	Norman Ross (USA) 22m 23.2s	George Vernot (Canada) 22m 36.4s	Frank Beaurepaire (Australia) 23m 04.0s
1924	Andrew Charlton (Australia) 20m 06.6s	Arne Borg (Sweden) 20m 41.4s	Frank Beaurepaire (Australia) 20m 48.4s
1928	Arne Borg (Sweden) 19m 51.8s	Andrew Charlton (Australia) 20m 02.6s	Clarence Crabbe (USA) 20m 28.8s
1932	Kusuo Kitamura (Japan) 19m 12.4s	Shozo Makino (Japan) 19m 14.1s	James Christy (USA) 19m 39.5s
1936	Norboru Terada (Japan) 19m 13.7s	Jack Medica (USA) 19m 34.0s	Shumpei Uto (Japan) 19m 34.5s
1948	James McLane (USA) 19m 18.5s	John Marshall (Australia) 19m 31.3s	Gyorgy Mitro (Hungary) 19m 43.2s
1952	Ford Konno (USA) 18m 30.3s	Shiro Hashizume (Japan) 18m 41.4s	Tetsuo Okamoto (Brazil) 18m 51.3s
1956	Murray Rose (Australia) 17m 58.9s	Tsuyoshi Yamanaka (Japan) 18m 00.3s	George Breen (USA) 18m 08.2s
1960	John Konrads (Australia) 17m 19.6s	Murray Rose (Australia) 17m 21.7s	George Breen (USA) 17m 30.6s
1964	Robert Windle (Australia) 17m 01.7s	John Nelson (USA) 17m 03.0s	Allan Wood (Australia) 17m 07.7s
1968	Michael Burton (USA) 16m 38.9s	John Kinsella (USA) 16m 57.3s	Greg Brough (Australia) 17m 04.7s
1972	Michael Burton (USA) 15m 52.58s	Graham Windeatt (Australia) 15m 58.48s	Douglas Northway (USA) 16m 09.25s
1976	Brian Goodell (USA) 15m 2.40s	Bobby Hackett (USA) 15m 3.91s	Stephen Holland (Australia) 15m 4.66s
1980			

* One mile

100 METRES BACKSTROKE

1904*	Walter Brack (Germany) 1m 16.8s	Georg Hoffmann (Germany)	Georg Zacharias (Germany)
1908	Arno Bieberstein (Germany) 1m 24.6s	Ludwig Dam (Denmark) 1m 26.6s	Herbert Haresnape (GB) 1m 27.0s
1912	Harry Hebner (USA) 1m 21.2s	Otto Fahr (Germany) 1m 22.4s	Paul Kellner (Germany) 1m 24.0s
1920	Warren Kealoha (USA) 1m 15.2s	Raymond Kegeris (USA) 1m 16.2s	Gerard Blitz (Belgium) 1m 19.0s
1924	Warren Kealoha (USA) 1m 13.2s	Paul Wyatt (USA) 1m 15.4s	Karoly Bartha (Hungary) 1m 17.8s
1928	George Kojac (USA) 1m 08.2s	Walter Laufer (USA) 1m 10.0s	Paul Wyatt (USA) 1m 12.0s
1932	Masaji Kiyokawa (Japan) 1m 08.6s	Toshio Irie (Japan) 1m 09.8s	Kentaro Kawatsu (Japan) 1m 10.0s
1936	Adolph Kiefer (USA) 1m 05.9s	Albert van de Weghe (USA) 1m 07.7s	Masaji Kiyokawa (Japan) 1m 08.4s
1948	Allen Stack (USA) 1m 06.4s	Robert Cowell (USA) 1m 06.5s	Georges Vallery (France) 1m 07.8s
1952	Yoshinobu Oyakawa (USA) 1m 05.4s	Gilbert Bozon (France) 1m 06.2s	Jack Taylor (USA) 1m 06.4s
1956	David Theile (Australia) 1m 02.2s	John Monckton (Australia) 1m 03.2s	Frank McKinney (USA) 1m 04.5s
1960	David Theile (Australia) 1m 01.9s	Frank McKinney (USA) 1m 02.1s	Robert Bennett (USA) 1m 02.3s
1968	Roland Matthes (E.Germany) 58.7s	Charles Hickcox (USA) 1m 00.2s	Ronald Mills (USA) 1m 00.5s
1972	Roland Matthes (E. Germany) 56.58s	Mike Stamm (USA) 57.70s	John Murphy (USA) 58.35s

*100 yards

200 METRES BACKSTROKE (continued)

Year	Gold	Silver	Bronze
1976	John Naber (USA) 55.49s	Peter Rocca (USA) 56.34s	Roland Matthes (E. Germany) 57.22s
1980			

200 METRES BACKSTROKE

Year	Gold	Silver	Bronze
1900	Ernst Hoppenberg (Germany) 2m 47.0s	Karl Ruberl (Austria) 2m 56.0s	Johannes Drost (Neths) 3m 01.0s
1964	Jed Graef (USA) 2m 10.3s	Gary Dilley (USA) 2m 10.5s	Robert Bennett (USA) 2m 13.1s
1968	Roland Matthes (E Germany) 2m 09.6s	Mitchell Ivey (USA) 2m 10.6s	Jack Horsley (USA) 2m 10.9s
1972	Roland Matthes (E. Germany) 2m 02.82s	Mike Stamm (USA) 2m 04.09s	Mitchell Ivey (USA) 2m 04.33s
1976	John Naber (USA) 1m 59.19s	Peter Rocca (USA) 2m 00.55s	Dan Harrigan (USA) 2m 1.35s
1980			

100 METRES BREASTSTROKE

Year	Gold	Silver	Bronze
1968	Donald McKenzie (USA) 1m 07.7s	Vladimir Kosinski (USSR) 1m 08.0s	Nicolai Pankin (USSR) 1m 08.0s
1972	Nobutaka Taguchi (Japan) 1m 04.94s	Tom Bruce (USA) 1m 05.43s	John Hencken (USA) 1m 05.61s
1976	John Hencken (USA) 1m 03.11s	David Wilkie (GB) 1m 03.43s	Arvidas Iouzaytis (USSR) 1m 04.23s
1980			

200 METRES BREASTSTROKE

Year	Gold	Silver	Bronze
1908	Frederick Holman (GB) 3m 09.2s	William Robinson (GB) 3m 12.8s	Pontus Hansson (Sweden) 3m 14.6s
1912	Walter Bathe (Germany) 3m 01.8s	Wilhelm Lutzow (Germany) 3m 05.0s	Kurt Malisch (Germany) 3m 08.0s
1920	Hakan Malmroth (Sweden) 3m 04.4s	Thor Henning (Sweden) 3m 09.2s	Arvo Aaltonen (Finland) 3m 12.2s
1924	Robert Skelton (USA) 2m 56.6s	Joseph de Combe (Belgium) 2m 59.2s	William Kirschbaum (USA) 3m 01.0s
1928	Yoshiyuki Tsuruta (Japan) 2m 48.8s	Erich Rademacher (Germany) 2m 50.6s	Teofilo Yldefonso (Philippines) 2m 56.4s
1932	Yoshiyuki Tsuruta (Japan) 2m 45.4s	Reizo Koike (Japan) 2m 46.6s	Teofilo Yldefonso (Philippines) 2m 47.1s
1936	Tetsuo Hamuro (Japan) 2m 42.5s	Erwin Sietas (Germany) 2m 42.9s	Reizo Koike (Japan) 2m 44.2s
1948	Joseph Verdeur (USA) 2m 39.3s	Keith Carter (USA) 2m 40.2s	Robert Sohl (USA) 2m 43.9s
1952	John Davies (Australia) 2m 34.4s	Bowen Stassforth (USA) 2m 34.7s	Herbert Klein (W.Germany) 2m 35.9s
1956	Masura Furukawa (Japan) 2m 34.7s	Masahiro Yoshimura (Japan) 2m 36.7s	Kharis Yunishev (USSR) 2m 36.8s
1960	William Mulliken (USA) 2m 37.4s	Yoshihiko Osaki (Japan) 2m 38.0s	Wieger Mensonides (Neths) 2m 39.7s
1964	Ian O'Brien (Australia) 2m 27.8s	Georgy Prokopenko (USSR) 2m 28.2s	Chet Jastremski (USA) 2m 29.6s
1968	Felipe Munoz (Mexico) 2m 28.7s	Vladimir Kosinski (USSR) 2m 29.2s	Brian Job (USA) 2m 29.9s
1972	John Hencken (USA) 2m 21.55s	David Wilkie (GB) 2m 23.67s	Nobutaka Taguchi (Japan) 2m 23.88s
1976	David Wilkie (GB) 2m 15.11s	John Hencken (USA) 2m 17.26s	Rick Colella (USA) 2m 19.20s
1980			

100 METRES BUTTERFLY

Year	Gold	Silver	Bronze
1968	Douglas Russell (USA) 55.9s	Mark Spitz (USA) 56.4s	Ross Wales (USA) 57.2s
1972	Mark Spitz (USA) 54.27s	Bruce Robertson (Canada) 55.56s	Jerry Heidenreich (USA) 55.74
1976	Matt Vogel (USA) 54.35s	Joe Bottom (USA) 54.50s	Gary Hall (USA) 54.65s
1980			

200 METRES BUTTERFLY

Year	Gold	Silver	Bronze
1956	William Yorzyk (USA) 2m 19.3s	Takashi Ishimoto (Japan) 2m 23.8s	Gyorgy Tumpek (Hungary) 2m 23.9s
1960	Michael Troy (USA) 2m 12.8s	Neville Hayes (Australia) 2m 14.6s	David Gillanders (USA) 2m 15.3s
1964	Kevin Berry (Australia) 2m 06.6s	Carl Robie (USA) 2m 07.5s	Fred Schmidt (USA) 2m 09.3s
1968	Carl Robie (USA) 2m 08.7s	Martyn Woodroffe (GB) 2m 09.0s	John Ferris (USA) 2m 09.3s
1972	Mark Spitz (USA) 2m 00.70s	Gary Hall (USA) 2m 02.86s	Robin Backhaus (USA) 2m 03.23s
1976	Mike Bruner (USA) 1m 59.23s	Steve Gregg (USA) 1m 59.54s	Bill Forrester (USA) 1m 59.96s
1980			

400 METRES INDIVIDUAL MEDLEY

Year	Gold	Silver	Bronze
1964	Richard Roth (USA) 4m 45.5s	Roy Saari (USA) 4m 47.1s	Gerhard Hetz (Germany) 4m 51.0s
1968	Charles Hickcox (USA) 4m 48.4s	Gary Hall (USA) 4m 48.7s	Michael Holthaus (W.Germany) 4m 51.4s
1972	Gunnar Larsson (Sweden) 4m 31.981s	Tim McKee (USA) 4m 31.983s	Andras Hargity (Hungary) 4m 32.70s
1976	Rod Strachan (USA) 4m 23.68s	Tom McKee (USA) 4m 24.62s	Andrey Smirnov (USSR) 4m 26.90s
1980			

4 × 200 METRES FREESTYLE RELAY

Year	Gold	Silver	Bronze
1908	Great Britain 10m 55.6s	Hungary 10m 59.0s	USA 11m 02.8s
1912	Australia 10m 11.2s	USA 10m 20.2s	GB 10m 28.2s
1920	USA 10m 04.4s	Australia 10m 25.4s	GB 10m 37.2s
1924	USA 9m 53.4s	Australia 10m 02.2s	Sweden 10m 06.8s
1928	USA 9m 36.2s	Japan 9m 41.4s	Canada 9m 47.8s
1932	Japan 8m 58.4s	USA 9m 10.5s	Hungary 9m 31.4s
1936	Japan 8m 51.5s	USA 9m 03.0s	Hungary 9m 12.3s
1948	USA 8m 46.0s	Hungary 8m 48.4s	France 9m 08.0s
1952	USA 8m 31.1s	Japan 8m 33.5s	France 8m 45.9s
1956	Australia 8m 23.6s	USA 8m 31.5s	USSR 8m 34.7s
1960	USA 8m 10.2s	Japan 8m 13.2s	Australia 8m 13.8s
1964	USA 7m 52.1s	Germany 7m 59.3s	Japan 8m 03.8s
1968	USA 7m 52.3s	Australia 7m 53.7s	USSR 8m 01.6s
1972	USA 7m 35.78s	W. Germany 7m 41.69s	USSR 7m 45.76s
1976	USA 7m 23.22s	USSR 7m 27.97s	GB 7m 32.11s
1980			

4 × 100 METRES MEDLEY RELAY

Year	Gold	Silver	Bronze
1960	USA 4m 05.4s	Australia 4m 12.0s	Japan 4m 12.2s
1964	USA 3m 58.4s	Germany 4m 01.6s	Australia 4m 02.3s
1968	USA 3m 54.9s	E. Germany 3m 57.5s	USSR 4m 00.7s
1972	USA 3m 48.16s	E. Germany 3m 52.12s	Canada 3m 52.26s
1976	USA 3m 42.22s	Canada 3m 45.94s	W. Germany 3m 47.29s
1980			

DIVING (MEN)
SPRINGBOARD

Year	Gold	Silver	Bronze
1908	Albert Zurner (Germany) 85.5pts	Kurt Behrens (Germany) 85.3	George Gaidzik (USA) 80.8 / Gottlob Walz (Germany) 80.8
1912	Paul Gunther (Germany) 79.23pts	Hans Luber (Germany) 76.78	Kurt Behrens (Germany) 73.75
1920	Louis Kuehn (USA) 675.00pts	Clarence Pinkston (USA) 655.30	Louis Balbach (USA) 649.50
1924	Albert White (USA) 696.40pts	Pete Desjardins (USA) 693.20	Clarence Pinkston (USA) 653.00
1928	Pete Desjardins (USA) 185.04pts	Michael Galitzen (USA) 174.06	Farid Simaika (Egypt) 172.46
1932	Michael Galitzen (USA) 161.38pts	Harold Smith (USA) 158.54	Richard Degener (USA) 151.82
1936	Richard Degener (USA) 163.57pts	Marshall Wayne (USA) 159.56	Albert Greene (USA) 146.29
1948	Bruce Harlan (USA) 163.64pts	Miller Anderson (USA) 157.29	Samuel Lee (USA) 145.52
1952	David Browning (USA) 205.29pts	Miller Anderson (USA) 199.84	Robert Clotworthy (USA) 184.92
1956	Robert Clotworthy (USA) 159.56pts	Donald Harper (USA) 156.23	Joaquin Capilla (Mexico) 150.69
1960	Gary Tobian (USA) 170.00pts	Samuel Hall (USA) 167.08	Juan Botella (Mexico) 162.30
1964	Ken Sitzberger (USA) 159.90pts	Frank Gorman (USA) 157.63	Larry Andreasen (USA) 143.77
1968	Bernard Wrightson (USA) 170.15pts	Klaus Dibiasi (Italy) 159.74	James Henry (USA) 159.09
1972	Franco Cagnotto (Italy) 400.95pts	Viacheslav Strahov (USSR) 392.10	Vladimir Vasin (USSR) 387.72
1976	Philip Boggs (USA) 619.05pts	Franco Cagnotto (Italy) 570.48	Alexandr Kosenkov (USSR) 567.24
1980			

PLATFORM DIVING

Year	Gold	Silver	Bronze
1908	Hjalmar Johansson (Sweden) 83.75pts	Karl Malmstrom (Sweden) 78.73	Arvid Spangberg (Sweden) 74.00
1912	Erik Adlerz (Sweden) 73.94pts	Albert Zurner (Germany) 72.60	Gustaf Blomgren (Sweden) 69.56
1920	Clarence Pinkston (USA) 100.67pts	Erik Adlerz (Sweden) 99.08	Harry Prieste (USA) 93.73
1924	Albert White (USA) 487.30pts	David Fall (USA) 486.50	Clarence Pinkston (USA) 473.00
1928	Pete Desjardins (USA) 98.74pts	Farid Simaika (Egypt) 98.58	Michael Galitzen (USA) 92.34
1932	Harold Smith (USA) 124.80pts	Michael Galitzen (USA) 124.28	Frank Kurtz (USA) 121.98
1936	Marshall Wayne (USA) 113.58pts	Albert Root (USA) 110.60	Hermann Stork (Germany) 110.31
1948	Samuel Lee (USA) 130.05pts	Bruce Harlan (USA) 122.30	Joaquin Capilla (Mexico) 113.52
1952	Samuel Lee (USA) 156.28pts	Joaquin Capilla (Mexico) 145.21	Gunther Haase (W.Germany) 141.31
1956	Joaquin Capilla (Mexico) 152.44pts	Gary Tobian (USA) 152.41	Richard Connor (USA) 149.79
1960	Robert Webster (USA) 165.56pts	Gary Tobian (USA) 165.25	Brian Phelps (GB) 157.13
1964	Robert Webster (USA) 148.58pts	Klaus Dibiasi (Italy) 147.54	Tom Gompf (USA) 146.57
1968	Klaus Dibiasi (Italy) 164.18pts	Alvaro Gaxiola (Mexico) 154.49	Edwin Young (USA) 153.93
1972	Klaus Dibiasi (Italy) 338.25pts	David Ambarcumian (USSR) 314.31	Franco Cagnotto (Italy) 312.93
1976	Klaus Dibiasi (Italy) 600.51pts	Gregory Lousanis (USA) 576.99	Vladimir Aleynik (USSR) 548.61
1980			

SWIMMING AND DIVING (WOMEN)

100 METRES FREESTYLE

1912	Fanny Durack (Australia) 1m 22.2s	Wilhelmina Wylie (Australia) 1m 25.4s	Jennie Fletcher (GB) 1m 27.0s
1920	Ethelda Bleibtrey (USA) 1m 13.6s	Irene Guest (USA) 1m 17.0s	Frances Schroth (USA) 1m 17.2s
1924	Ethel Lackie (USA) 1m 12.4s	Mariechen Wehselau (USA) 1m 12.8s	Gertrude Ederle (USA) 1m 14.2s
1928	Albina Osipowich (USA) 1m 11.0s	Eleonor Garatti (USA) 1m 11.4s	Joyce Cooper (GB) 1m 13.6s
1932	Helene Madison (USA) 1m 06.8s	Willy den Ouden (Netherlands) 1m 07.8s	Eleonor Garatti-Saville (USA) 1m 08.2s
1936	Rie Mastenbroek (Netherlands) 1m 05.9s	Jeanette Campbell (Argentina) 1m 06.4s	Gisela Arendt (Germany) 1m 06.6s
1948	Greta Andersen (Denmark) 1m 06.3s	Ann Curtis (USA) 1m 06.5s	Marie-Louise Vaessen (Netherlands) 1m 07.6s
1952	Katalin Szoke (Hungary) 1m 06.8s	Hanny Termeulen (Netherlands) 1m 07.0s	Judit Temes (Hungary) 1m 07.1s
1956	Dawn Fraser (Australia) 1m 02.0s	Lorraine Crapp (Australia) 1m 02.3s	Faith Leech (Australia) 1m 05.1s
1960	Dawn Fraser (Australia) 1m 01.2s	Chris von Saltza (USA) 1m 02.8s	Natalie Steward (GB) 1m 03.1s
1964	Dawn Fraser (Australia) 59.9s	Sharon Stouder (USA) 59.9s	Kathleen Ellis (USA) 1m 00.8s
1968	Jan Henne (USA) 1m 00.0s	Susan Pedersen (USA) 1m 00.3s	Linda Gustavson (USA) 1m 00.3s
1972	Sandra Neilson (USA) 58.59s	Shirley Babashoff (USA) 59.02s	Shane Gould (Australi) 59.06s
1976	Kornelia Ender (E. Germany) 55.65s	Petra Priemer (E. Germany) 56.49s	Brigitha Enith (Netherlands) 65.65s
1980			

200 METRES FREESTYLE

1968	Debbie Meyer (USA) 2m 10.5s	Jan Henne (USA) 2m 11.0s	Jane Barkman (USA) 2m 11.2s
1972	Shane Gould (Australia) 2m 03.56s	Shirley Babashoff (USA) 2m 04.33s	Keena Rothhammer (USA) 2m 04.92s
1976	Kornelia Ender (E. Germany) 1m 59.26s	Shirley Babashoff (USA) 2m 1.22s	Brigitha Enith (Netherlands) 2m 1.40s
1980			

400 METRES FREESTYLE

1924	Martha Norelius (USA) 6m 02.2s	Helen Wainwright (USA) 6m 03.8s	Gertrude Ederle (USA) 6m 04.8s
1928	Martha Norelius (USA) 5m 42.8s	Marie Braun (Netherlands) 5m 57.8s	Josephine McKim (USA) 6m 00.2s
1932	Helene Madison (USA) 5m 28.5s	Lenore Kight (USA) 5m 28.6s	Jennie Maakal (S.Africa) 5m 47.3s
1936	Rie Mastenbroek (Netherlands) 5m 26.4s	Ragnhild Hveger (Denmark) 5m 27.5s	Lenore Wingard (USA) 5m 29.0s
1948	Ann Curtis (USA) 5m 17.8s	Karen Harup (Denmark) 5m 21.2s	Cathie Gibson (GB) 5m 22.5s
1952	Valeria Gyenge (Hungary) 5m 12.1s	Eva Novak (Hungary) 5m 13.7s	Evelyn Kawamoto (USA) 5m 14.6s
1956	Lorraine Crapp (Australia) 4m 54.6s	Dawn Fraser (Australia) 5m 02.5s	Sylvia Ruuska (USA) 5m 07.1s
1960	Chris von Saltza (USA) 4m 50.6s	Jane Cederqvist (Sweden) 4m 53.9s	Tineke Lagerberg (Netherlands) 4m 56.9s
1964	Virginia Duekel (USA) 4m 43.3s	Marilyn Ramenofsky (USA) 4m 44.6s	Terri Stickles (USA) 4m 47.2s
1968	Debbie Meyer (USA) 4m 31.8s	Linda Gustavson (USA) 4m 35.5s	Karen Moras (Australia) 4m 37.0s
1972	Shane Gould (Australia) 4m 19.04s	Novella Calligaris (Italy) 4m 22.44s	Gudrun Wegner (E. Germany) 4m 23.11s
1976	Petra Thumer (E. Germany) 4m 8.89s	Shirley Babashoff (USA) 4m 10.46s	Shannon Smith (Canada) 4m 14.60s
1980			

800 METRES FREESTYLE

1968	Debbie Meyer (USA) 9m 24.0s	Pamela Kruse (USA) 9m 35.7s	Maria-Teresa Ramirez (Mexico) 9m 38.5s
1972	Keena Rothhammer (USA) 8m 53.68s	Shane Gould (Australia) 8m 56.39s	Novella Calligaris (Italy) 8m 57.46s
1976	Petra Thumer (E. Germany) 8m 20.59s	Shirley Babashoff (USA) 8m 37.59s	Wendy Weinberg (USA) 8m 42.60s
1980			

100 METRES BACKSTROKE

1924	Sybil Bauer (USA) 1m 23.2s	Phyllis Harding (GB) 1m 27.4s	Aileen Riggin (USA) 1m 28.2s
1928	Marie Braun (Netherlands) 1m 22.0s	Ellen King (GB) 1m 22.2s	Joyce Cooper (GB) 1m 22.8s
1932	Eleanor Holm (USA) 1m 19.4s	Philomena Mealing (Australia) 1m 21.3s	Valerie Davies (GB) 1m 22.5s
1936	Nina Senff (Netherlands) 1m 18.9s	Rie Mastenbroek (Netherlands) 1m 19.2s	Alice Bridges (USA) 1m 19.4s
1948	Karen Harup (Denmark) 1m 14.4s	Suzanne Zimmermann (USA) 1m 16.0s	Judy Joy Davies (Australia) 1m 16.7s
1952	Joan Harrison (S.Africa) 1m 14.3s	Geertje Wielema (Netherlands) 1m 14.5s	Jean Stewart (N.Z.) 1m 15.8s
1956	Judy Grinham (GB) 1m 12.9s	Carin Cone (USA) 1m 12.9s	Margaret Edwards (GB) 1m 13.1s
1960	Lynn Burke (USA) 1m 09.3s	Natalie Steward (GB) 1m 10.8s	Satoko Tanaka (Japan) 1m 11.4s
1964	Cathy Ferguson (USA) 1m 07.7s	Christine Caron (France) 1m 07.9s	Virginia Duenkel (USA) 1m 08.0s
1968	Kaye Hall (USA) 1m 06.2s	Elaine Tanner (Canada) 1m 06.7s	Jane Swagerty (USA) 1m 08.1s
1972	Melissa Belote (USA) 1m 05.78s	Andrea Gyarmati (Hungary) 1m 06.26s	Susie Atwood (USA) 1m 06.34s
1976	Ulrike Richter (E. Germany) 1m 0.83s	Birgit Treiber (E. Germany) 1m 3.41s	Nancy Garapick (Canada) 1m 3.71s
1980			

200 METRES BACKSTROKE

1968	Lillian Watson (USA) 2m 24.8s	Elaine Tanner (Canada) 2m 27.4s	Kaye Hall (USA) 2m 28.9s
1972	Melissa Belote (USA) 2m 19.19s	Susie Atwood (USA) 2m 20.38s	Donna Gurr (Canada) 2m 23.22s
1976	Ulrike Richter (E. Germany) 2m 13.43s	Birgit Treiber (E. Germany) 2m 14.97s	Nancy Garapick (Canada) 2m 15.60s
1980			

100 METRES BREASTROKE

1968	Djurdjica Bjedov (Yugoslavia) 1m 15.8s	Galina Prosumenschikova (USSR) 1m 15.9s	Sharon Wichman (USA) 1m 16.1s
1972	Catherine Carr (USA) 1m 13.58s	Galina Stepanova (USSR) 1m 14.99s	Beverley Whitfield (Australia) 1m 15.73s
1976	Hannelore Anke (E. Germany) 1m 11.16s	Liubov Rusanova (USSR) 1m 13.40s	Marina Koshevaia (USSR) 1m 13.30s
1980			

200 METRES BREASTROKE

1924	Lucy Morton (GB) 3m 33.2s	Agnes Geraghty (USA) 3m 34.0s	Gladys Carson (GB) 3m 35.4s
1928	Hilde Schrader (Germany) 3m 12.6s	Marie Baron (Netherlands) 3m 15.2s	Lotte Hildensheim (Germany) 3m 17.6s
1932	Clare Dennis (Australia) 3m 06.3s	Hideko Maehata (Japan) 3m 06.4s	Else Jacobson (Denmark) 3m 07.1s
1936	Hideko Maehata (Japan) 3m 03.6s	Martha Genenger (Germany) 3m 04.2s	Inge Sorensen (Denmark) 3m 07.8s
1948	Nel van Vliet (Netherlands) 2m 57.2s	Beatrice Lyons (Australia) 2m 57.7s	Eva Novak (Hungary) 3m 00.2s
1952	Eva Szekely (Hungary) 2m 51.7s	Eva Novak (Hungary) 2m 54.4s	Elenor Gordon (GB) 2m 57.6s
1956	Ursula Happe (W.Germany) 2m 53.1s	Eva Szekely (Hungary) 2m 54.8s	Eva-Maria ten Elsen (W.Germany) 2m 55.1s
1960	Anita Lonsbrough (GB) 2m 49.5s	Wiltrud Urselmann (Germany) 2m 50.0s	Barbara Gobel (Germany) 2m 53.6s
1964	Galina Prosumenschikova (USSR) 2m 46.4s	Claudia Kolb (USA) 2m 47.6s	Svetlana Babanina (USSR) 2m 48.6s
1968	Sharon Wichman (USA) 2m 44.4s	Djurdjica Bjedov (Yugoslavia) 2m 46.4s	G. Prosumenschikova (USSR) 2m 47.0s
1972	Beverley Whitfield (Australia) 2m 41.71s	Dana Schoenfield (USA) 2m 42.05s	Galina Stepanova (USSR) 2m 42.36s
1976	Marina Koshevaia (USSR) 2m 33.35s	Marina Iurchenia (USSR) 2m 36.08s	Liubov Rusanova (USSR) 2m 36.22s
1980			

100 METRES BUTTERFLY

1956	Shelley Mann (USA) 1m 11.0s	Nancy Ramey (USA) 1m 11.9s	Mary-Jane Sears (USA) 1m 14.4s
1960	Carolyn Schuler (USA) 1m 09.5s	Marianne Heemskerk (Netherlands) 1m 10.4s	Jan Andrew (Australia) 1m 12.2s
1964	Sharon Stouder (USA) 1m 04.7s	Ada Kok (Netherlands) 1m 05.6s	Kathleen Ellis (USA) 1m 06.0s
1968	Lyn McClements (Australia) 1m 05.5s	Ellie Daniel (USA) 1m 05.8s	Susan Shields (USA) 1m 06.2s
1972	Mayumi Aoki (Japan) 1m 03.34s	Roswitha Beier (E. Germany) 1m 03.61s	Andrea Gyarmati (Hungary) 1m 03.73s
1976	Kornelia Ender (E. Germany) 1m 0.13s	Andrea Pollack (E. Germany) 1m 0.98s	Wendy Boglioli (USA) 1m 1.17s
1980			

200 METRES BUTTERFLY

1968	Ada Kok (Netherlands) 2m 24.7s	Helga Lindner (E. Germany) 2m 24.8s	Ellie Daniel (USA) 2m 25.9s
1972	Karen Moe (USA) 2m 15.57s	Lynn Colella (USA) 2m 13.34s	Ellie Daniel (USA) 2m 16.74s
1976	Andrea Pollack (E. Germany) 2m 11.41s	Ulrike Tauber (E. Germany) 2m 12.50s	Rosemarie Gabriel (E. Germany) 2m 12.86s
1980			

400 METRES INDIVIDUAL MEDLEY

1964	Donna de Varona (USA) 5m 18.7s	Sharon Finneran (USA) 5m 24.1s	Martha Randall (USA) 5m 24.2s
1968	Claudia Kolb (USA) 5m 08.5s	Lynn Vidali (USA) 5m 22.2s	Sabine Steinbach (E. Germany) 5m 25.3s
1972	Gail Neall (Australia) 5m 02.97s	Leslie Cliff (Canada) 5m 03.57s	Novella Calligaris (Italy) 5m 03.99s
1976	Ulrike Tauber (E. Germany) 4m 42.77s	Cheryl Gibson (Canada) 4m 48.10s	Becky Smith (Canada) 4m 50.48s
1980			

4 × 100 METRES FREESTYLE RELAY

1912	GB 5m 52.8s	Germany 6m 04.6s	Austria 6m 17.0s
1920	USA 5m 11.6s	GB 5m 40.8s	Sweden 5m 43.6s
1924	USA 4m 58.8s	GB 5m 17.0s	Sweden 5m 35.8s
1928	USA 4m 47.6s	GB 5m 02.8s	S Africa 5m 13.4s

| 1976 | John Naber (USA) 55.49s | Peter Rocca (USA) 56.34s | Roland Matthes (E. Germany) 57.22s |
| 1980 | | | |

200 METRES BACKSTROKE

1900	Ernst Hoppenberg (Germany) 2m 47.0s	Karl Ruberl (Austria) 2m 56.0s	Johannes Drost (Neths) 3m 01.0s
1964	Jed Graef (USA) 2m 10.3s	Gary Dilley (USA) 2m 10.5s	Robert Bennett (USA) 2m 13.1s
1968	Roland Matthes (E.Germany) 2m 09.6s	Mitchell Ivey (USA) 2m 10.6s	Jack Horsley (USA) 2m 10.9s
1972	Roland Matthes (E. Germany) 2m 02.82s	Mike Stamm (USA) 2m 04.09s	Mitchell Ivey (USA) 2m 04.33s
1976	John Naber (USA) 1m 59.19s	Peter Rocca (USA) 2m 00.55s	Dan Harrigan (USA) 2m 1.35s
1980			

100 METRES BREASTSTROKE

1968	Donald McKenzie (USA) 1m 07.7s	Vladimir Kosinski (USSR) 1m 08.0s	Nicolai Pankin (USSR) 1m 08.0s
1972	Nobutaka Taguchi (Japan) 1m 04.94s	Tom Bruce (USA) 1m 05.43s	John Hencken (USA) 1m 05.61s
1976	John Hencken (USA) 1m 03.11s	David Wilkie (GB) 1m 03.43s	Arvidas Iouzaytis (USSR) 1m 04.23s
1980			

200 METRES BREASTSTROKE

1908	Frederick Holman (GB) 3m 09.2s	William Robinson (GB) 3m 12.8s	Pontus Hansson (Sweden) 3m 14.6s
1912	Walter Bathe (Germany) 3m 01.8s	Wilhelm Lutzow (Germany) 3m 05.0s	Kurt Malisch (Germany) 3m 08.0s
1920	Hakan Malmroth (Sweden) 3m 04.4s	Thor Henning (Sweden) 3m 09.2s	Arvo Aaltonen (Finland) 3m 12.2s
1924	Robert Skelton (USA) 2m 56.6s	Joseph de Combe (Belgium) 2m 59.2s	William Kirschbaum (USA) 3m 01.0s
1928	Yoshiyuki Tsuruta (Japan) 2m 48.8s	Erich Rademacher (Germany) 2m 50.6s	Teofilo Yldefonso (Philippines) 2m 56.4s
1932	Yoshiyuki Tsuruta (Japan) 2m 45.4s	Reizo Koike (Japan) 2m 46.6s	Teofilo Yldefonso (Philippines) 2m 47.1s
1936	Tetsuo Hamuro (Japan) 2m 42.5s	Erwin Sietas (Germany) 2m 42.9s	Reizo Koike (Japan) 2m 44.2s
1948	Joseph Verdeur (USA) 2m 39.3s	Keith Carter (USA) 2m 40.2s	Robert Sohl (USA) 2m 43.9s
1952	John Davies (Australia) 2m 34.4s	Bowen Stassforth (USA) 2m 34.7s	Herbert Klein (W.Germany) 2m 35.9s
1956	Masura Furukawa (Japan) 2m 34.7s	Masahiro Yoshimura (Japan) 2m 36.7s	Kharis Yunishev (USSR) 2m 36.8s
1960	William Mulliken (USA) 2m 37.4s	Yoshihiko Osaki (Japan) 2m 38.0s	Wieger Mensonides (Neths) 2m 39.7s
1964	Ian O'Brien (Australia) 2m 27.8s	Georgy Prokopenko (USSR) 2m 28.2s	Chet Jastremski (USA) 2m 29.6s
1968	Felipe Munoz (Mexico) 2m 28.7s	Vladimir Kosinski (USSR) 2m 29.2s	Brian Job (USA) 2m 29.9s
1972	John Hencken (USA) 2m 21.55s	David Wilkie (GB) 2m 23.67s	Nobutaka Taguchi (Japan) 2m 23.88s
1976	David Wilkie (GB) 2m 15.11s	John Hencken (USA) 2m 17.26s	Rick Colella (USA) 2m 19.20s
1980			

100 METRES BUTTERFLY

1968	Douglas Russell (USA) 55.9s	Mark Spitz (USA) 56.4s	Ross Wales (USA) 57.2s
1972	Mark Spitz (USA) 54.27s	Bruce Robertson (Canada) 55.56s	Jerry Heidenreich (USA) 55.74
1976	Matt Vogel (USA) 54.35s	Joe Bottom (USA) 54.50s	Gary Hall (USA) 54.65s
1980			

200 METRES BUTTERFLY

1956	William Yorzyk (USA) 2m 19.3s	Takashi Ishimoto (Japan) 2m 23.8s	Gyorgy Tumpek (Hungary) 2m 23.9s
1960	Michael Troy (USA) 2m 12.8s	Neville Hayes (Australia) 2m 14.6s	David Gillanders (USA) 2m 15.3s
1964	Kevin Berry (Australia) 2m 06.6s	Carl Robie (USA) 2m 07.5s	Fred Schmidt (USA) 2m 09.3s
1968	Carl Robie (USA) 2m 08.7s	Martyn Woodroffe (GB) 2m 09.0s	John Ferris (USA) 2m 09.3s
1972	Mark Spitz (USA) 2m 00.70s	Gary Hall (USA) 2m 02.86s	Robin Backhaus (USA) 2m 03.23s
1976	Mike Bruner (USA) 1m 59.23s	Steve Gregg (USA) 1m 59.54s	Bill Forrester (USA) 1m 59.96s
1980			

400 METRES INDIVIDUAL MEDLEY

1964	Richard Roth (USA) 4m 45.5s	Roy Saari (USA) 4m 47.1s	Gerhard Hetz (Germany) 4m 51.0s
1968	Charles Hickcox (USA) 4m 48.4s	Gary Hall (USA) 4m 48.7s	Michael Holthaus (W.Germany) 4m 51.4s
1972	Gunnar Larsson (Sweden) 4m 31.981s	Tim McKee (USA) 4m 31.983s	Andras Hargity (Hungary) 4m 32.70s
1976	Rod Strachan (USA) 4m 23.68s	Tom McKee (USA) 4m 24.62s	Andrey Smirnov (USSR) 4m 26.90s
1980			

4×200 METRES FREESTYLE RELAY

1908	Great Britain 10m 55.6s	Hungary 10m 59.0s	USA 11m 02.8s
1912	Australia 10m 11.2s	USA 10m 20.2s	GB 10m 28.2s
1920	USA 10m 04.4s	Australia 10m 25.4s	GB 10m 37.2s
1924	USA 9m 53.4s	Australia 10m 02.2s	Sweden 10m 06.8s
1928	USA 9m 36.2s	Japan 9m 41.4s	Canada 9m 47.8s
1932	Japan 8m 58.4s	USA 9m 10.5s	Hungary 9m 31.4s
1936	Japan 8m 51.5s	USA 9m 03.0s	Hungary 9m 12.3s
1948	USA 8m 46.0s	Hungary 8m 48.4s	France 9m 08.0s
1952	USA 8m 31.1s	Japan 8m 33.5s	France 8m 45.9s
1956	Australia 8m 23.6s	USA 8m 31.5s	USSR 8m 34.7s
1960	USA 8m 10.2s	Japan 8m 13.2s	Australia 8m 13.8s
1964	USA 7m 52.1s	Germany 7m 59.3s	Japan 8m 03.8s
1968	USA 7m 52.3s	Australia 7m 53.7s	USSR 8m 01.6s
1972	USA 7m 35.78s	W. Germany 7m 41.69s	USSR 7m 45.76s
1976	USA 7m 23.22s	USSR 7m 27.97s	GB 7m 32.11s
1980			

4×100 METRES MEDLEY RELAY

1960	USA 4m 05.4s	Australia 4m 12.0s	Japan 4m 12.2s
1964	USA 3m 58.4s	Germany 4m 01.6s	Australia 4m 02.3s
1968	USA 3m 54.9s	E.Germany 3m 57.5s	USSR 4m 00.7s
1972	USA 3m 48.16s	E. Germany 3m 52.12s	Canada 3m 52.26s
1976	USA 3m 42.22s	Canada 3m 45.94s	W. Germany 3m 47.29s
1980			

DIVING (MEN)
SPRINGBOARD

1908	Albert Zurner (Germany) 85.5pts	Kurt Behrens (Germany) 85.3	George Gaidzik (USA) 80.8 / Gottlob Walz (Germany) 80.8
1912	Paul Gunther (Germany) 79.23pts	Hans Luber (Germany) 76.78	Kurt Behrens (Germany) 73.75
1920	Louis Kuehn (USA) 675.00pts	Clarence Pinkston (USA) 655.30	Louis Balbach (USA) 649.50
1924	Albert White (USA) 696.40pts	Pete Desjardins (USA) 693.20	Clarence Pinkston (USA) 653.00
1928	Pete Desjardins (USA) 185.04pts	Michael Galitzen (USA) 174.06	Farid Simaika (Egypt) 172.46
1932	Michael Galitzen (USA) 161.38pts	Harold Smith (USA) 158.54	Richard Degener (USA) 151.82
1936	Richard Degener (USA) 163.57pts	Marshall Wayne (USA) 159.56	Albert Greene (USA) 146.29
1948	Bruce Harlan (USA) 163.64pts	Miller Anderson (USA) 157.29	Samuel Lee (USA) 145.52
1952	David Browning (USA) 205.29pts	Miller Anderson (USA) 199.84	Robert Clotworthy (USA) 184.92
1956	Robert Clotworthy (USA) 159.56pts	Donald Harper (USA) 156.23	Joaquin Capilla (Mexico) 150.69
1960	Gary Tobian (USA) 170.00pts	Samuel Hall (USA) 167.08	Juan Botella (Mexico) 162.30
1964	Ken Sitzberger (USA) 159.90pts	Frank Gorman (USA) 157.63	Larry Andreasen (USA) 143.77
1968	Bernard Wrightson (USA) 170.15pts	Klaus Dibiasi (Italy) 159.74	James Henry (USA) 159.09
1972	Franco Cagnotto (Italy) 400.95pts	Viacheslav Strahov (USSR) 392.10	Vladamir Vasin (USSR) 387.72
1976	Philip Boggs (USA) 619.05pts	Franco Cagnotto (Italy) 570.48	Alexandr Kosenkov (USSR) 567.24
1980			

PLATFORM DIVING

1908	Hjalmar Johansson (Sweden) 83.75pts	Karl Malmstrom (Sweden) 78.73	Arvid Spangberg (Sweden) 74.00
1912	Erik Adlerz (Sweden) 73.94pts	Albert Zurner (Germany) 72.60	Gustaf Blomgren (Sweden) 69.56
1920	Clarence Pinkston (USA) 100.67pts	Erik Adlerz (Sweden) 99.08	Harry Prieste (USA) 93.73
1924	Albert White (USA) 487.30pts	David Fall (USA) 486.50	Clarence Pinkston (USA) 473.00
1928	Pete Desjardins (USA) 98.74pts	Farid Simaika (Egypt) 98.58	Michael Galitzen (USA) 92.34
1932	Harold Smith (USA) 124.80pts	Michael Galitzen (USA) 124.28	Frank Kurtz (USA) 121.98
1936	Marshall Wayne (USA) 113.58pts	Albert Root (USA) 110.60	Hermann Stork (Germany) 110.31
1948	Samuel Lee (USA) 130.05pts	Bruce Harlan (USA) 122.30	Joaquin Capilla (Mexico) 113.52
1952	Samuel Lee (USA) 156.28pts	Joaquin Capilla (Mexico) 145.21	Gunther Haase (W.Germany) 141.31
1956	Joaquin Capilla* (Mexico) 152.44pts	Gary Tobian (USA) 152.41	Richard Connor (USA) 149.79
1960	Robert Webster (USA) 165.56pts	Gary Tobian (USA) 165.25	Brian Phelps (GB) 157.13
1964	Robert Webster (USA) 148.58pts	Klaus Dibiasi (Italy) 147.54	Tom Gompf (USA) 146.57
1968	Klaus Dibiasi (Italy) 164.18pts	Alvaro Gaxiola (Mexico) 154.49	Edwin Young (USA) 153.93
1972	Klaus Dibiasi (Italy) 338.25pts	David Ambarcumian (USSR) 314.31	Franco Cagnotto (Italy) 312.93
1976	Klaus Dibiasi (Italy) 600.51pts	Gregory Lousanis (USA) 576.99	Vladimir Aleynik (USSR) 548.61
1980			

SWIMMING AND DIVING (WOMEN)

100 METRES FREESTYLE

1912	Fanny Durack (Australia) 1m 22.2s	Wilhelmina Wylie (Australia) 1m 25.4s	Jennie Fletcher (GB) 1m 27.0s
1920	Ethelda Bleibtrey (USA) 1m 13.6s	Irene Guest (USA) 1m 17.0s	Frances Schroth (USA) 1m 17.2s
1924	Ethel Lackie (USA) 1m 12.4s	Mariechen Wehselau (USA) 1m 12.8s	Gertrude Ederle (USA) 1m 14.2s
1928	Albina Osipowich (USA) 1m 11.0s	Eleonor Garatti (USA) 1m 11.4s	Joyce Cooper (GB) 1m 13.6s
1932	Helene Madison (USA) 1m 06.8s	Willy den Ouden (Netherlands) 1m 07.8s	Eleonor Garatti-Saville (USA) 1m 08.2s
1936	Rie Mastenbroek (Netherlands) 1m 05.9s	Jeanette Campbell (Argentina) 1m 06.4s	Gisela Arendt (Germany) 1m 06.6s
1948	Greta Andersen (Denmark) 1m 06.3s	Ann Curtis (USA) 1m 06.5s	Marie-Louise Vaessen (Netherlands) 1m 07.6s
1952	Katalin Szoke (Hungary) 1m 06.8s	Hanny Termeulen (Netherlands) 1m 07.0s	Judit Temes (Hungary) 1m 07.1s
1956	Dawn Fraser (Australia) 1m 02.0s	Lorraine Crapp (Australia) 1m 02.3s	Faith Leech (Australia) 1m 05.1s
1960	Dawn Fraser (Australia) 1m 01.2s	Chris von Saltza (USA) 1m 02.8s	Natalie Steward (GB) 1m 03.1s
1964	Dawn Fraser (Australia) 59.9s	Sharon Stouder (USA) 59.9s	Kathleen Ellis (USA) 1m 00.8s
1968	Jan Henne (USA) 1m 00.0s	Susan Pedersen (USA) 1m 00.3s	Linda Gustavson (USA) 1m 00.3s
1972	Sandra Neilson (USA) 58.59s	Shirley Babashoff (USA) 59.02s	Shane Gould (Australi) 59.06s
1976	Kornelia Ender (E. Germany) 55.65s	Petra Priemer (E. Germany) 56.49s	Brigitha Enith (Netherlands) 65.65s
1980			

200 METRES FREESTYLE

1968	Debbie Meyer (USA) 2m 10.5s	Jan Henne (USA) 2m 11.0s	Jane Barkman (USA) 2m 11.2s
1972	Shane Gould (Australia) 2m 03.56s	Shirley Babashoff (USA) 2m 04.33s	Keena Rothhammer (USA) 2m 04.92s
1976	Kornelia Ender (E. Germany) 1m 59.26s	Shirley Babashoff (USA) 2m 1.22s	Brigitha Enith (Netherlands) 2m 1.40s
1980			

400 METRES FREESTYLE

1924	Martha Norelius (USA) 6m 02.2s	Helen Wainwright (USA) 6m 03.8s	Gertrude Ederle (USA) 6m 04.8s
1928	Martha Norelius (USA) 5m 42.8s	Marie Braun (Netherlands) 5m 57.8s	Josephine McKim (USA) 6m 00.2s
1932	Helene Madison (USA) 5m 28.5s	Lenore Kight (USA) 5m 28.6s	Jennie Maakal (S.Africa) 5m 47.3s
1936	Rie Mastenbroek (Netherlands) 5m 26.4s	Ragnhild Hveger (Denmark) 5m 27.5s	Lenore Wingard (USA) 5m 29.0s
1948	Ann Curtis (USA) 5m 17.8s	Karen Harup (Denmark) 5m 21.2s	Cathie Gibson (GB) 5m 22.5s
1952	Valeria Gyenge (Hungary) 5m 12.1s	Eva Novak (Hungary) 5m 13.7s	Evelyn Kawamoto (USA) 5m 14.6s
1956	Lorraine Crapp (Australia) 4m 54.6s	Dawn Fraser (Australia) 5m 02.5s	Sylvia Ruuska (USA) 5m 07.1s
1960	Chris von Saltza (USA) 4m 50.6s	Jane Cederqvist (Sweden) 4m 53.9s	Tineke Lagerberg (Netherlands) 4m 56.9s
1964	Virginia Duekel (USA) 4m 43.3s	Marilyn Ramenofsky (USA) 4m 44.6s	Terri Stickles (USA) 4m 47.2s
1968	Debbie Meyer (USA) 4m 31.8s	Linda Gustavson (USA) 4m 35.5s	Karen Moras (Australia) 4m 37.0s
1972	Shane Gould (Australia) 4m 19.04s	Novella Calligaris (Italy) 4m 22.44s	Gudrun Wegner (E. Germany) 4m 23.11s
1976	Petra Thumer (E. Germany) 4m 8.89s	Shirley Babashoff (USA) 4m 10.46s	Shannon Smith (Canada) 4m 14.60s
1980			

800 METRES FREESTYLE

1968	Debbie Meyer (USA) 9m 24.0s	Pamela Kruse (USA) 9m 35.7s	Maria-Teresa Ramirez (Mexico) 9m 38.5s
1972	Keena Rothhammer (USA) 8m 53.68s	Shane Gould (Australia) 8m 56.39s	Novella Calligaris (Italy) 8m 57.46s
1976	Petra Thumer (E. Germany) 8m 20.59s	Shirley Babashoff (USA) 8m 37.59s	Wendy Weinberg (USA) 8m 42.60s
1980			

100 METRES BACKSTROKE

1924	Sybil Bauer (USA) 1m 23.2s	Phyllis Harding (GB) 1m 27.4s	Aileen Riggin (USA) 1m 28.2s
1928	Marie Braun (Netherlands) 1m 22.0s	Ellen King (GB) 1m 22.2s	Joyce Cooper (GB) 1m 22.8s
1932	Eleanor Holm (USA) 1m 19.4s	Philomena Mealing (Australia) 1m 21.3s	Valerie Davies (GB) 1m 22.5s
1936	Nina Senff (Netherlands) 1m 18.9s	Rie Mastenbroek (Netherlands) 1m 19.2s	Alice Bridges (USA) 1m 19.4s
1948	Karen Harup (Denmark) 1m 14.4s	Suzanne Zimmermann (USA) 1m 16.0s	Judy Joy Davies (Australia) 1m 16.7s
1952	Joan Harrison (S.Africa) 1m 14.3s	Geertje Wielema (Netherlands) 1m 14.5s	Jean Stewart (N.Z.) 1m 15.8s
1956	Judy Grinham (GB) 1m 12.9s	Carin Cone (USA) 1m 12.9s	Margaret Edwards (GB) 1m 13.1s
1960	Lynn Burke (USA) 1m 09.3s	Natalie Steward (GB) 1m 10.8s	Satoko Tanaka (Japan) 1m 11.4s
1964	Cathy Ferguson (USA) 1m 07.7s	Christine Caron (France) 1m 07.9s	Virginia Duenkel (USA) 1m 08.0s
1968	Kaye Hall (USA) 1m 06.2s	Elaine Tanner (Canada) 1m 06.7s	Jane Swagerty (USA) 1m 08.1s
1972	Melissa Belote (USA) 1m 05.78s	Andrea Gyarmati (Hungary) 1m 06.26s	Susie Atwood (USA) 1m 06.34s
1976	Ulrike Richter (E. Germany) 1m 0.83s	Birgit Treiber (E. Germany) 1m 3.41s	Nancy Garapick (Canada) 1m 3.71s
1980			

200 METRES BACKSTROKE

1968	Lillian Watson (USA) 2m 24.8s	Elaine Tanner (Canada) 2m 27.4s	Kaye Hall (USA) 2m 28.9s
1972	Melissa Belote (USA) 2m 19.19s	Susie Atwood (USA) 2m 20.38s	Donna Gurr (Canada) 2m 23.22s
1976	Ulrike Richter (E. Germany) 2m 13.43s	Birgit Treiber (E. Germany) 2m 14.97s	Nancy Garapick (Canada) 2m 15.60s
1980			

100 METRES BREASTSTROKE

1968	Djurdjica Bjedov (Yugoslavia) 1m 15.8s	Galina Prosumenschikova (USSR) 1m 15.9s	Sharon Wichman (USA) 1m 16.1s
1972	Catherine Carr (USA) 1m 13.58s	Galina Stepanova (USSR) 1m 14.99s	Beverley Whitfield (Australia) 1m 15.73s
1976	Hannelore Anke (E. Germany) 1m 11.16s	Liubov Rusanova (USSR) 1m 13.40s	Marina Koshevaia (USSR) 1m 13.30s
1980			

200 METRES BREASTSTROKE

1924	Lucy Morton (GB) 3m 33.2s	Agnes Geraghty (USA) 3m 34.0s	Gladys Carson (GB) 3m 35.4s
1928	Hilde Schrader (Germany) 3m 12.6s	Marie Baron (Netherlands) 3m 15.2s	Lotte Hildensheim (Germany) 3m 17.6s
1932	Clare Dennis (Australia) 3m 06.3s	Hideko Maehata (Japan) 3m 06.4s	Else Jacobson (Denmark) 3m 07.1s
1936	Hideko Maehata (Japan) 3m 03.6s	Martha Genenger (Germany) 3m 04.2s	Inge Sorensen (Denmark) 3m 07.8s
1948	Nel van Vliet (Netherlands) 2m 57.2s	Beatrice Lyons (Australia) 2m 57.7s	Eva Novak (Hungary) 3m 00.2s
1952	Eva Szekely (Hungary) 2m 51.7s	Eva Novak (Hungary) 2m 54.4s	Elenor Gordon (GB) 2m 57.6s
1956	Ursula Happe (W.Germany) 2m 53.1s	Eva Szekely (Hungary) 2m 54.8s	Eva-Maria ten Elsen (W.Germany) 2m 55.1s
1960	Anita Lonsbrough (GB) 2m 49.5s	Wiltrud Urselmann (Germany) 2m 50.0s	Barbara Gobel (Germany) 2m 53.6s
1964	Galina Prosumenschikova (USSR) 2m 46.4s	Claudia Kolb (USA) 2m 47.6s	Svetlana Babanina (USSR) 2m 48.6s
1968	Sharon Wichman (USA) 2m 44 4s	Djurdjica Bjedov (Yugoslavia) 2m 46.4s	G. Prosumenschikova (USSR) 2m 47.0s
1972	Beverley Whitfield (Australia) 2m 41.71s	Dana Schoenfield (USA) 2m 42.05s	Galina Stepanova (USSR) 2m 42.36s
1976	Marina Koshevaia (USSR) 2m 33.35s	Marina Iurchenia (USSR) 2m 36.08s	Liubov Rusanova (USSR) 2m 36.22s
1980			

100 METRES BUTTERFLY

1956	Shelley Mann (USA) 1m 11.0s	Nancy Ramey (USA) 1m 11.9s	Mary-Jane Sears (USA) 1m 14.4s
1960	Carolyn Schuler (USA) 1m 09.5s	Marianne Heemskerk (Netherlands) 1m 10.4s	Jan Andrew (Australia) 1m 12.2s
1964	Sharon Stouder (USA) 1m 04.7s	Ada Kok (Netherlands) 1m 05.6s	Kathleen Ellis (USA) 1m 06.0s
1968	Lyn McClements (Australia) 1m 05.5s	Ellie Daniel (USA) 1m 05.8s	Susan Shields (USA) 1m 06.2s
1972	Mayumi Aoki (Japan) 1m 03.34s	Roswitha Beier (E. Germany) 1m 03.61s	Andrea Gyarmati (Hungary) 1m 03.73s
1976	Kornelia Ender (E. Germany) 1m 0.13s	Andrea Pollack (E. Germany) 1m 0.98s	Wendy Boglioli (USA) 1m 1.17s
1980			

200 METRES BUTTERFLY

1968	Ada Kok (Netherlands) 2m 24.7s	Helga Lindner (E.Germany) 2m 24.8s	Ellie Daniel (USA) 2m 25.9s
1972	Karen Moe (USA) 2m 15.57s	Lynn Colella (USA) 2m 13.34s	Ellie Daniel (USA) 2m 16.74s
1976	Andrea Pollack (E. Germany) 2m 11.41s	Ulrike Tauber (E. Germany) 2m 12.50s	Rosemarie Gabriel (E. Germany) 2m 12.86s
1980			

400 METRES INDIVIDUAL MEDLEY

1964	Donna de Varona (USA) 5m 18.7s	Sharon Finneran (USA) 5m 24.1s	Martha Randall (USA) 5m 24.2s
1968	Claudia Kolb (USA) 5m 08.5s	Lynn Vidali (USA) 5m 22.2s	Sabine Steinbach (E. Germany) 5m 25.3s
1972	Gail Neall (Australia) 5m 02.97s	Leslie Cliff (Canada) 5m 03.57s	Novella Calligaris (Italy) 5m 03.99s
1976	Ulrike Tauber (E. Germany) 4m 42.77s	Cheryl Gibson (Canada) 4m 48.10s	Becky Smith (Canada) 4m 50.48s
1980			

4 × 100 METRES FREESTYLE RELAY

1912	GB 5m 52.8s	Germany 6m 04.6s	Austria 6m 17.0s
1920	USA 5m 11.6s	GB 5m 40.8s	Sweden 5m 43.6s
1924	USA 4m 58.8s	GB 5m 17.0s	Sweden 5m 35.8s
1928	USA 4m 47.6s	GB 5m 02.8s	S.Africa 5m 13.4s

1932	USA 4m 38.0s	Netherlands 4m 47.5s	GB 4m 52.4s
1936	Netherlands 4m 36.0s	Germany 4m 36.8s	USA 4m 40.2s
1948	USA 4m 29.2s	Denmark 4m 29.6s	Netherlands 4m 31.6s
1952	Hungary 4m 24.4s	Netherlands 4m 29.0s	USA 4m 30.1s
1956	Australia 4m 17.1s	USA 4m 19.2s	S.Africa 4m 25.7s
1960	USA 4m 08.9s	Australia 4m 11.3s	Germany 4m 19.7s
1964	USA 4m 03.8s	Australia 4m 06.9s	Netherlands 4m 12.0s
1968	USA 4m 02.5s	E.Germany 4m 05.7s	Canada 4m 07.2s
1972	USA 3m 55.19s	E.Germany 3m 55.55s	W.Germany 3m 57.93s
1976	USA 3m 44.82s	E.Germany 3m 45.50s	Canada 3m 48.81s
1980			

4×100 METRES MEDLEY RELAY

1960	USA 4m 41.1s	Australia 4m 45.9s	Germany 4m 47.6s
1964	USA 4m 33.9s	Netherlands 4m 37.0s	USSR 4m 39.2s
1968	USA 4m 28.3s	Australia 4m 30.0s	W.Germany 4m 36.4s
1972	USA 4m 20.75s	E.Germany 4m 24.91s	W.Germany 4m 26.46s
1976	E.Germany 4m 7.95s	USA 4m 14.55s	Canada 4m 15.22s
1980			

SPRINGBOARD DIVING

1920	Aileen Riggin (USA) 539.90pts	Helen Wainwright (USA) 534.80	Thelma Payne (USA) 534.10
1924	Betty Becker (USA) 474.50pts	Aileen Riggin (USA) 460.40	Caroline Fletcher (USA) 434.40
1928	Helen Meany (USA) 78.62pts	Dorothy Poynton (USA) 75.62	Georgia Coleman (USA) 73.38
1932	Georgia Coleman (USA) 87.52pts	Katherine Rawls (USA) 82.56	Jane Fauntz (USA) 81.12
1936	Marjorie Gestring (USA) 89.27pts	Katherine Rawls (USA) 88.35	Dorothy Poynton-Hill (USA) 82.36
1948	Victoria Draves (USA) 108.74pts	Zoe-Ann Olson (USA) 108.23	Patricia Elsener (USA) 101.30
1952	Patricia McCormick (USA) 147.30pts	Mady Moreau (France) 139.34	Zoe-Ann Olson-Jensen (USA) 127.57
1956	Patricia McCormick (USA) 142.36pts	Jeanne Stunyo (USA) 125.89	Irene MacDonald (Canada) 121.40
1960	Ingrid Kramer (Germany) 155.81pts	Paula-Jean Myers-Pope (USA) 141.24	Elizabeth Ferris (GB) 139.09
1964	Ingrid Engel-Kramer (Germany) 145.00pts	Jeanne Collier (USA) 138.36	Patricia Willard (USA) 138.18
1968	Susan Gossick (USA) 150.77pts	Tamara Pogosheva (USSR) 145.30	Keala O'Sullivan (USA) 145.23
1972	Micki King (USA) 450.03pts	Ulrika Knape (Sweden) 434.19	Marina Janicke (E.Germany) 430.92
1976	Jennifer Chandler (USA) 506.19pts	Christa Kohler (E.Germany) 469.41	Cynthia McIngvale (USA) 466.83
1980			

PLATFORM DIVING

1912	Greta Johansson (Sweden) 39.90pts	Lisa Regnell (Sweden) 36.00	Belle White (GB) 34.00
1920	Stefani Fryland-Clausen (Denmark) 34.60pts	Eileen Armstrong (GB) 33.30	Eva Ollivier (Sweden) 32.60
1924	Caroline Smith (USA) 166.00pts	Betty Becker (USA) 167.00	Hjordis Topel (Sweden) 164.00
1928	Betty Becker-Pinkston (USA) 31.60pts	Georgia Coleman (USA) 30.60	Lala Sjoqvist (Sweden) 29.20
1932	Dorothy Poynton (USA) 40.26pts	Georgia Coleman (USA) 35.56	Marion Roper (USA) 35.22
1936	Dorothy Poynton-Hill (USA) 33.93pts	Velma Dunn (USA) 33.63	Kathe Kohler (Germany) 33.43
1948	Victoria Draves (USA) 68.87pts	Patricia Elsener (USA) 66.28	Birte Christoffersen (Denmark) 66.04
1952	Patricia McCormick (USA) 79.37pts	Paula-Jean Myers (USA) 71.63	Juno Irwin (USA) 70.49
1956	Patricia McCormick (USA) 84.85pts	Juno Irwin (USA) 81.64	Paula-Jean Myers (USA) 81.58
1960	Ingrid Kramer (Germany) 91.28pts	Paula-Jean Myers-Pope (USA) 88.94	Ninel Krutova (USSR) 86.99
1964	Lesley Bush (USA) 99.80pts	Ingrid Engel-Kramer (Germany) 98.45	Galina Alekseyeva (USSR) 97.60
1968	Milena Duchkova (Czech) 109.59pts	Natalya Lobanova (USSR) 105.14	Ann Peterson (USA) 101.11
1972	Ulrika Knape (Sweden) 390.00pts	Milena Duchkova (Czech) 370.92	Marina Janicke (E.Germany) 360.54
1976	Elena Vayswhkovskaia (USSR) 406.59pts	Ulrika Knape (Sweden) 402.60	Debby Wilson (Canada) 401.07
1980			

WATER POLO

1900	GB	Belgium	France
1904	USA	USA	USA
1908	GB	Belgium	Sweden
1912	GB	Sweden	Belgium
1920	GB	Belgium	Sweden
1924	France	Belgium	USA
1928	Germany	Hungary	France
1932	Hungary 8pts	Germany 5	USA 5
1936	Hungary 5pts	Germany 5	Belgium 2
1948	Italy 6pts	Hungary 3	Netherlands 2
1952	Hungary 5pts	Yugoslavia 5	Italy 2
1956	Hungary 10pts	Yugoslavia 7	USSR 6
1960	Italy 5pts	USSR 3	Hungary 2
1964	Hungary 5pts	Yugoslavia	USSR 2
1968	Yugoslavia 8pts	USSR 8	Hungary 6
1972	USSR	Hungary	USA
1976	Hungary	Italy	Holland
1980			

WEIGHT-LIFTING

Weights are given in pounds until 1972 and thereafter in kilos.

UNDER 52 KILOS (FLYWEIGHT)

1972	Zygmunt Smalcerz (Poland) 337.5	Lajos Szeucs (Hungary) 330	Sandor Holczreiter (Hungary) 327.5
1976	Alexandr Voronin (USSR) 242.5kgs	Gyorgy Koszegi (Hungary) 237.5kgs	Mohammed Nassiri (Iran) 235.0kgs
1980			

UNDER 56 KILOS (BANTAMWEIGHT)

1948	Joseph de Pietro (USA) 307.5	Julian Creus (GB) 297.5	Richard Tom (USA) 295
1952	Ivan Udodov (USSR) 315	Mahmound Namdjou (Iran) 307.5	Ali Mirzai (Iran) 300
1956	Charles Vinci (USA) 342.5	Vladimir Stogov (USSR) 337.5	Mahmoud Namdjou (Iran) 332.5
1960	Charles Vinci (USA) 345	Joshinobu Miyake (Japan) 337.5	Ismail Khan (Iran) 330
1964	Alexey Vakhonin (USSR) 357.5	Imre Földi (Hungary) 355	Shiro Ichinoseki (Japan) 347.5
1968	Mohamed Nassiri (Iran) 367.5	Imre Földi (Hungary) 367.5	Henryk Trebicki (Poland) 357.5
1972	Imre Földi (Hungary) 377.5	Mohamed Nassiri (Iran) 370.0	Gennadi Chetin (USSR) 367.5
1976	Norair Nurikian (Bulgaria) 262.5kgs	Grzegorz Cziura (Poland) 252.5kgs	Kenchiki Ando (Japan) 250.0kgs
1980			

UNDER 60 KILOS (FEATHERWEIGHT)

1920	Francois de Haes (Belgium) 220	Alfred Schmidt (Estonia) 212.5	E. Ritter (Switz) 210
1924	Pierino Gabetti (Italy) 402.5	Andreas Stadler (Austria) 385	A. Reinmann (Switzerland) 382.5
1928	Franz Andrysek (Austria) 287.5	Pierino Gabetti (Italy) 282.5	Hans Wölpert (Germany) 282.5
1932	Raymond Suvigny (France) 287.5	Hans Wölpert (Germany) 282.5	Anthony Terlazzo (USA) 280
1936	Anthony Terlazzo (USA) 312.5	Saleh Soliman (Egupt) 305	Ibrahim Shams (Egypt) 300
1948	Mahmoud Fayed (Egypt) 332.5	Rodney Wilkes (Trinidad) 317.5	Jaffar Salmassi (Iran) 312.5
1952	Rafael Chimishkian (USSR) 337.5	Nikolay Saksonov (USSR) 332.5	Rodney Wilkes (Trinidad) 322.5
1956	Isaac Berger (USA) 352.5	Evgeniy Minayev (USSR) 342.5	Marian Zielinski (Poland) 335
1960	Evgeniy Minayev (USSR) 372.5	Isaac Berger (USA) 362.5	Sebastiano Mannironi (Italy) 352.5
1964	Yoshinobu Miyake (Japan) 397.5	Isaac Berger (USA) 382.5	Mieczyslaw Nowak (Poland) 377.5
1968	Yoshinobu Miyake (Japan) 392.5	Dimitri Zhanidze (USSR) 387.5	Yoshiyuki Miyake (Japan) 385
1972	Norair Nourikian (Bulgaria) 402.5	Dimitri Zhanidze (USSR) 400.0	Janos Benedek (Hungary) 390.0
1976	Nikolai Koleshikov (USSR) 285kgs	Georgi Todorov (Bulgaria) 280kgs	Kazamusa Hirai (Japan) 275.0kgs
1980			

UNDER 67.5 KILOS (LIGHTWEIGHT)

1920	Alfred Neuland (Estonia) 257.5	Louis Williquet (Belgium) 240	Florimond Rooms (Belgium) 230
1924	Edmond Decottignies (France) 440	Anton Zwerina (Austria) 427.5	Bohumil Durdis (Czech) 425
1928	Kurg Helbig & Hans Haas (Germany) (Austria) 322.5		Fernand Arnout (France) 302.5
1932	Rene Duverger (France) 325	Hans Haas (Austria) 307.5	Gastone Pierini (Italy) 302.5
1936	Mohammed Mesbah & Robert Fein (Egypt) (Austria) 342.5		Karl Jansen (Germany) 327.5
1948	Ibrahim Shams (Egypt) 360	Appia Hammouda (Egypt) 360	James Halliday (GB) 340
1952	Thomas Kono (USA) 362.5	Yevgeniy Lopatin (USSR) 350	Verdi Barberis (Australia) 350
1956	Igor Rybak (USSR) 380	Ravil Shabutdinov (USSR) 372.5	Kim Hee (Korea) 370
1960	Viktor Bushuyev (USSR) 397.5	Tan Howe Liang (Singapore) 380	Abdul Aziz (Iraq) 380
1964	Waldemar Baszanowski (Poland) 432.5	Vladimir Kaplunov (USSR) 432.5	Marian Zielinski (Poland) 420
1968	Waldemar Baszanowski (Poland) 437.5	Parviz Jalayer (Iran) 422.5	Marian Zielinski (Poland) 420
1972	Mukharbi Kirzhinov (USSR) 460.0	Mladen Koutchev (Bulgaria) 450.0	Zbigniew Kaczmarek (Poland) 437.5
1976	Piotr Korol (USSR) 305kgs	Daniel Senet (France) 300kgs	Kazimierz Czarnecki (Poland) 295.0kgs
1980			

UNDER 75 KILOS (MIDDLEWEIGHT)

1920	Henri Gance (France) 245	Ubaldo Bianchi (Italy) 237.5	Albert Pettersson (Sweden) 237.5

1924	Carlo Galimberti (Italy) 492.5	Alfred Neuland (Estonia) 455	J. Kikkas (Estonia) 450
1928	Roger Francois (France) 335	Carlo Galimberti (Italy) 332.5	August Scheffer (Netherlands) 327.5
1932	Rudolf Ismayr (Germany) 345	Carlo Galimberti (Italy) 340	Karl Hipfinger (Austria) 337.5
1936	Khadr El Thouni (Egypt) 387.5	Rudolf Ismayr (Germany) 352.5	Adolf Wagner (Germany) 352.5
1948	Frank Spellman (USA) 390	Peter George (USA) 382.5	Sung Kim (Korea) 380
1952	Peter George (USA) 400	Gerald Gratton (Canada) 390	Sung Kim (South Korea) 382.5
1956	Fyeodor Bagdanovskiy (USSR) 420	Peter George (USA) 412.5	Ermanno Pignatti (Italy) 382.5
1960	Aleksandr Kurynov (USSR) 472.5	Thomas Kono (USA) 427.5	Gyözö Veres (Hungary) 405
1964	Hans Zdrazila (Czechoslavakia) 445	Viktor Kurentsov (USSR) 440	Masashi Ohuchi (Japan) 437.5
1968	Victor Kurentsov (USSR) 475	Masashi Ohuchi (Japan) 455	Karoly Bakos (Hungary) 440
1972	Yordan Bikov (Bulgaria) 485.0	Mohamed Trabulsi (Lebanon) 472.5	Anselmo Silvino (Italy) 470.0
1976	Yordan Mitkov (Bulgaria) 335.0kgs	Vartan Militsyan (USSR) 330.0kgs	Peter Wenzel (E. Germany) 327.5kgs
1980			

UNDER 82.5 KILOS (LIGHT HEAVYWEIGHT)

1920	Ernest Cadine (France) 290	Fritz Hünenberger (Switzerland) 275	Erik Pettersson (Sweden) 272.5
1924	Charles Rigoulot (France) 502.5	Fritz Hünenberger (Switzerland) 490	Leopold Friedrich (Austria) 490
1928	Sayed Nosseir (Egypt) 355	Louis Hostin (France) 352.5	Johannes Verheyen (Netherlands) 337.5
1932	Louis Hostin (France) 365	Svend Olsen (Denmark) 360	Henry Duey (USA) 330
1936	Louis Hostin (France) 372.5	Eugen Duetsch (Germany) 365	Ibrahim Wasif (Egypt) 360
1948	Stanley Stanczyk (USA) 417.5	Harold Sakata (USA) 380	Gosta Magnusson (Sweden) 375
1952	Trofim Lomakin (USSR) 417.5	Stanley Stancyzk (USA) 415	Arkhadiy Vorobyev (USSR) 407.5
1956	Thomas Kono (USA) 447.5	Vasiliy Stepanov (USSR) 427.5	James George (USA) 417.5
1960	Ireneusz Palinski (Poland) 442.5	James George (USA) 430	Jan Bochenek (Poland) 420
1964	Rudolf Plyukfelder (USSR) 475	Geza Toth (Hungary) 467.5	Gyözö Veres (Hungary) 467.5
1968	Boris Selitsky (USSR) 485	Vladimir Belyaev (USSR) 485	Norbert Ozimek (Poland) 472.5
1972	Leif Jenssen (Norway) 507.5	Norbert Ozimek (Poland) 497.5	Gyoergy Horvath (Hungary) 495.0
1976	Valeri Shary (USSR) 365kgs	Trendafil Stoichev (Bulgaria) 360kgs	Peter Baczako (Hungary) 345kgs
1980			

UNDER 90 KILOS (MID-HEAVYWEIGHT)

1952	Norbert Schemansky (USA) 445	Grigoriy Novak (USSR) 410	Lennox Kilgour (Trinidad) 402.5
1956	Arkhadiy Vorobyev (USSR) 462.5	David Sheppard (USA) 442.5	Jean Debuf (France) 425
1960	Arkhadiy Vorobyev (USSR) 472.5	Trofim Lomakin (USSR) 457.5	Louis Martin (GB) 445
1964	Vladimir Golovanov (USSR) 487.5	Louis Martin (GB) 475	Ireneusz Palinski (Poland) 467.5
1968	Kaarlo Kangasniemi (Finland) 517.5	Yan Talts (USSR) 507.5	Marek Golab (Poland) 495
1972	Andon Nikolov (Bulgaria) 525.0	Atanass Chopov (Bulgaria) 517.5	Hans Bettembourg (Sweden) 512.5
1976	David Rigert (USSR) 382.5kgs	Lee James (USA) 362.5kgs	Atanas Shopov (USSR) 360.0kgs
1980			

UNDER 110 KILOS (HEAVYWEIGHT)

1920	Filippo Bottino (Italy) 270	Joseph Alzin (Luxembourg) 255	L. Bernot (France) 250
1924	Giuseppe Tonani (Italy) 517.5	Franz Aigner (Austria) 515	Harald Tammer (Estonia) 497.5
1928	Josef Strassberger (Germany) 372.5	Arnold Luhäär (Estonia) 360	Jaroslav Skobla (Czechoslovakia) 357.5
1932	Jaroslav Skobla (Czechoslovakia) 380	Vaclav Psenicka (Czechoslovakia) 377.5	Josef Strassberger (Germany) 377.5
1936	Josef Manger (Austria) 410	Vaclav Psenicka (Czechoslovakia) 402.5	Arnold Luhäär (Estonia) 400
1948	John Davis (USA) 452.5	Norbert Schemansky (USA) 425	Abraham Charite (Netherlands) 412.5
1952	John Davis (USA) 460	James Bradford (USA) 437.5	Humberto Selvetti (Argentina) 432.5
1956	Paul Anderson (USA) 500	Humberto Selvetti (Argentina) 500	Alberto Pigaiani (Italy) 452.5
1960	Yuriy Vlasov (USSR) 537.5	James Bradford (USA) 512.5	Norbert Schemansky (USA) 500
1964	Leonid Zhabotinsky (USSR) 572.5	Yuriy Vlasov (USSR) 570	Norbert Schemansky (USA) 537.5
1968	Leonid Zhabotinsky (USSR) 572.5	Serge Reding (Belgium) 555	Joseph Dube (USA) 555
1972	Yan Talts (USSR) 580.0	Alexandre Kraitchev (Bulgaria) 562.5	Stefan Gruetzner (E. Germany) 555.0

1976	Yuri Zaitsev (USSR) 385kgs	Krastio Semerdjiev (Bulgaria) 385kgs	Tadeusz Rutkowski (Poland) 377.5kgs
1980			

OVER 110 KILOS (SUPER-HEAVYWEIGHT)

1972	Vassili Alexeev (USSR) 640.0	Rudolf Mang (W. Germany) 610.0	Gerd Bonk (E. Germany) 572.5
1976	Vasili Alexeev (USSR) 440.0kgs	Gerd Bonk (E. Germany) 405.0kgs	Helmut Losch (E. Germany) 387.5kgs
1980			

WRESTLING
FREESTYLE—UNDER 48 KILOS (LIGHT FLYWEIGHT)

1904	Robert Curry (USA)	John Heim (USA)	Gustav Thiefenthaler (USA)
1976	Khassan Issaev (Bulgaria)	Roman Dnietrev (USSR)	Akira Kudo (Japan)
1980			

UNDER 52 KILOS (FLYWEIGHT)

1904	Robert Curry (USA)	John Heim (USA)	Gustav Thiefenthaler (USA)
1948	Lennart Viitala (Finland)	Halit Balamir (Turkey)	Thure Johansson (Sweden)
1952	Hasan Gemici (Turkey)	Yushu-Kitano (Japan)	Mahmoud Mollaghassemi (Iran)
1956	Mirian Tsalkalamanidze (USSR)	Mohamed Khojastehpour (Iran)	Huseyin Akbas (Turkey)
1960	Ahmed Bilek (Turkey)	Masayuki Matsubara (Japan)	Saidabadi Safepour (Iran)
1964	Yoshikatsu Yoshida (Japan)	Chang Sun Chang (Korea)	Ali Akbar Said (Iran)
1968	Shigeo Nakata (Japan)	Dick Sanders (USA)	Sukhbaatar Bazyrin (Mongolia)
1972	Kiyomi Kato (Japan)	Arsen Alakhverdiev (USSR)	Hyong Kim Gwong (North Korea)
1976	Yuji Takada (Japan)	Alexandr Ivanov (USSR)	Haez Sup Jeon (S. Korea)
1980			

UNDER 57 KILOS (BANTAMWEIGHT)

1904	George Mehnert (USA)	August Wester (USA)	Z. Strebler (USA)
1908	George Mehnert (USA)	W. J. Press (GB)	B. A. Cote (Canada)
1924	Kustaa Pihlajamaki (Finland)	Kaarlo Mäkinen (Finland)	Bryant Hines (USA)
1928	Kaarlo Mäkinen (Finland)	Edmond Spapen (Belgium)	James Trifonov (Canada)
1932	Robert Pearce (USA)	Odön Zombori (Hungary)	Aatos Jaskari (Finland)
1936	Odön Zombori (Hungary)	Ross Flood (USA)	Johannes Herbert (Germany)
1948	Nasuk Akkar (Turkey)	Gerald Leeman (USA)	Charles Kouyos (France)
1952	Shohachi Ishii (Japan)	Rashid Mamedbekov (USSR)	K. D. Jadav (India)
1956	Mustafa Dagistanli (Turkey)	Mohamed Yaghoubi (Iran)	Mihkail Chakhov (USSR)
1960	Terence McCann (USA)	Madjet Zalev (Bulgaria)	Tadeusz Trojanowski (Poland)
1964	Yojiro Uetake (Japan)	Huseyin Akbas (Turkey)	Aidyn Ibragimov (USSR)
1968	Yojiro Uetake (Japan)	Donald Behm (USA)	Gorgori Abutaleb (Iran)
1972	Hideaki Yanagida (Japan)	Richard Sanders (USA)	Laszlo Klinga (Hungary)
1975	Vladimir Umin (USSR)	Hans Bruchert (E. Germany)	Masao Arai (Japan)
1980			

UNDER 62 KILOS (FEATHERWEIGHT)

1904	B. Bradshaw (USA)	T. McLeer (USA)	B. C. Clapper (USA)
1908	George Dole (USA)	J. Slim (GB)	W. McKie (GB)
1920	Charles Ackerley (USA)	Samuel Gerson (USA)	S. Bernard (GB)
1924	Robin Reed (USA)	Chester Newton (USA)	Katsutoshi Naitoh (Japan)
1928	Allie Morrison (USA)	Kustäa Pihlajamaki (Finland)	Hans Minder (Switzerland)
1932	Kustäa Pihlajamäki (Finland)	Edgar Nemir (USA)	Einar Karlsson (Sweden)
1936	Kustäa Pihlajamäki (Finland)	Francis Millard (USA)	Gösta Jönsson (Sweden)
1948	Gazanfer Bilge (Turkey)	Iva Sjölin (Sweden)	Adölf Muller (Switzerland)
1952	Bayram Sit (Turkey)	Nasser Guivethchi (Iran)	Josiah Henson (USA)
1956	Shozo Sasahara (Japan)	Joseph Mewis (Belgium)	Erkki Penttila (Finland)
1960	Mustafa Dagistanli (Turkey)	Stojan Ivanov (Bulgaria)	Vladimir Rubashvili (USSR)

1964	Osamu Watanabe (Japan)	Stantcho Ivanov (Bulgaria)	Nodar Khokhashvili (USSR)
1968	Masaaki Kaneko (Japan)	Todorov Enio (Bulgaria)	Seyed Abassy (Iran)
1972	Zagalav Abdulbekov (USSR)	Vehbi Akdag (Turkey)	Ivan Krastev (Bulgaria)
1976	Jung-Mo Yang (S. Korea)	Zeveg Oidov (Mongolia)	Gene Davis (USA)
1980			

UNDER 68 KILOS (LIGHTWEIGHT)

1904	O. Roehm (USA)	S. R. Tesing (USA)	Albert Zukel (USA)
1908	G. de Relwyskow (GB)	W. Wood (GB)	A. Gingell (GB)
1920	Kalle Antilla (Finland)	Gottfrid Svensson (Sweden)	P. Wright (GB)
1924	Russel Vis (USA)	Volmar Wickström (Finland)	Arve Haavisto (Finland)
1928	Osvald Kapp (Estonia)	Charles Pacome (France)	Eino Leino (Finland)
1932	Charles Pacome (France)	Karoly Karpati (Hungary)	Gustaf Klaren (Sweden)
1936	Karoly Karpati (Hungary)	Wolfgang Ehrl (Finland)	Hermanni Pihlajamäki (Finland)
1948	Celal Atik (Turkey)	Gösta Frändförs (Sweden)	Hermann Baumann (Switzerland)
1952	Olle Anderberg (Sweden)	Thomas Evans (USA)	Djahanbakte Tovighe (Iran)
1956	Emamali Habibi (Iran)	Shigeru Kasahara (Japan)	Alimbert Bestayev (USSR)
1960	Shelby Wilson (USA)	Viktor Sinyavskiy (USSR)	Enio Dimow (Bulgaria)
1964	Enio Kimor (Bulgaria)	Klaus Rost (Germany)	Iwao Horiuchi (Japan)
1968	Abdullah Movahed (Iran)	Valychev Enio (Bulgaria)	Sereeter Danzandarjaa (Mongolia)
1972	Dan Gable (USA)	Kikuo Wada (Japan)	Ruslan Ashuraliev (USSR)
1976	Pavel Pinigin (USSR)	Lloyd Keaser (USA)	Yasaburo Sugawara (Japan)
1980			

UNDER 74 KILOS (WELTERWEIGHT)

1904	Charles Erickson (USA)	William Beckmann (USA)	J. Winholtz (USA)
1928	Arvo Haavisto (Finland)	Lloyd Appleton (USA)	Morris Letchford (Canada)
1932	Jack van Bebber (USA)	Daniel MacDonald (Canada)	Eino Leino (Finland)
1936	Frank Lewis (USA)	Ture Andersson (Sweden)	Joseph Schleimer (Canada)
1948	Yasar Dogu (Turkey)	Richard Garrard (Australia)	Leland Merrill (USA)
1952	William Smith (USA)	Per Berlin (Sweden)	Abdullah Modjtavabi (Iran)
1956	Mitsuo Ikeda (Japan)	Ibrahim Zengin (Turkey)	Vakhtang Balavadze (USSR)
1960	Douglas Blubaugh (USA)	Ismail Ogan (Turkey)	Muhammad Bashir (Pakistan)
1964	Ismail Ogan (Turkey)	Guliko Sagaradze (USSR)	Mohamad-Ali Sanatkaran (Iran)
1968	Mahmut Atalay (Turkey)	Daniel Robin (France)	Dagvas Purev (Mongolia)
1972	Wayne Wells (USA)	Jan Karlsson (Sweden)	Adolf Seger (W. Germany)
1976	Jiichiro Date (Japan)	Mansour Barzegar (Iran)	Stanley Dziedzic (USA)
1980			

UNDER 82 KILOS (MIDDLEWEIGHT)

1908	Stanley Bacon (GB)	G. de Relwyskow (GB)	F. Beck (GB)
1920	Eino Leino (Finland)	Väinö Penttala (Finland)	Charles Johnson (USA)
1924	Fritz Haggmann (Switzerland)	Pierre Olivier (Belgium)	Vilho Pekkala (Finland)
1928	Ernst Kyburz (Switzerland)	Donald Stockton (Canada)	S. Rabin (GB)
1932	Ivar Johansson (Sweden)	Kyosti Luukko (Finland)	Jozsef Tunyogi (Hungary)
1936	Emile Poilve (France)	Richard Voliva (USA)	Ahmet Kirecci (Turkey)
1948	Glen Brand (USA)	Adil Candemir (Turkey)	Erik Linden (Sweden)
1952	David Zimakuridze (USSR)	Gholamreza Takhti (Iran)	György Gurics (Hungary)
1956	Nikola Stanchev (Bulgaria)	Daniel Hodge (USA)	Georgiy Skhirladze (USSR)
1960	Hassan Gungor (Turkey)	Georgiy Skhirtladze (USSR)	Hans Antonsson (Sweden)
1964	Prodan Gardjev (Bulgaria)	Hassan Güngör (Turkey)	Daniel Brand (USA)
1968	Boris Gurevitch (USSR)	Munkbhat Jigjid (Mongolia)	Prodan Gardjev (Bulgaria)
1972	Levan Tediashvili (USSR)	John Peterson (USA)	Vasile Jorga (Rumania)

1976	John Peterson (USA)	Viktor Novojilov (USSR)	Adolf Seger (W. Germany)
1980			

UNDER 90 KILOS (LIGHT-HEAVYWEIGHT)

1904	B. Hansen (USA)	Frank Kungler (USA)	F. C. Warmbold (USA)
1920	Anders Larsson (Sweden)	Charles Courant (Switzerland)	Walter Maurer (USA)
1924	John Spellman (USA)	Rudolf Svensson (Sweden)	Charles Courant (Switzerland)
1928	Thure Sjöstedt (Sweden)	Anton Bögli (Switzerland)	Henri Lefevre (France)
1932	Peter Mehringer (USA)	Thure Sjöstedt (Sweden)	Eddie Scarf (Australia)
1936	Knut Fridell (Sweden)	August Neo (Estonia)	Erich Siebert (Germany)
1948	Henry Wittenberg (USA)	Fritz Stöckli (Switzerland)	Bengt Fahlkvist (Sweden)
1952	Viking Palm (Sweden)	Henry Wittenberg (USA)	Adil Atam (Turkey)
1956	Gholamreza Takhti (Iran)	Boris Koulayev (USSR)	Peter Blair (USA)
1960	Ismet Atli (Turkey)	Gholamreza Takhti (Iran)	Anatoliy Albul (USSR)
1964	Alexander Medved (USSR)	Ahmed Ayuk (Turkey)	Said Mustavow (Bulgaria)
1968	Ahmed Ayuk (Turkey)	Shota Lomidze (USSR)	Jozsef Csatari (Hungary)
1972	Ben Peterson (USA)	Gennadi Strakhov (USSR)	Karoly Bajko (Hungary)
1976	Levan Tediashvili (USSR)	Ben Peterson (USA)	Stelica Morcov (Rumania)
1980			

UNDER 100 KILOS (HEAVYWEIGHT)

1896	Karl Schumann (Germany)	Georges Tsitas (Greece)	Stephanos Christopulos (Greece)
1904	B. Hansen (USA)	Frank Kungler (USA)	F. Warmbold (USA)
1908	G. O'Kelly (GB)	Jacob Gundersen (Norway)	Edward Barrett (GB)
1920	Robert Roth (Switzerland)	Nathan Pendleton (USA)	Ernst Nilsson (Sweden) & Frederick Meyer (USA)
1924	Harry Steele (USA)	Henry Wernli (Switzerland)	A. McDonald (GB)
1928	Johan Richthoff (Sweden)	Aukusti Sihvola (Finland)	Edmond Dame (France)
1932	Johan Richthoff (Sweden)	John Riley (USA)	Nikolaus Hirschl (Austria)
1936	Kristjan Palusalu (Estonia)	Josef Klapuch (Czechoslovakia)	Hjalmar Nyström (Finland)
1948	Gyula Bobis (Hungary)	Bertil Antonsson (Sweden)	John Armstrong (Australia)
1952	Arsen Mekokishvili (USSR)	Bertil Antonsson (Sweden)	Ken Richmond (GB)
1956	Hamit Kaplan (Turkey)	Hussein Alicher (Bulgaria)	Taisto Kangasniemi (Finland)
1960	Wilfried Dietrich (Germany)	Hamit Kaplan (Turkey)	Sergey Sarasov (USSR)
1964	Alexander Ivanitsky (USSR)	Liutvi Djiber (Bulgaria)	Hamit Kaplan (Turkey)
1968	Alexandr Medved (USSR)	Osman Douraliev (Bulgaria)	Wilfried Dietrich (W. Germany)
1972	Ivan Yarygin (USSR)	Khorloo Baianmunkh (Mongolia)	Jozsef Csatari (Hungary)
1976	Ivan Yarygin (USSR)	Russell Hellickson (USA)	Dimo Kostov (Bulgaria)
1980			

OVER 100 KILOS (SUPER-HEAVYWEIGHT)

1972	Alexandr Medved (USSR)	Osman Douraliev (Bulgaria)	Chris Taylor (USA)
1976	Soslan Andiev (USSR)	Joszef Balla (Hungary)	Laidslau Simon (Rumania)
1980			

GRECO ROMAN—UNDER 48 KILOS (LIGHT-FLYWEIGHT)

1972	Gheorghe Berceanu (Rumania)	Rahim Aliabadi (Iran)	Stefan Anghelov (Bulgaria)
1976	Alexey Shumakov (USSR)	Gheorghe Berceanu (Rumania)	Stefan Anghelov (Bulgaria)
1980			

UNDER 52 KILOS (FLYWEIGHT)

1948	Pietro Lombardi (Italy)	Kenan Olcay (Turkey)	Reino Kangasmäki (Finland)
1952	Boris Gurevich (USSR)	Ignazio Fabra (Italy)	Leo Honkala (Finland)
1956	Nikolay Solovyev (USSR)	Ignazio Fabra (Italy)	Dursan Egribas (Turkey)
1960	Dumitru Pirvulescu (Rumania)	Ossman Sayed (UAR)	Mohamed Paziraye (Iran)
1964	Tsutomu Hanahara (Japan)	Angel Kerezov (Bulgaria)	Dumitru Pirvulescu (Rumania)

1968	Petar Kirov (Bulgaria)	Vladimir Bakulin (USSR)	Miroslav Seman (Czechoslovakia)
1972	Petar Kirov (Bulgaria)	Koichiro Hirayama (Japan)	Giuseppe Bognanni (Italy)
1976	Vitaly Konstantinov (USSR)	Nicu Ginga (Rumania)	Koichiro Hirayama (Japan)
1980			

UNDER 57 KILOS (BANTAMWEIGHT)

1924	Eduard Putsep (Estonia)	Änseim Ähifors (Finland)	Vaino Ikonen (Finland)
1928	Kurt Leucht (Germany)	Josef Maudr (Czechoslovakia)	Giovanni Gozzi (Italy)
1932	Jakob Brendel (Germany)	Marcello Nizzola (Italy)	Louis Francois (France)
1936	Marton Lorinc (Hungary)	Egon Svensson (Sweden)	Jakob Brendel (Germany)
1948	Kurt Pettersson (Sweden)	Mahmoud Hassan Aly (Egypt)	Hamit Kaya (Turkey)
1952	Imre Hodos (Hungary)	Zakaria Khihab (Lebanon)	Artem Teryan (USSR)
1956	Konstantin Vyrupayev (USSR)	Edvin Vesterby (Sweden)	Francisc Horvat (Rumania)
1960	Olyeg Karavayev (USSR)	Ion Cernea (Rumania)	Dinko Petrov (Bulgaria)
1964	Masamitsu Ichiguchi (Japan)	Vladlen Trostjanski (USSR)	Ion Cernea (Rumania)
1968	Janos Varga (Hungary)	Ion Baciu (Rumania)	Ivan Kochergin (USSR)
1972	Rustem Kazakov (USSR)	Hans Veil (W. Germany)	Risto Björlin (Finland)
1976	Pertti Ukkola (Finland)	Ivan Grgic (Yugoslavia)	Farhat Mustafin (USSR)
1980			

UNDER 62 KILOS (FEATHERWEIGHT)

1912	Kalle Koskelo (Finland)	Georg Gerstäcker (Germany)	Otton Lasanen (Finland)
1920	Oskari Friman (Finland)	Heikki Kähkönen (Finland)	Fridjof Svensson (Sweden)
1924	Kalle Anttila (Finland)	Aleksanteri Toivola (Finland)	Erik Malmberg (Sweden)
1928	Voldemar Vali (Estonia)	Erik Malmberg (Sweden)	Giacomo Quaglia (Italy)
1932	Giovanni Gozzi (Italy)	Wolfgang Ehrl (Germany)	Lauri Koskela (Finland)
1936	Yasar Erkan (Turkey)	Aarne Reini (Finland)	Einar Karlsson (Sweden)
1948	Mohammed Oktav (Turkey)	Olle Anderberg (Sweden)	Ferenc Toth (Hungary)
1952	Yakov Punkin (USSR)	Imre Polyak (Hungary)	Abdel Rashed (Egypt)
1956	Räuno Makinen (Finland)	Imre Polyak (Hungary)	Roman Dzneladze (USSR)
1960	Muzanir Sille (Turkey)	Imre Polyak (Hungary)	Konstantin Vyrupayev (USSR)
1964	Imre Polyak (Hungary)	Roman Rurura (USSR)	Branko Martinovic (Yugoslavia)
1968	Roman Rurura (USSR)	Ideo Fujimoto (Japan)	Simion Popescu (Rumania)
1972	Gheorghi Markov (Bulgaria)	Heinz Wehling (W. Germany)	Kazimierz Lipien (Poland)
1976	Kazimierz Lipien (Poland)	Nelson Davidian (USSR)	Laszlo Reczi (Hungary)
1980			

UNDER 68 KILOS (LIGHTWEIGHT)

1908	Enrico Porro (Italy)	Nikolav Orlov (Russia)	Arvo Linden-Linko (Finland)
1912	Eemil Ware (Finland)	Gustaf Malmstrom (Sweden)	Edvin Matiasson (Sweden)
1920	Eemil Ware (Finland)	Taavi Tamminen (Finland)	Fritjof Andersen (Norway)
1924	Oskari Friman (Finland)	Lajos Keresztes (Hungary)	Kalle Westerlund (Finland)
1928	Lajos Keresztes (Hungary)	Edvard Sperling (Germany)	Edvard Westerlund (Finland)
1932	Erik Malmberg (Sweden)	Abraham Kurland (Denmark)	Edvard Sperling (Germany)
1936	Lauri Koskela (Finland)	Josef Herda (Czechoslovakia)	Voldemar Väli (Estonia)
1948	Karl Freij (Sweden)	Aage Eriksen (Norway)	Karoly Ferencz (Hungary)
1952	Khasame Safin (USSR)	Karl Freij (Sweden)	Mikulas Athansov (Czechoslovakia)
1956	Kyösti Lehtonen (Finland)	Riza Dogan (Turkey)	Gyula Tóth (Hungary)
1960	Avtandil Koridze (USSR)	Bosidar Martinovic (Sweden)	Gustaf Freij (Yugoslavia)
1964	Kazim Ayvas (Turkey)	Valeriu Bularca (Rumania)	David Gvantseladze (USSR)
1968	Muneji Munemura (Japan)	Stevan Horvat (Yugoslavia)	Petros Galaktopoulos (Greece)
1972	Shamil Khisamutdinov (USSR)	Stoyan Apostolov (Bulgaria)	Gian Ranzi (Italy)

| 1976 | Suren Nalbandyan (USSR) | Stefan Rusu (Rumania) | Heinz Wehling (E. Germany) |
| 1980 | | | |

UNDER 74 KILOS (WELTERWEIGHT)

1932	Ivan Johansson (Sweden)	Vaino Kajander-Kajukorpi (Finland)	Ercole Gallegatti (Italy)
1936	Rudolf Svedberg (Sweden)	Fritz Schäfer (Germany)	Eina Virtanen (Finland)
1948	Gösta Andersson (Sweden)	Miklos Szilvasi (Hungary)	Carl Hansen (Denmark)
1952	Miklos Szilvasi (Hungary)	Gösta Andersson (Sweden)	Khalil Taha (Lebanon)
1956	Mithat Bayrak (Turkey)	Vladimir Manayev (USSR)	Per Berlin (Sweden)
1960	Mithat Bayrak (Turkey)	Günther Maritschnigg (Germany)	Rene Schiermeyer (France)
1964	Anatoly Koleslov (USSR)	Cyril Pethov (Bulgaria)	Bertil Nyström (Sweden)
1968	Rudolf Vesper (E. Germany)	Daniel Robin (France)	Karoly Bajiko (Hungary)
1972	Vitezslav Macha (Czechoslovakia)	Petros Galaktopoulos (Greece)	Jan Karlsson (Sweden)
1976	Anatoliy Bykov (USSR)	Viteszlav Macha (Czechoslovakia)	Karl Helbing (W. Germany)
1980			

UNDER 82 KILOS (MIDDLEWEIGHT)

1908	Fritjof Martensson (Sweden)	Mauritz Ansson (Sweden)	Anders Andersen (Denmark)
1912	Claes Johansson (Sweden)	Max Klein (Russia)	Alfred Asikainen (Finland)
1920	Carl Westergren (Sweden)	Artur Lindfors (Finland)	Mätta Perttilä (Finland)
1924	Edvard Westerlund (Finland)	Artur Lindfors (Finland)	Roman Steinberg (Estonia)
1928	Väinö Kokkinen (Finland)	Laszlo Papp (Hungary)	Albert Kusnetz (Estonia)
1932	Väinö Kokkinen (Finland)	Johann Foldeak (Germany)	Axel Cadier (Sweden)
1936	Ivar Johansson (Sweden)	Ludwig Schweikert (Germany)	Joszef Paiotas (Hungary)
1948	Axel Grönberg (Sweden)	Muhlin Tayfur (Turkey)	Ercole Gallegatti (Italy)
1952	Axel Grönberg (Sweden)	Kalervo Rauhala (Finland)	Nikolay Belov (USSR)
1956	Guivi Kartozia (USSR)	Dimitar Dobrev (Bulgaria)	Karl Jansson (Sweden)
1960	Dimitar Dobrev (Bulgaria)	Lothar Metz (E. Germany)	Ion Taranu (Rumania)
1964	Branislav Simic (Yugoslavia)	Jiri Kormanik (Czechoslovakia)	Lothar Metz (Germany)
1968	Lothat Metz (E. Germany)	Valentin Olenik (USSR)	Branislav Simic (Yugoslavia)
1972	Csaba Hegedus (Hungary)	Anatoli Nazarenko (USSR)	Milan Nenadic (Jugoslavia)
1976	Momir Petkovic (Yugoslavia)	Vladimir Cheboksarov (USSR)	Ivan Kolev (Bulgaria)
1980			

UNDER 90 KILOS (LIGHT HEAVYWEIGHT)

1908	Werener Weckman (Finland)	Yrjö Saarela (Finland)	Karl Jensen (Denmark)
1912	Anders Ahlgren (Sweden)	Ivar Bohling (Finland)	Bela Vargya (Hungary)
1920	Claes Johansson (Sweden)	Edil Rosenqvist (Finland)	Johnsen Eriksen (Denmark)
1924	Carl Westergren (Sweden)	Rudolf Svensson (Sweden)	Onni Pellinen (Finland)
1928	Ibrahim Moustafa (Egypt)	Adolf Rieger (Germany)	Onni Pellinen (Finland)
1932	Rydolf Svensson (Sweden)	Onni Pellinen (Finland)	Mario Gruppioni (Italy)
1936	Axel Cadier (Sweden)	Edwins Bietags (Lithuania)	August Neo (Estonia)
1948	Karl Nilsson (Sweden)	Kaelpo Gröndahl (Finland)	Ibrahim Orabi (Egypt)
1952	Kaelpo Gröndahl (Finland)	Shalva Shikladze (USSR)	Karl Nilsson (Sweden)
1956	Valentin Nikolayev (USSR)	Petko Sirakov (Bulgaria)	Karl Nilsson (Sweden)
1960	Teviic Kis (Turkey)	Kraliu Bimbalov (Bulgaria)	Guivi Kartozia (USSR)
1964	Boyan Radev (Bulgaria)	Pev Svensson (Sweden)	Heinz Kiehl (Germany)
1968	Boyan Radev (Bulgaria)	Nikolai Yakovenko (USSR)	Nicolae Martinescu (Rumania)
1972	Valeri Rezantsev (USSR)	Josip Corak (Yugoslavia)	Czeslaw Kwiecinski (Poland)
1976	Valeri Rezantsev (USSR)	Stoyan Ivanon (Bulgaria)	Czeslaw Kwiecinski (Poland)
1980			

UNDER 100 KILOS (HEAVYWEIGHT)

1908	Richard Weisz (Hungary)	Aleksandr Petrov (Russia)	Sören Jensen (Denmark)
1912	Yrjö Saarela (Finland)	Johan Olin (Finland)	Sören Jensen (Denmark)
1920	Adolf Lindfors (Finland)	Paul Hansen (Denmark)	Marti Nieminen (Finland)
1924	Henry Deglane (France)	Edil Rosenqvist (Finland)	Raymund Bado (Hungary)
1928	Rudolf Svensson (Sweden)	Hjalmar Vyström (Finland)	Georg Gehring (Germany)
1932	Carl Westergren (Sweden)	Josef Urban (Czechoslovakia)	Nikolaus Hirschl (Austria)
1936	Kristjan Palusalu (Estonia)	John Nyman (Sweden)	Kurt Hornfischer (Germany)
1948	Ahmed Kirecci (Turkey)	Tor Nilsson (Sweden)	Guido Fantoni (Italy)
1952	Johannes Kotkas (USSR)	Josef Ruzicka (Czechoslovakia)	Tauro Kovanen (Finland)
1956	Anatoliy Pafenyov (USSR)	Wilfried Dietrich (Germany)	Adelmo Bulgarelli (Italy)
1960	Ivan Bogdan (USSR)	Wilfried Dietrich (Germany)	Bohumil Kubat (Czechoslovakia)
1964	Istvan Kozma (Hungary)	Anatoly Roskin (USSR)	Wilfried Dietrich (Germany)
1968	Istvan Kozma (Hungary)	Anatoly Roskin (USSR)	Petr Kment (Czechoslovakia)
1972	Nicolae Martinescu (Rumania)	Nikolai Iakovenko (USSR)	Ferenc Kiss (Hungary)
1976	Nikolai Bolboshin (USSR)	Kamen Goranov (Bulgaria)	Andrzej Skrylewski (Poland)
1980			

OVER 100 KILOS (SUPER HEAVYWEIGHT)

1972	Anatoly Rushin (USSR)	Alexandre Tomov (Bulgaria)	Victor Dolipschi (Rumania)
1976	Alexandr Kolchinski (USSR)	Alexandr Tomov (Bulgaria))	Roman Codreanu (Rumania)
1980			

YACHTING

STAR

1932	USA 46pts	GB 35	Sweden 25
1936	Germany 80pts	Sweden 64	Netherlands 63
1948	USA 5,828pts	Cuba 4,849	Netherlands 4,731
1952	Italy 7,635pts	USA 7,216	Portugal 4,903
1956	USA 5,876pts	Italy 5,649	Bahamas 5,223
1960	USSR 7,619pts	Portugal 6,665	USA 6,269
1964	Bahamas 5,664pts	USA 5,585	Sweden 5,527
1968	USA 14.4pts	Norway 43.7	Italy 44.7
1972	Australia 28.1pts	Sweden 44.0	W. Germany 44.4
1976	Not held		
1980			

FLYING DUTCHMAN

1960	Norway 6,774pts	Denmark 5,991	Germany 5,882
1964	New Zealand 6,255pts	GB 5,556	USA 5,158
1968	GB 3.0pts	W.Germany 43.7	Brazil 48.4
1972	GB 22.7pts	France 40.7	W. Germany 51.1
1976	W. Germany 34.70pts	GB 51.70	Brazil 52.10
1980			

FINN

1956	Paul Elvström (Denmark) 7,509pts	Andre Nelis (Belgium) 6,254	John Marvin (USA) 5,953
1960	Paul Elvström (Denmark) 8,171pts	Aleksandr Tyukelov (USSR) 6,250	Andre Nelis (Belgium) 5,934
1964	Willi Kuhweide (Germany) 7,638pts	Peter Barrett (USA) 6,373pts	Henning Wind (Denmark) 6,190
1968	Valentin Mankin (USSR) 11.7pts	Hubert Raudasche (Austria) 53.4	Fabio Albarelli (Italy) 55.1
1972	Serge Maury (France) 58.0pts	Ilias Hatzipavlis (Greece) 71.0	Victor Potapov (USSR) 74.7
1976	E. Germany 35.40pts	USSR 39.70	Australia 46.40
1980			

TEMPEST

1972	USSR 28.1pts	GB 34.4	USA 47.7
1976	Sweden 14pts	USSR 30.40	USA 32.70

SOLING

1972	USA 8.7pts	Sweden 31.7	Canada 47.1
1976	Denmark 46.70pts	USA 47.40	E. Germany 47.40
1980			

470

1976	W. Germany 42.40pts	Spain 49.70	Australia 57.00
1980			

TORNADOS

1976	GB 18pts	USA 36.00	W. Germany 37.70
1980			

VOLLEYBALL (MEN)

1964	USSR 17pts	Czechoslovakia 17	Japan 16
1968	USSR 17pts	Japan 16	Czechoslovakia 16
1972	Japan	East Germany	USSR
1976	Poland	USSR	Cuba
1980			

VOLLEYBALL (WOMEN)

1964	Japan 10pts	USSR 9	Poland 8
1968	USSR 14pts	Japan 13	Poland 12
1972	USSR	Japan	North Korea
1976	Japan	USSR	S. Korea
1980			

WINTER OLYMPIC GAMES

500 METRES SPEED SKATING

1924	Charles Jewtraw (USA) 44s	Oskar Olsen (Norway) 44.2s	Roald Larsen (Norway) & Clas Thunberg (Finland) 44.8s
1928	Clas Thunberg (Finland) & Bernt Evensen (Norway) 43.4s		John Farrell (USA), Roald Larsen (Norway), Jaakko Friman (Finland) 43.6s
1932	John Shea (USA) 43.4s	Bernt Evensen (Norway)	Alexander Hurd (Canada)
1936	Ivar Ballangrud (Norway) 43.4s	Georg Krog (Norway) 43.5s	Leo Freisinger (USA) 44s
1948	Finn Helgesen (Norway) 43.1s	Ken Bartholomew (USA), Thomas Byberg (Norway), Robert Fitzgerald (USA) 43.2s	
1952	Kenneth Henry (USA) 43.2s	Don McDermott (USA) 43.9s	Arne Johansen (Nor) Gorden Audley (Can) 44s
1956	Eugeniy Grischin (USSR) 40.2s	Rafael Gratsch (USSR) 40.8s	Alv Gjestvang (Norway) 41s
1960	Eugeniy Grischin (USSR) 40.2s	William Disney (USA) 40.3s	Rafael Gratsch (USSR) 40.4s
1964	Dick McDermott (USA) 40.1s	Eugeniy Grischin (USSR), Alv Gjestvang (Norway), & Vladimir Orlov (Poland) 40.6s	
1968	Erhard Keller (W.Germany) 40.3s	Magne Thomassen (Norway) 40.5s	Dick McDermott (USA) 40.5s
1972	Erhard Keller (W. Germany) 39.44s	Hasse Borjes (Sweden) 39.69s	Valery Muratov (USSR) 39.80s
1976	Eugeny Kulikov (USSR) 39.17s	Valery Muratov (USSR) 39.25s	Dan Immerfall (USA) 39.54s
1980			

1500 METRES SPEED SKATING

1924	Clas Thunberg (Finland) 2m 20.8s	Roald Larsen (Norway) 2m 22s	Sigurd Moen (Norway) 2m 25.6s
1928	Clas Thunberg (Finland) 2m 21.1s	Bernt Evensen (Norway) 2m 21.9s	Ivar Ballangrud (Norway) 2m 22.6s
1932	John Shea (USA) 2m 57.5s	Alexander Hurd (Canada)	William Logan (Canada)
1936	Charles Mathiesen (Norway) 2m 19.2s	Ivar Ballangrud (Norway) 2m 20.2s	Birger Vasenius (Finland) 2m 20.9s
1948	Sverre Farstad (Norway) 2m 17.6s	Ake Seyffarth (Sweden) 2m 18.1s	Odd Lundberg (Norway) 2m 18.9s
1952	Hjalmar Andersen (Norway) 2m 20.4s	Willem van der Voort (Netherlands) 2m 10.6s	Roald Aas (Norway) 2m 21.6s
1956	Eugeniy Grischin & Yuri Michailov (USSR) 2m 8.6s		Toivo Salonen (Finland) 2m 9.4s
1960	Roald Aas (Norway) & Eugeniy Grischin (USSR) 2m 10.4s		Boris Stenin (USSR) 2m 11.5s
1964	Ants Antson (USSR) 2m 10.3s	Cornelis Verkerk (Netherlands) 2m 10.6s	Villy Haugen (Norway) 2m 11.2s
1968	Cornelis Verkerk (Netherlands) 2m 3.4s	Ard Schenk (Netherlands) & Ivar Eriksen (Norway) 2m 5s	
1972	Ard Schenk (Netherlands) 2m 2.96s	Roar Grönvald (Norway) 2m 4.26s	Goran Claesson (Sweden) 2m 5.89s
1976	Jan Egil Storholt (Norway) 1m 59.38s	Yuri Kondakov (USSR) 1m 59.97s	Hans van Helden (Netherlands) 2m 00.87s
1980			

5000 METRES SPEED SKATING

1924	Clas Thunberg (Finland) 8m 39s	Julius Skutnabb (Finland) 8m 48.4s	Roald Larsen (Norway) 8m 50.2s
1928	Ivar Ballangrud (Norway) 8m 50.5s	Julius Skutnabb (Finland) 8m 59.1s	Bernt Evensen (Norway) 9m 1.1s
1932	Irving Jaffee (USA) 9m 40.8s	Edward Murphy (USA)	William Logan (Canada)
1936	Ivar Ballangrud (Norway) 8m 19.6s	Birger Vasenius (Finland) 8m 23.3s	Antero Ojala (Finland) 8m 30.1s
1948	Reidar Liaklev (Norway) 8m 29.4s	Odd Lundberg (Norway 8m 32.7s	Göthe Hedlund (Sweden) 8m 34.8s
1952	Hjalmar Andersen (Norway) 8m 10.6s	Cornelis Broekman (Netherlands) 8m 21.6s	Sverre Haugli (Norway) 8m 22.4s
1956	Boris Schilkov (USSR) 7m 48.7s	Sigvard Ericsson (Sweden) 7m 56.7s	Oleg Gontscharenko (USSR) 7m 57.5s
1960	Viktor Kositschkin (USSR) 7m 51.3s	Knut Johannesen (Norway) 8m 0.8s	Jan Pesman (Netherlands) 8m 5.1s
1964	Knut Johannesen (Norway) 7m 38.4s	Per-Ivar Moe (Norway) 7m 38.6s	Fred Maier (Norway) 7m 42s

1968	Fred Maier (Norway) 7m 22.4s	Cornelis Verkerk (Netherlands) 7m 23.2s	Petrus Nottet (Netherlands) 7m 25.5s
1972	Ard Schenk (Netherlands) 7m 23.61s	Roar Grönvold (Norway) 7m 28.18s	Sten Stensen (Norway) 7m 33.39s
1976	Sten Stensen (Norway) 7m 24.48s	Piet Kleine (Netherlands) 7m 26.47s	Hans van Helden (Netherlands) 7m 26.54s
1980			

10000 METRES SPEED SKATING

1924	Julius Skutnabb (Finland) 18m 4.8s	Clas Thunberg (Finland) 18m 7.8s	Roald Larsen (Norway) 18m 12.2s
1932	Irving Jaffee (USA) 19m 13.6s	Ivar Ballangrud (Norway)	Frank Stack (Canada)
1936	Ivar Ballangrud (Norway) 17m 24.3s	Birger Vasenius (Finland) 17m 28.2s	Max Stiepl (Austria) 17m 30s
1948	Ake Seyffarth (Sweden) 17m 26.3s	Lauri Parkkinen (Finland) 17m 36s	Pentti Lammio (Finland) 17m 42.7s
1952	Hjalmar Andersen (Norway) 16m 45.8s	Cornelis Broekman (Netherlands) 17m 10.6s	Carl-Erik Asplund (Sweden) 17m 16.6s
1956	Sigvard Ericsson (Sweden) 16m 35.9s	Knut Johannesen (Norway) 16m 36.9s	Oleg Gontscharenko (USSR) 16m 42.3s
1960	Knut Johannesen (Norway) 15m 46.6s	Viktor Kositschkin (USSR) 15m 49.2s	Kjell Bäckman (Sweden) 16m 14.2s
1964	Johnny Nilsson (Sweden) 15m 50.1s	Fred Maier (Norway) 16m 6s	Knut Johannesen (Norway) 16m 6.3s
1968	Johnny Höeglin (Sweden) 15m 23.6s	Fred Maier (Norway) 15m 23.9s	Orjan Sandler (Sweden) 15m 31.8s
1972	Ard Schenk (Netherlands) 15m 1.35s	Kees Verkerk (Netherlands) 15m 4.70s	Sten Stensen (Norway) 15m 7.08s
1976	Piet Kleine (Netherlands) 14m 50.59s	Sten Stensen (Norway) 14m 53.30s	Hans van Helden (Netherlands) 15m 02.02s
1980			

WOMEN'S 500 METRES SPEED SKATING

1960	Helga Haase (Germany) 45.9s	Natalia Dontschenko (USSR) 46s	Jeanne Ashworth (USA) 46.1s
1964	Lydia Skoblikova (USSR) 45s	Irina Jegorova (USSR) 45.4s	Tatyana Sidorova (USSR) 45.5s
1968	Ludmilla Titova (USSR) 46.1s	Mary Meyers (USA) 46.3s	Diane Holum (USA) 46.3s
1972	Anne Henning (USA) 43.44s	Vera Krasnova (USSR) 44.01s	Ljudmila Titova (USSR) 44.45s
1976	Sheila Young (USA) 42.76s	Catherine Priestner (Canada) 43.12s	Tatiana Averina (USSR) 43.17s
1980			

1000 METRES SPEED SKATING

1960	Klara Guseva (USSR) 1m 34.1s	Helga Haase (Germany) 1m 34.3s	Tamara Rylova (USSR) 1m 34.8s
1964	Lydia Skoblikova (USSR) 1m 33.2s	Irina Yegorova (USSR) 1m 34.3s	Kaija Mustonen (Finland) 1m 34.8s
1968	Carolina Geijssen (Netherlands) 1m 32.6s	Ludmilla Titova (USSR) 1m 32.9s	Diane Holum (USA) 1m 33.4s
1972	Monika Pflug (W. Germany) 1m 31.4s	Atje Keulen-Deetstra (Netherlands) 1m 31.6s	Anne Henning (USA) 1m 31.6s
1976	Tatiana Averina (USSR) 1m 28.43s	Leah Poulos (USA) 1m 28.57	Sheila Young (USA) 1m 29.14s
1980			

1500 METRES SPEED SKATING

1960	Lydia Skoblikova (USSR) 2m 25.2s	Elvira Seroczynska (Poland) 2m 25.7s	Helena Pilejczyk (Poland) 2m 27.1s
1964	Lydia Skoblikova (USSR) 2, 22.6s	Kaija Mustonen (Finland) 2m 25.5s	Berta Kolokoltzeva (USSR) 2m 27.1s
1968	Kaija Mustonen (Finland) 2m 22.4s	Carolina Geijssen (Netherlands) 2m 22.7s	Christina Kaiser (Netherlands) 2m 24.5s
1972	Dianne Holum (USA) 2m 20.85s	Stien Baas-Kaiker (Netherlands) 2m 21.05s	Atje Keulen-Deelstra (Netherlands) 2m 22.05s
1976	Galina Stepanskaya (USSR) 2m 16.58s	Sheila Young (USA) 2m 17.06s	Tatiana Averina (USSR) 2m 17.96s
1980			

3000 METRES SPEEDSKATING

1960	Lydia Skoblikova (USSR) 5m 14.3s	Valentina Stenina (USSR) 5m 16.9s	Eevi Huttunen (Finland) 5m 21s
1964	Lydia Skoblikova (USSR) 5m 14.9s	Valentina Stenina (USSR) & Pil Hwa Han (N.Korea) 5m 18.5s	
1968	Johanna Schut (Netherlands) 4m 56.2s	Kaija Mustonen (Finland) 5m 1s	Christina Kaiser (Netherlands) 5m 1.3s
1972	Stien Baas-Kaiser (Netherlands) 4m 52.14s	Diane Holum (USA) 4m 58.67s	Atje Keulen-Deelstra (Netherlands) 4m 59.91s
1976	Tatiana Averina (USSR) 4m 45.19s	Andrea Mitscherlich (E. Germany) 4m 45.23s	Lisbeth Korsmo (Norway) 4m 45.24s
1980			

ICE HOCKEY

1920	Canada	USA	Czechoslovakia
1924	Canada	USA	GB
1928	Canada	Sweden	Switzerland
1932	Canada	USA	Germany
1936	GB	Canada	USA
1948	Canada	Czechoslovakia	Switzerland
1952	Canada	USA	Sweden
1956	USSR	USA	Canada
1960	USA	Canada	USSR
1964	USSR	Sweden	Czechoslovakia
1968	USSR	Czechoslovakia	Canada
1972	USSR	USA	Czechoslovakia
1976	USSR	Czechoslovakia	W. Germany
1980			

FIGURE SKATING (MEN)

1908	Ulrich Salchow (Sweden) 1,886.5	Richard Johansson (Sweden) 1,826	Per Thoren (Sweden) 1,787
1920	Gillis Grafström (Sweden) 2,575.25	Andreas Krogh (Norway) 2,634	Martin Stuxrud (Norway) 2,561
1924	Gillis Grafström (Sweden) 2,575.25	Willy Böckl (Austria) 2,518.75	Geo Gautschi (Switzerland) 2,223.5
1928	Gillis Grafström (Sweden) 2,698.25	Willy Böckl (Austria) 2,682.50	Robert van Zeebröck (Belgium) 2,578.75
1932	Karl Schäfer (Austria) 2,602	Gillis Grafström (Sweden) 2,514.5	Montgomery Wilson (Canada) 2,448.3
1936	Karl Schäfer (Austria) 2,959	Ernst Baier (Germany) 2,805.3	Felix Kaspar (Austria) 2,801
1948	Dick Button (USA) 1,720.6	Hans Gerschwiler (Switzerland) 1,630.1	Edi Rada (Austria) 1,603.2
1952	Dick Button (USA) 1,730.3	Helmut Seibt (Austria) 1,621.3	Jim Grogan (USA) 1,627.4
1956	Hayes Jenkins (USA) 1,497.75	Ronald Robertson (USA) 1,492.15	David Jenkins (USA) 1,465.41
1960	David Jenkins (USA) 1,440.2	Karol Divin (Czechoslovakia) 1,414.3	Donald Jackson (Canada) 1,401
1964	Manfred Schnelldorfer (Germany) 1,916.9	Alain Calmat (France) 1,876.5	Scott Allen (USA) 1,873.6
1968	Wolfgang Schwartz (Austria) 1,904.1	Tim Wood (USA) 1,891.6	Patrick Pera (France) 1,864.5
1972	Ondrej Nepela (Czech) 2,739.1	Sergei Chetverukhin (USSR) 2,672.4	Patrick Pera (France) 2,653.1
1976	John Curry (GB) 192.74	Vladimir Kovalev (USSR) 187.64	Toller Cranston (Canada) 187.38
1980			

FIGURE SKATING (WOMEN)

1908	Madge Syers (GB) 1,262.5pts	Elsa Rendschmidt (Germany) 1,055.0	D. Greenough-Smith (GB) 960.5
1920	Magda Julin (Sweden) 887.75	Svea Noren (Sweden) 887.75	Theresa Weld (USA) 890.0
1924	Herma Planck-Szabo (Austria) 2,094.25	Beatrix Loughran (USA) 1,959.0	Ethel Muckelt (GB) 1,750.50
1928	Sonja Henie (Norway) 2,452.25	Fritzi Burger (Austria) 2,248.50	Beatrix Loughran (USA) 2,254.50
1932	Sonja Henie (Norway) 2,302.5	Fritzi Burger (Austria) 2,167.1	Maribel Vinson (USA) 2,158.5
1936	Sonja Henie (Norway) 2,971.4	Cecilia Colledge (GB) 2,926.8	Vivi-Anne Hulten (Sweden) 2,763.2
1948	Barbara Scott (Canada) 1,467.7	Eva Pawlik (Austria) 1,418.3	Jeanette Altwegg (GB) 1,405.5
1952	Jeanette Altwegg (GB) 1,455.8	Tenley Albright (USA) 1,432.2	Jacqueline du Bief (France) 1,422.0
1956	Tenley Albright (USA) 1,866.39	Carol Heiss (USA) 1,848.24	Ingrid Wendl (Austria) 1,753.91
1960	Carol Heiss (USA) 1,490.1	Sjoukje Dijkstra (Netherlands) 1,424.8	Barbara Roles (USA) 1,414.9
1964	Sjoukje Dijkstra (Netherlands) 2,018.5	Regine Heitzer (Austria) 1,945.5	Petra Burka (Canada) 1,940.0
1968	Peggy Fleming (USA) 1,970.5	Gabriele Seyfert (E.Germany) 1,882.3	Hana Maskova (Czech) 1,828.8
1972	Trixi Schuba (Austria) 2,751.5	Karen Magnussen (Canada) 2,673.2	Janet Lynn Holmes (USA) 2,663.1
1976	Dorothy Hamill (USA) 193.80pts	Dianne de Leeuw (Netherlands) 190.24	Christine Errath (E. Germany) 188.16
1980			

PAIRS

1908	Germany 56.0pts	GB 51.5	GB 48.0
1920	Finland 80.75pts	Norway 72.75	GB 66.25
1924	Austria 74.50pts	Finland 71.75	France 69.25
1928	France 100.50pts	Austria 99.25	Austria 93.25
1932	France 78.7pts	USA 77.5	Hungary 76.4
1936	Germany 103.3pts	Austria 102.7	Hungary 97.6
1948	Belgium 123.5pts	Hungary 122.2	Canada 121.0
1952	Germany 102.6pts	USA 100.6	Hungary 97.4
1956	Austria 101.8pts	Canada 101.7	Hungary 99.3
1960	Canada 80.4pts	Germany 76.8	USA 76.2
1964	USSR 104.4pts		Canada 98.5
1968	USSR 315.2pts	USSR 312.3	W.Germany 304.4
1972	USSR 420.4pts	USSR 419.4	E. Germany 411.8
1976	USSR 140.54pts	E. Germany 136.35	E. Germany 134.57
1980			

ICE DANCING

1976 Ljudmila Pakhomova Alexandr Gorshkov (USSR) 209.92pts	Irina Moiseeva Andrei Minenkov (USSR) 204.88	Colleen O'Connor Jim Millns (USA) 202.64
1980		

15 KMS–CROSS-COUNTRY

1960 Haakon Bursveen (Norway) 51m 55.5s	Sixten Jernberg (Sweden) 51m 58.6s	Veikko Hakulinen (Finland) 52m 03.0s
1964 Eero Mäntyranta (Finland) 50m 54.1s	Harald Grönningen (Norway) 51m 34.8s	Sixten Jernberg (Sweden) 51m 42.2s
1968 Harald Grönningen (Norway) 47m 54.2s	Eero Mäntyranta (Finland) 47m 56.1s	Gunnar Larsson (Sweden) 48m 33.7s
1972 Sven Ake Lundback (Sweden) 45m 28.24s	Fedor Simaschov (USSR) 46m 00.84s	Ivar Formo (Norway) 46m 2.68s
1976 Nicolai Bajukov (USSR) 43m 58.47s	Evgeniy Beliaev (USSR) 44m 01.10	Arto Koivisto (Finland) 44m 19.25s
1980		

30 KMS–CROSS-COUNTRY

1956 Veikko Hakulinen (Finland) 1h 44m 06.0s	Sixten Jernberg (Sweden) 1h 44m 30.0s	Pavel Koltschin (USSR) 1h 45m 45.0s
1960 Sixten Jernberg (Sweden) 1h 51m 03.9s	Rolf Rämgard (Sweden) 1h 51m 16.9s	Nikolay Anikin (USSR) 1h 52m 28.2s
1964 Eero Mäntyranta (Finland) 1h 30m 50.7s	Harald Gronningen (Norway) 1h 32m 02.3s	Isor Voronchikin (USSR) 1h 32m 15.8s
1968 Franco Nones (Italy) 1h 35m 39.2s	Odd Martinsen (Norway) 1h 36m 28.9s	Eero Mäntyranta (Finland) 1h 36m 55.3s
1972 Vyacheslav Vedenin (USSR) 1h 36m 31.15s	Paul Tyldum (Norway) 1h 37m 25.30s	Johs Harviken (Norway) 1h 37m 32.24s
1976 Sergei Saveliev (USSR) 1h 30m 29.38s	Bill Koch (USA) 1h 30m 57.84s	Ivan Garanin (USSR) 1h 31m 09.29s
1980		

50 KMS–CROSS-COUNTRY

1924 Thorleif Haug (Norway) 3h 44m 32.0s	Thoralf Stromstad (Norway) 3h 46m 23.0s	Johan Gröttumsbraaten (Norway) 3h 47m 46.0s
1928 Per Erik Hedlund (Sweden) 4h 52m 03.3s	Gustaf Jonsson (Sweden) 5h 05m 30.0s	Volger Andersson (Sweden) 5h 05m 46.0s
1932 Veli Saarinen (Finland) 4h 28m 00.0s	Väinö Likkanen (Finland) 4h 28m 20.0s	Arne Rustadstuen (Norway) 4h 31m 53s
1936 Elis Wiklund (Sweden) 3h 30m 11.0s	Axel Wikström (Sweden) 3h 33m 20.0s	Nils-Joel Englund (Sweden) 3h 34m 10.0s
1948 Nils Karlsson (Sweden) 3h 47m 48.0s	Harald Eriksson (Sweden) 3h 52m 20.0s	Benjamin Vanninen (Finland) 3h 57m 28.0s
1952 Veikko Hakulinen (Finland) 3h 33m 33.0s	Eero Kolehmainen (Finland) 3h 38m 11.0s	Majnar Estenstad (Norway) 3h 38m 28.0s
1956 Sixten Jernberg (Sweden) 2h 50m 27.0s	Veikko Hakulinen (Finland) 2h 51m 45.0s	Fyedor Terentyev (USSR) 2h 53m 32.0s
1960 Kalevi Hämäläinen (Finland) 2h 59m 06.3s	Veikko Hakulinen (Finland) 2h 59m 26.7s	Rolf Ramgard (Sweden) 3h 02m 46.7s
1964 Sixten Jernberg (Sweden) 2h 43m 52.6s	Assar Ronnlund (Sweden) 2h 44m 58.2s	Arto Tiainen (Finland) 2h 45m 30.4s
1968 Ole Ellefsater (Norway) 2h 28m 45.8s	Viatches Bedenin (USSR) 2h 29m 02.5s	Josef Haas (Switz) 2h 29m 14.8s
1972 Paul Tyldum (Norway) 2h 43m 14.75s	Magne Myrmo (Norway) 2h 43m 29.45s	Vyacheslav Vedenin (USSR) 2h 44m 0.19s
1976 Ivar Formo (Norway) (2h 37m 30.05s	Gert-Dietmar Klause (E. Germany) 2h 38m 13.21s	Benny Södergren (Sweden) 2h 39m 39.21s
1980		

RELAY RACE 4×10 KMS

1936 Finland 2h 41m 33.0s	Norway 2h 41m 39.0s	Sweden 2h 43m 03.0s
1948 Sweden 2h 32m 08.0s	Finland 2h 41m 06.0s	Norway 2h 44m 33.0s
1952 Finland 2h 20m 16.0s	Norway 2h 23m 13.0s	Sweden 2h 24m 13.0s
1956 USSR 2h 15m 30.0s	Finland 2h 16m 31.0s	Sweden 2h 17m 42.0s
1960 Finland 2h 18m 45.6s	Norway 2h 18m 46.4s	USSR 2h 21m 21.6s
1964 Sweden 2h 18m 34.6s	Finland 2h 18m 42.4s	USSR 2h 18m 46.4s
1968 Norway 2h 8m 33.5s	Sweden 2h 10m 13.2s	Finland 2h 10m 56.7s
1972 USSR 2h 4m 47.94s	Norway 2h 4m 57.06s	Switzerland 2h 7m 0.06s
1976 Finland 2h 7m 59.72s	Norway 2h 9m 58.36s	USSR 2h 10m 51.46s
1980		

5 KMS–CROSS-COUNTRY (WOMEN)

1964 Klaudia Boyerskikh (USSR) 17m 50.5s	Mirja Lehtonen (Finland) 17m 52.9s	Alevtina Koltchina (USSR) 18m 08.4s
1968 Toini Gustafsson (Sweden) 16m 45.2s	Galina Koulakova (USSR) 16m 48.4s	Alevtina Koltchina (USSR) 16m 51.6s
1972 Galina Koulakova (USSR) 17m 0.50s	Marjatta Kajosmaa (Finland) 17m 5.50s	Helena Sikolova (Czech) 17m 7.32s
1976 Helena Takalo (Finland) 15m 48.69	Raisa Smetanina (USSR) 15m 49.73s	Galina Koulakora (USSR) 16m 07.36s
1980		

10 KMS–CROSS-COUNTRY (WOMEN)

1952 Lydia Wideman (Finland) 41m 40.0s	Mirja Heitamies (Finland) 42m 39.0s	Siiri Rantanen (Finland) 42m 50.0s
1956 Lyubov Kosyryeva (USSR) 38m 11.0s	Radya Yeroschina (USSR) 38m 16.0s	Sonja Edstrom (Sweden) 38m 32.0s
1960 Maria Gusakova (USSR) 39m 46.6s	Lyubov Baranova (USSR) 40m 04.2s	Radya Yeroschina (USSR) 40m 06.0s
1964 Klaudia Boyarskikh (USSR) 40m 24.3s	Judokija Mekshilo (USSR) 40m 26.6s	Maria Gusakova (USSR) 40m 46.6s
1968 Toini Gustafsson (Sweden) 36m 46.5s	Berit Mördre (Sweden) 37m 54.6s	Inger Aufles (Norway) 37m 59.9s
1972 Galina Koulakova (USSR) 34m 17.82s	Alevtina Olunina (USSR) 34m 54.11s	Marjatta Kajosmaa (Finland) 34m 56.45s
1976 Raisa Smetanina (USSR) 30m 13.41s	Helena Takalo (Finland) 30m 14.28s	Galina Koulakova (USSR) 30m 38.61s
1980		

3×5 KMS–RELAY

1956 Finland 1h 9m 01.0s	USSR 1h 9m 28.0s	Sweden 1h 9m 48.0s
1960 Sweden 1h 4m 21.4s	USSR 1h 5m 2.6s	Finland 1h 6m 27.5s
1964 USSR 59m 20.2s	Sweden 1h 1m 27.0s	Finland 1h 2m 45.1s
1968 Norway 57m 30.0s	Sweden 57m 51.0s	USSR 58m 13.6s
1972 USSR 48m 46.15s	Finland 49m 19.37s	Norway 49m 51.49s

RELAY RACE 4×5 KMS

1976 USSR 1h 7m 49.75s	Finland 1h 8m 36.57s	E. Ger 1h 9m 57.95s
1980		

ALPINE SKI-ING (MEN)
GIANT SLALOM

1952 Stein Eriksen (Norway) 2m 25.0s	Christian Pravda (Austria) 2m 26.9s	Toni Spiess (Austria) 2m 28.8s
1956 Anton Sailer (Austria) 3m 00.1s	Andreas Molterer (Austria) 3m 0.63s	Walter Schuster (Austria) 3m 07.2s
1960 Roger Staub (Switzerland) 1m 48.3s	Josef Stiegler (Austria) 1m 48.7s	Ernst Hinterseer (Austria) 1m 49.1s
1964 Francois Bonlieu (France) 1m 46.71s	Karl Schranz (Austria) 1m 47.09s	Josef Stiegler (Austria) 1m 48.05s
1968 Jean-Claude Killy (France) 3m 29.28s	Willy Favre (Switzerland) 3m 31.50s	Heinrich Messner (Austria) 3m 31.83s
1972 Gustavo Thoeni (Italy) 3m 9.62s	Edmund Bruggman (Switzerland) 3m 10.75s	Werner Mattle (Switzerland) 3m 10.90s
1976 Heini Hemmi (Switzerland) 3m 26.97s	Ernst Good (Switzerland) 3m 27.17s	Ingemar Stenmark (Sweden) 3m 27.41s
1980		

SLALOM

1948 Edi Reinalter (Switzerland) 2m 10.3s	James Couttet (France) 2m 10.8s	Henri Oreiller (France) 2m 12.8s
1952 Othmar Schneider (Austria) 2m 00.0s	Stein Eriksen (Norway) 2m 01.2s	Guttorm Berge (Norway) 2m 01.7s
1956 Anton Sailer (Austria) 3m 14.7s	Schiharu Igaya (Japan) 3m 18.7s	Stig Sollander (Sweden) 3m 20.2s
1960 Ernst Hinterseer (Austria) 2m 08.9s	Matthias Leitner (Austria) 2m 10.3s	Charles Bozon (France) 2m 10.4s
1964 Josef Stiegler (Austria) 2m 11.13s	William Kidd (USA) 2m 11.27s	James Heuga (USA) 2m 11.52s
1968 Jean-Claude Killy (France) 1m 39.73s	Herbert Huber (Austria) 1m 39.82s	Alfred Matt (Austria) 1m 40.09s
1972 Francisco Ochoa (Spain) 1m 49.27s	Gustavo Thoeni (Italy) 1m 50.28s	Rolando Thoeni (Italy) 1m 50.30s
1976 Piero Gros (Italy) 2m 03.29s	Gustavo Thoeni (Italy) 2m 03.73s	Willy Frommelt (Liechtenstein) 2m 04.28s
1980		

DOWNHILL

1948 Henri Oreiller (France) 2m 55.0s	Franz Gabl (Austria) 2m 59.1s	K. Molitor & R. Olinger (Switzerland) 3m 00.3s
1952 Zeno Colo (Italy) 2m 30.8s	Othmar Schneider (Austria) 2m 32.0s	Christian Pravda (Austria) 2m 32.4s
1956 Anton Sailer (Austria) 2m 52.2s	Raymond Fellay (Switzerland) 2m 55.7s	Andreas Molterer (Austria) 2m 56.2s
1960 Jean Vuarnet (France) 2m 06.0s	Hans-Peter Lanig (Germany) 2m 06.5s	Guy Perillat (France) 2m 06.9s
1964 Egon Zimmermann (Austria) 2m 18.16s	Leo Lacroix (France) 2m 18.90s	Wolfgang Bartels (Germany) 2m 19.48s
1968 Jean-Claude Killy (France) 1m 59.85s	Guy Perillat (France) 1m 59.93s	Jean-Daniel Dätwyler (Switzerland) 2m 00.32s
1972 Bernhard Russi (Switzerland) 1m 51.43s	Roland Collombin (Switzerland) 1m 52.07s	Heinrich Messner (Austria) 1m 52.40s
1976 Franz Klammer (Austria) 1m 46.73s	Bernhard Russi (Switzerland) 1m 46.06s	Herbert Plank (Italy) 1m 46.59s
1980		

ALPINE SKI-ING (WOMEN)
GIANT SLALOM

1952 Andrea Lawrence (USA) 2m 06.8s	Dagmar Rom (Austria) 2m 09.0s	Annemarie Buchner (Germany) 2m 10s
1956 Ossi Reichert (Germany) 1m 56.5s	Josefine Frandl (Austria) 1m 57.8s	Dorothea Hochleitner (Austria) 1m 58.2s
1960 Yvonne Ruegg (Switzerland) 1m 39.9s	Penelope Pitou (USA) 1m 40.0s	Giuliana Minuzzo (Italy) 1m 40.2s
1964 Marielle Goitschel (France) 1m 52.24s	Christine Goitschel & Jean Saubert (France) (USA) 1m 53.11s	
1968 Nancy Greene (Canada) 1m 51.97s	Annie Famose (France) 1m 54.61s	Fernande Bochatay (Switzerland) 1m 54.74s

1972	Marie Therese Nadig (Switzerland) 1m 29.90s	Annemarie Proell (Austria) 1m 30.75s	Wiltrud Drexel (Austria) 1m 32.35s
1976	Kathy Kreiner (Canada) 1m 29.13s	Rosi Mittermaier (W. Germany) 1m 29.25s	Danielle Debernard (France) 1m 29.95s
1980			

SLALOM

1948	Gretchen Frazer (USA) 1m 57.2s	Antoinette Meyer (Switzerland) 1m 57.7s	Erika Mahringer (Austria) 1m 58.0s
1952	Andrea Lawrence (USA) 2m 10.6s	Ossi Reichert (Germany) 2m 11.4s	Annemarie Buchner (Germany) 2m 13.3s
1956	Renée Colliard (Switzerland) 1m 2.3s	Regina Schöpf (Austria) 1m 55.4s	Evginija Sidorova (USSR) 1m 56.7s
1960	Ann Heggtveit (Canada) 1m 49.6s	Betsy Snite (USA) 1m 52.9s	Barbara Henneberger (Germany) 1m 56.6s
1964	Christine Goitschel (France) 1m 29.86s	Marielle Goitschel (France) 1m 30.77s	Jean Saubert (USA) 1m 31.36s
1968	Marielle Goitschel (France) 1m 25.86s	Nancy Greene (Canada) 1m 26.15s	Annie Famose (France) 1m 27.89s
1972	Barbara Cochran (USA) 91.24s	Danielle Debernard (France) 91.26s	Florence Steurer (France) 92.69s
1976	Rosi Mittermaier (W. Germany) 1m 30.54s	C. Giordani (Italy) 1m 30.87s	Hanni Wenzel (Liechtenstein) 1m 32.20s
1980			

DOWNHILL

1948	Hedy Schlunegger (Switzerland) 2m 28.3s	Trude Beiser (Austria) 2m 29.1s	Resi Hammerer (Austria) 2m 30.2s
1952	Trude Beiser (Austria) 1m 47.1s	Annemarie Buchner (Germany) 1m 48.0s	Giuliana Minuzzo (Italy) 1m 49.0s
1956	Madeleine Berthod (Switzerland) 1m 40.7s	Frieda Dänzer (Switzerland) 1m 45.4s	Lucile Wheeler (Canada) 1m 45.9s
1960	Heidi Biebl (Germany) 1m 37.6s	Penelope Pitou (USA) 1m 38.6s	Gertrud Hecher (Austria) 1m 38.9s
1964	Christl Haas (Austria) 1m 55.39s	Edith Zimmerman (Austria) 1m 56.42s	Gertrud Hecher (Austria) 1m 56.66s
1968	Olga Pall (Austria) 1m 40.87s	Isabelle Mir (France) 1m 41.33s	Christl Haas (Austria) 1m 41.44s
1972	Marie-Therese Nadig (Switzerland) 1m 36.68s	Annemarie Proell (Austria) 1m 37s	Susan Corrock (USA) 1m 37.68s
1976	Rosi Mittermaier (W. Germany) 1m 46.16s	Brigitte Totschnig (Austria) 1m 46.68s	Cynthia Nelson (USA) 1m 47.50s
1980			

SKI JUMPING
SMALL HILL (70 METRES)

1964	Veikko Kankkonen (Finland) 229.90pts	Toralf Engan (Norway) 226.30	Torgeir Brandtzäg (Norway) 222.90
1968	Jiri Raska (Czech) 216.5pts	Reinhold Bachler (Austria) 214.2	Baldur Preiml (Austria) 212.6
1972	Yukio Kasaya (Japan) 244.2pts	Akitsugu Konno (Japan) 234.8	Seiji Aochi (Japan) 229.5
1976	Hans-Georg Aschenbach (E. Germany) 252.0pts	Jochen Danneberg (E. Germany) 246.0	Karl Schnabl (Austria) 242.0
1980			

BIG HILL (90 METRES)

1964	Toralf Engan (Norway) 230.7pts	Veikko Kankkonen (Finland) 228.9	Torgeir Brantzäs (Norway) 227.2
1968	Valdimir Beloussov (USSR) 231.3pts	Jiri Raska (Czech) 229.4	Lars Grini (Norway) 214.3
1972	Wojciech Fortuna (Poland) 219.9pts	Walter Steiner (Switzerland) 219.8	Rainer Schmidt (E. Germany) 219.3
1976	Karl Schnabel (Austria) 234.8pts	Anton Innauer (Austria) 232.9	Henry Glass (E. Germany) 221.7
1980			

NORDIC COMBINED
(CROSS-COUNTRY AND JUMPING)

1924	Thorleif Haug (Norway) 18,906pts	Thoralf Strömstad (Norway) 18,219	Johan Gröttumsbraaten (Norway) 17,854
1928	Johan Gröttumsbraaten (Norway) 17,833pts	Hans Vinjarengen (Norway) 15,303	John Snersrud (Norway) 15,021
1932	Johan Gröttumsbraaten (Norway) 446.0pts	Olex Stenen (Norway) 436.05	Hans Vinjarengen (Norway) 434.60
1936	Oddbjörn Hagen (Norway) 430.30pts	Olaf Hoffsbakken (Norway) 419.80	Sverre Brodahl (Norway) 408.10
1948	Heikki Hasu (Finland) 448.80pts	Martti Huhtala (Finland) 433.65	Sfen Israelsson (Sweden) 433.40
1952	Simon Slättvik (Norway) 451.62pts	Heikki Hasu (Finland) 447.5	Sverre Stenersen (Norway) 436.335
1956	Sverre Stenersen (Norway) 454.0pts	Bengt Eriksson (Sweden) 437.4	F. Gron-Gasienica (Poland) 436.8
1960	Georg Thoma (Germany) 457.952pts	Tormod Knutsen (Norway) 453.0	Nikolay Gusokaw (USSR) 452.0
1964	Tormod Knutsen (Norway) 469.28pts	Nikolai Kiselev (USSR) 453.04	Georg Thoma (Germany) 452.88
1968	Franz Keller (W.Germany) 449.04pts	Alois Kälin (Switzerland) 447.94	Andreas Kunz (E.Germany) 444.10
1972	Ulrich Wehling (E. Germany) 413.34pts	Rauno Miettinen (Finland) 405.50	Karl Luck (E. Germany) 398.80
1976	Ulrich Wehling (E. Germany) 423.39pts	Urban Hettich (W. Germany) 419.90	Konrad Winkler (E. Germany) 417.47
1980			

BIATHLON

1960	Klas Lestander (Sweden) 1h 33m 21.6s	Antti Tyrvainen (Finland) 1h 33m 57.7s	Aleksandr Privalov (USSR) 1h 34m 54.2s
1964	Vladimir Melyanin (USSR) 1h 20m 26.0s	Aleksandr Privalov (USSR) 1h 23m 42.5s	Olav Jordet (Norway) 1h 24m 38.8s
1968	Magnar Solberg (Norway) 1h 13m 45.9s	Alexandr Tikhonov (USSR) 1h 14m 40.4s	Vladimir Goundartsev (USSR) 1h 18m 27.4s
1972	Magnar Solberg (Norway) 1h 15m 55.50s	Hansjorg Knauthe (E. Ger) 1h 16m 7.60s	Lars Arvidson (Sweden) 1h 16m 27.03s
1976	Nicolai Kruglov (USSR) 1h 14m 12.26s	Hokki Ikola (Finland) 1h 15m 54.10s	Alexander Elizarov (USSR) 1h 16m 5.57s
1980			

BIATHLON—RELAY

1968	USSR 2h 13m 2.4s	Norway 2h 14m 50.2s	Sweden 2h 17m 26.3s
1972	USSR 1h 51m 44.92s	Finland 1h 54m 37.25s	E. Ger 1h 54m 37.67s
1976	USSR 1h 57m 55.64s	Finland 2h 1m 45.58s	E. Ger 2h 4m 8.61s
1980			

BOBSLEIGH
2—MAN BOB

1932	USA 8m 14.74s	Switzerland 8m 16.28s	USA 8m 29.15s
1936	USA 5m 29.29s	Switzerland 5m 30.64s	USA 5m 33.96s
1948	Switzerland 5m 29.2s	Switzerland 5m 30.4s	USA 5m 35.3s
1952	Germany 5m 24.54s	USA 5m 26.89s	Switzerland 5m 27.71s
1956	Italy 5m 30.14s	Italy 5m 31.45s	Switzerland 5m 37.46s
1964	GB 4m 21.90s	Italy 4m 22.02s	Italy 4m 22.63s
1968	Italy 4m 41.54s	Germany 4m 41.54s	Rumania 4m 44.46s
1972	W. Germany 4m 57.07s	W. Germany 4m 58.84s	Switzerland 4m 59.33s
1976	E. Germany 3m 44.42s	W. Germany 3m 44.99s	Austria 3m 45.70s
1980			

4—MAN BOB

1924	Switzerland 5m 45.54s	GB 5m 48.83s	Belgium 6m 02.29s
1928	USA 3m 20.5s	USA 3m 21.0s	Germany 3m 21.9s
1932	USA 7m 53.68s	USA 7m 55.70s	Germany 8m 00.04s
1936	Switzerland 5m 19.85s	Switzerland 5m 22.73s	GB 5m 23.41s
1948	USA 5m 20.1s	Belgium 5m 21.3	USA 5m 21.5
1952	Germany 5m 07.84s	USA 5m 10.48s	Switzerland 5m 11.70s
1956	Switzerland 5m 10.44s	Italy 5m 12.10s	USA 5m 12.39s
1964	Canada 4m 14.46s	Austria 4m 15.48s	Italy 4m 15.60
1968	Italy 2m 17.39s	Austria 2m 17.48s	Switzerland 2m 18.04s
1972	Switzerland 3m 32.36s	Italy 3m 32.91s	W. Germany 3m 33.23s
1976	E. Germany 3m 40.43s	Switzerland 3m 40.89s	W. Germany 3m 41.37s
1980			

TOBOGGANING—SINGLE SEATER (MEN)

1964	Thomas Kohler (Germany) 3m 26.77s	Klaus Bonsack (E.Germany) 3m 27.04s	Hans Plenk (Germany) 3m 30.15s
1968	Manfred Schmid (Austria) 2m 52.48s	Thomas Kohler (E.Germany) 2m 52.66s	Klaus Bonsack (E.Germany) 2m 53.33s
1972	Wolfgang Sheidel (E. Germany) 3m 27.58s	Harald Ehrig (E. Germany) 3m 28.39s	Wolfram Fiedler (E. Germany) 3m 28.73s
1976	Detlef Guenther (E. Germany) 3m 27.69s	Josef Fendt (W. Germany) 3m 28.20s	Hans Rinn (E. Germany) 3m 28.57s
1980			

SINGLE SEATER (WOMEN)

1964	Ortrun Enderlein (Germany) 3m 24.67s	Lise Geisler (Germany) 3m 27.42s	Helene Thurner (Austria) 3m 29.06s
1968	Erica Lechner (Italy) 2m 28.66s	Christa Schmuck (W.Germany) 2m 29.37s	Angelika Dunhaupt (W.Germany) 2m 29.56s
1972	Anna Muller (E. Germany) 2m 59.18s	Ute Ruhrold (E. Germany) 2m 59.49s	Margit Schumann (E. Germany) 2m 59.54s
1976	Margit Schumann (E. Germany) 2m 50.62s	Ute Ruhrold (E. Germany) 2m 50.85s	E. Demleitner (W. Germany) 2m 51.06s
1980			

2 SEATER (MEN)

1964	Austria 1m 41.62s	Austria 1m 41.91s	Italy 1m 42.87s
1968	E.Germany 1m 35.85s	Austria 1m 36.34s	W.Germany 1m 37.29s
1972	Italy & E. Germany 1m 28.35s		E. Germany 1m 29.16s
1976	E. Germany 1m 25.60s	W. Germany 1m 25.89s	Austria 1m 25.92s
1980			